The Short Oxford History of Europe

General Editor: T. C. W. Blanning

The Sixteenth Century

Edited by Euan Cameron

OXFORD
UNIVERSITY PRESS

OXFORD
UNIVERSITY PRESS

Great Clarendon Street, Oxford OX2 6DP

Oxford University Press is a department of the University of Oxford.
It furthers the University's objective of excellence in research, scholarship,
and education by publishing worldwide in

Oxford New York

Auckland Cape Town Dar es Salaam Hong Kong Karachi
Kuala Lumpur Madrid Melbourne Mexico City Nairobi
New Delhi Shanghai Taipei Toronto

With offices in

Argentina Austria Brazil Chile Czech Republic France Greece
Guatemala Hungary Italy Japan Poland Portugal Singapore
South Korea Switzerland Thailand Turkey Ukraine Vietnam

Oxford is a registered trade mark of Oxford University Press
in the UK and in certain other countries

Published in the United States
by Oxford University Press Inc., New York

© The Several Contributors 2006

British Library Cataloguing in Publication Data

Data available

Library of Congress Cataloging in Publication Data

Data available

Typeset by RefineCatch Limited, Bungay, Suffolk
Printed in Great Britain
on acid-free paper by
Biddles Ltd., King's Lynn, Norfolk

ISBN 0–19–873188–4 978–0–19–873188–7
ISBN 0–19–873189–2 (Pbk.) 978–0–19–873189–4 (Pbk.)

1 3 5 7 9 10 8 6 4 2

General Editor's Preface

The problems of writing a satisfactory general history of Europe are many, but the most intractable is clearly the reconciliation of depth with breadth. The historian who can write with equal authority about every part of the continent in all its various aspects has not yet been born. Two main solutions have been tried in the past: either a single scholar has attempted to go it alone, presenting an unashamedly personal view of a period, or teams of specialists have been enlisted to write what are in effect anthologies. The first offers a coherent perspective but unequal coverage, the second sacrifices unity for the sake of expertise. This new series is underpinned by the belief that it is this second way that has the fewest disadvantages and that even those can be diminished if not neutralized by close cooperation between the individual contributors under the directing supervision of the volume editor. All the contributors to every volume in this series have read each other's chapters, have met to discuss problems of overlap and omission, and have then redrafted as part of a truly collective exercise. To strengthen coherence further, the editor has written an introduction and conclusion, weaving the separate strands together to form a single cord. In this exercise, the brevity promised by the adjective 'short' in the series' title has been an asset. The need to be concise has concentrated everyone's minds on what really mattered in the period. No attempt has been made to cover every angle of every topic in every country. What this volume does provide is a short but sharp and deep entry into the history of Europe in the period in all its most important aspects.

T. C. W. Blanning

Sidney Sussex College
Cambridge

Contents

List of Contributors

CHRISTOPHER BLACK is Professor of Italian History in the University of Glasgow. His interests include the social history of early modern Italy, notably confraternities and parish life. He started with a particular specialization in the city of Perugia, its politics, culture, and art, on which he published several articles. He is the author of *Italian Confraternities in the Sixteenth Century* (1989; repr. 2004), *Early Modern Italy: A Social History* (2000), and *Church, Religion and Society in Early Modern Italy* (2004).

D. A. BRADING, FBA, is Emeritus Professor of Mexican History, University of Cambridge, a former Director of the Centre of Latin American Studies, and fellow of Clare Hall, Cambridge. His research interests centre on the history of Latin America in the early modern era. His many publications include *Miners and Merchants in Bourbon Mexico, 1763–1810* (1971), *Haciendas and Ranchos in the Mexican Bajío, León, 1700–1860* (1978), *Prophecy and Myth in Mexican History* (1984), *The Origins of Mexican Nationalism* (1985), *The First America: The Spanish Monarchy, Creole Patriots and the Liberal State, 1492–1867* (1991), *Church and State in Bourbon Mexico: The Diocese of Michoacán, 1749–1810* (1994), and more recently *Mexican Phoenix: Our Lady of Guadalupe: Image and Tradition across Five Centuries* (2002).

EUAN CAMERON is Academic Dean and Henry Luce III Professor of Reformation Church History in Union Theological Seminary in New York City. His research interests revolve around religious difference, dissent, and division in the Middle Ages and early modern period in Europe. He is the author of *The Reformation of the Heretics: The Waldenses of the Alps 1480–1580* (1984), *The European Reformation* (1991), *Waldenses: Rejections of Holy Church in Medieval Europe* (2000), and *Interpreting Christian History: The Challenge of the Churches' Past* (2005). He also edited *Early Modern Europe: An Oxford History* (1999).

MARK GREENGRASS is Professor of History in the University of Sheffield. He has researched and published extensively in the history of France in the early modern period, and has also been Director of the Hartlib Papers Project which transcribed, edited, and published the unique manuscript collections of Samuel Hartlib (*c.*1600–62). He now directs for the University of Sheffield the British Academy John Foxe Project. His many publications include *France in the Age of Henri IV* (1984), *The French Reformation* (1987), *Conquest and Coalescence: The Shaping of the State in Early Modern Europe* (1990), and *The Longman Companion to the European Reformation, c.1500–1618* (1998). He has co-edited *Samuel Hartlib and Universal Reformation: Studies in Intellectual Communication* (1994), and *The Adventure of Religious Pluralism in Early Modern France,* (2000).

CHARLES G. NAUERT is Professor Emeritus of History at the University of Missouri-Columbia. His research interests include the history of relations between humanist culture and the scholastic culture of the universities in Northern Europe, and more generally, the history of ideas in the European Renaissance. A particular interest is the revival of interest in ancient scepticism during the sixteenth century. He is the author of *Agrippa and the Crisis of Renaissance Thought* (1965), *The Age of Renaissance and Reformation* (1977), and *Humanism and the Culture of Renaissance Europe* (1995), and a lengthy article on Renaissance commentaries on the *Natural History* of Pliny the Elder, published in *Catalogus Translationum et Commentariorum,* 4. He has also written a *Historical Dictionary of the Renaissance* (2004). He is the author of the introductions and notes for vols. xi and xii of *The Collected Works of Erasmus* published by the University of Toronto Press.

TOM SCOTT is Honorary Professor in the Reformation Studies Institute in the University of St Andrews. His research interests embrace town–country relations and regional identities in late medieval and early modern Germany, including many aspects of the Reformation at the grassroots and the German Peasants' War. His many publications in early modern economic and social history include *Freiburg and the Breisgau: Town–Country Relations in the Age of Reformation and Peasants' War* (1986), *Thomas Müntzer: Theology and Revolution in the German Reformation* (1989), *Regional Identity and Economic Change: The Upper Rhine, 1450–1600* (1997), *Society and Economy in Germany, 1300–1600* (2002), and *Town, Country, and Regions in Reformation Germany* (2005). He has also edited *The Peasantries of Europe from the Fourteenth to the Eighteenth Centuries* (1998) and co-edited *The German Peasants' War: A History in Documents* (1991).

Introduction

Euan Cameron

Few would doubt that the sixteenth century forms a turning-point in the history of Europe. The Europe of the later fifteenth century was a continent still defined by the political, intellectual, and spiritual inheritance of the Middle Ages. By 1600 all the reference-points had changed. Europeans had experienced the first great wave of techno-logical mass communication and the first phases of ideologically motivated change and conflict. They had seen the population and economy shift from gentle decline to structural and often painful growth. They had confronted a vastly enlarged world with a mixture of confused bewilderment and an aggressive determination to take their cultural values to the rest of humanity. In past historiography this transformation of European culture from a regional phenome-non to a dominant force in the whole world might have called forth much triumphalist rhetoric. That is no longer the case—and indeed, would ill reflect the atmosphere of the sixteenth century itself. The sixteenth century was an age of adjustment, a time when people were forced to think all kinds of things previously unthinkable. With such radical changes in the mental universe came all manner of traumas and conflicts, both for Europeans themselves and for those whom they encountered.

The scene in 1500

Economic historians traditionally analysed the vibrancy or activity in an economy in terms of cycles of growth and contraction. This dia-lectic did not reflect the economic perceptions of the time: the assumption then would rather have been of an ideal steady state of just prices and fixed relationships, where any dynamic processes were most likely the outcome of human sin and greed. Nevertheless, up to at least around 1470 Western Europe's economic life had been dominated by factors working towards contraction. The ruling trend was the cataclysmic population decline of the second half of the fourteenth century which did not begin to recover until the latter half of the fifteenth at the earliest. The market in basic foodstuffs was depressed because there were, quite simply, fewer mouths to feed. As a consequence, farming communities had diversified, establishing some areas of specialist production in vines, dyestuffs, and so forth. Already by 1500 Europe was living in an economy of regional and international trade rather than mere subsistence.

The patterns of trade had, however, necessarily shifted. The Mediterranean economy of the High Middle Ages was based on Latin and Byzantine control of the north and Muslim control of the south coast, with substantial Latin trading colonies of the Italian maritime powers, Venice and Genoa, in the islands in the Levant. By the second half of the fifteenth century the polarity had shifted from north–south to east–west, with the Ottoman conquest of the remainder of Asia Minor followed, after 1526, by that of all of Greece and the southern Balkans. This did not isolate the Eastern from the Western worlds: trade and all forms of exchange, peaceful and not so peaceful, continued. However, the rules and the players had changed, and the south-eastern margins of Europe had been moved far to the north-west of their traditional and historic location. This geopolitical shift established for the first time a certain ambiguity about the status of parts of the Balkans within the European world. That same ambiguity would cast a long shadow, seen in Tony Blair's 1999 observation that Kosovo, to the north-west of Greece, was on the 'doorstep of Europe'.[1]

In the political and military sphere, the middle fifteenth century had also seen the gradual closing of a distinct phase in European history. The centuries-old entanglement of the English and French monarchies on French soil came to an end with the final expulsion of the English from Gascony in 1453. The 1454 Peace of Lodi inaugurated a forty-year period of internal peace in central Italy, one that

---

[1] See http://www.pbs.org/wgbh/pages/frontline/shows/kosovo/interviews/blair.-html; also http://lrb.veriovps.co.uk/v21/no9/gleno1_.html.

would be brutally ended by the invasion of Charles VIII of France in 1494. In the rest of Europe the later fifteenth century saw the last gasp of a traditional feudal and chivalric warfare rapidly becoming obsolete. Artillery and Swiss infantry, paid for by the French King Louis XI, gradually whittled away the political power of the nascent quasi-state of Burgundy–Flanders, itself something of a self-conscious throwback to idealized medieval chivalry. After 1477 the possessions of the dukes of Burgundy were dismantled and shared between the Habsburgs and the kings of France. Amongst other things, this development signalled the military ascendancy of those powers that could deploy the largest numbers of field guns and pikes.

The social structure of the late medieval world was still to a large extent dominated by the class of military nobility that had formed Europe's aristocracy since around the year 1000. The distinctive cultural attributes of this elite class, vital to their fiscal and legal privileges as well as their right to be heard in political matters, remained as they had always been: sufficient landed wealth to exclude the need for productive gainful work of any kind; and the skills appropriate to serve one's suzerain in warfare. Even among the princes of the Church, secular and warlike factors counted: consider the case of Matthäus Lang von Wellenburg, archbishop of Salzburg (1468–1540), who long served as a political and military leader under Maximilian I, only receiving priest's orders the day before taking up his archbishopric in 1519. However, signs were emerging around 1500 that the future might belong to a political service elite characterized by something more than just idleness and violence. Courtier-books foreshadowed the need for a refined and cultured giver of counsel. Even Charles the Rash of Burgundy had tried governing through a 'great council' in his fragmented domains in Flanders. Increasingly the administration of policy, and in due course its formulation, would be influenced by a lay administrative class that included members drawn neither from the traditional military nobility nor from the clergy (though both the latter would remain important).

The slow and gradual rise of an administrative class accompanied a subtle but profound shift in the way in which government and politics worked. The fifteenth century was an age of gradually growing use of paper. Paper not only allowed the production of books to be vastly easier and cheaper than parchment, a costly substance that required hours of skilful preparation; it also made it realistic to record the ephemera of administration and casual correspondence in vastly greater detail and abundance than before. Government could record its own decisions and disputes; but individuals could also expose themselves to the risks of leaving written records of their thoughts. A historian of the Reformation era has remarked on how many (surviving!) letters bear the postscript 'burn after reading'. The sixteenth century would witness a continuing massive growth in the scale and variety of the written records of Europeans' activities.

Beneath the level of the governing elites, change was somewhat slower and less dramatic. One must remember that in this era stability and permanency in the social order represented the ideal. Change was at best an unavoidable and undesirable necessity. Perhaps the most important motifs to later medieval society were community and social differentiation. 'Community' meant the web of lateral and horizontal relationships that bound together those men and women who lived and worked as part of the same social organism, whether a rural village living by agriculture or a busy town or city parish. The sense of 'commune' in some parts of Europe (most famously in south-western Germany) could be remarkably strong, though it would suffer some strains and shocks under the pressures of the sixteenth century. By 'social differentiation' is meant the unquestioned assumption—shocking to some modern ears—that in the proper and divinely sanctioned order of society everyone should have a place in a system below some and above others. Class, generational, or gender equality was the last thing in the minds of the people of the late Middle Ages. Most lay societies were fairly clearly graduated into greater or lesser nobility, bourgeoisie, and artisans, greater and lesser tenant farmers down to labourers and servants. Alongside the laity, moreover, was the complex parallel society created within Europe by the clergy and priesthood, including monks, friars, and nuns and to some extent all those with the status of 'clerk' (the literate). In one sense the clergy was superior to all the rest of society by its privileged status, by its (sometimes theoretical) exemptions from the military and fiscal demands imposed on the laity, and by its sacramental authority. In another sense it was a parallel society, composed of its own nobility, middle class, and proletariat, consumed by the same political pressures and concerns as the rest, albeit in a distinct form.

A great deal about late medieval society was not comprehended within the laws and ethical norms set down by authority, secular or religious. Historians now acknowledge the importance of informal social bonds and norms of behaviour based on local tradition and convention. Even in areas such as sexual morality where both state and Church had a great deal to say about the approved modes of behaviour, custom and practice could be just as potent as the rules of one's betters. Family historians have observed how the medieval canon law of marriage tried to maintain a fragile web of contact between the theoretical rules of the Church and the more informal customs of village life. The often very high proportion of brides pregnant at marriage offers the most potent testimony to this struggle. In the bonds of society likewise, more ancient kinship and clan networks could at times rival and even trump the claims of settled community or social hierarchy.

The Europe of c.1500 was still coming to terms with the continent-wide dispersal of the literary, artistic, and philosophical phenomenon known as the Renaissance. For at least a century small cliques of scholars, literati, and artists had thought and argued that they had broken decisively with the previous few centuries of European taste, what they themselves called the 'Middle Ages', the inter-mediate time between Greek and Roman antiquity and their own 'modern' times. In turn they believed they had recovered the elegance, proportion, and ethical sensibilities of their ancient classical models. In Italy these Renaissance men and women were by the end of the fifteenth century already in the cultural ascendant: they represented the vogue and taste of the age. Renaissance taste affected such diverse issues as literary style, the priorities in the education of the young, aesthetics in painting, statuary, architecture, typography, and even arms and armour. It also encouraged discussion about the relative priority of the life of ascetic retreat and self-denial versus the life of purposive engagement in household and commonwealth.

In Italy the 'Gothic' style had never really reached the level of flourishing found in Northern Europe. North of the Alps matters were much more complex. The Renaissance represented a foreign, even exotic intrusion into a sophisticated and well-articulated literary and artistic culture. A handful of French, German, and English scholars and book-collectors had adopted this style by the middle of the fifteenth century. Nevertheless they did not represent a majority, and one could not even argue that they were necessarily the most powerful 'modern' forces in art and culture. Sometimes they pretentiously exaggerated their struggles with the 'barbarians' and 'detractors' of good letters, ascribing to themselves an imaginary or self-inflicted isolation that did not really reflect their academic or cultural standing. In poetry, rhetoric, and ancient classical philology the scholars of the Renaissance were starting to carve a reputable niche for themselves by c.1500, even as professors in traditional universities. It remained to be seen how they would be integrated into the wider cultural world of Europe beyond Italy.

Europe on the eve of the Reformation was, to all outward appearances, not just a very religious culture, but a very conformist culture. Overwhelming evidence argues for the enthusiasm of Europe's peoples towards their Church life. Cathedrals and parish churches were rebuilt or embellished in the latest mode of the Gothic style. Altarpieces, carved, painted, or both, were commissioned in great numbers. From all ranks of society Christians craved physical and sensory contact with the sacred in the form of relics and images. Above all, masses for the souls of the recently departed were cumulated by the faithful in ever-increasing quantities. At the same time, the evidence of organized heresy, of obstinate dissent and separation from the official Church, had diminished markedly from the levels seen 200–250 years before. England and Bohemia were significant exceptions, but only in certain ways. In other words, there was little to forewarn the people of Europe that a major upheaval in the teachings and worship practices of Catholic Christianity was in any way imminent. On the other hand, the challenges that there were, the criticisms of the moral and disciplinary failings of many priests, the resentment of its legal immunities and political interventions, had been in a sense internalized. That is, significant leaders of the clergy themselves acknowledged the need for improvements and were seriously striving to bring those about.

The diversity that really divided Christians from each other lay along a vertical axis from the theologians at one extreme to the least educated laity at the opposite extreme. At the lowest educational level, ritual was a mechanism for exerting pressure on the invisible world. Religious and parareligious practices helped people with their everyday concerns. Amongst the most learned and thoughtful, all address to the divine depended to some extent on the right intention, on the abasement of the fallen mortal and the exaltation of the holy and the sacred. Learned people were troubled by and frequently discussed the casual use of 'superstitious' techniques by the masses, but had little idea of what to do about them; even to preach too hard against them endangered the preacher's credibility. Some theologians may not even have realized quite how far up the social and intellectual scale the 'superstitious' attitude already reached.

To a very perceptive eye, certain dangers might have been apparent. Controlling or oppressive systems become vulnerable when those who exercise control cease fully to believe in them. Here one needs to be very cautious. The intellectuals of the northern Renaissance were for the most part conventionally devout Christians by their lights. However, some of these refined souls, including many in the highest offices of the Church, had real difficulty in believing that the eternal destiny of a human soul could literally depend on the numbers of masses said, on the pilgrimages travelled, or the rituals of penance undergone. In the thirteenth century this sacramental economy of salvation was fresh and vibrant. By the late fifteenth it was still very strong and formally unchallenged. However, the elites of Europe had become, at the very least, disenchanted with the claims of an inelegantly expressed and crabby theology, combined with an overwrought mass of rituals, to offer the only description of and access to the divine. As yet these critiques were unformed; they had little or no agreed dogmatic (as opposed to aesthetic) content, and their exponents were not seeking to subvert established religious authority. However, if an alternative interpretation of the redemption of the individual soul were to have been offered, who knows where such restless and inquiring souls might turn?

The year 1500 is even more obviously the cusp of momentous change in regard to Europeans' visions of the outside world. For most of the Middle Ages the European vision of the world was shaped by a very limited and incomplete perspective determined by fable and legend as much as by correct information. In the fourteenth and fifteenth centuries one of the most successful and most widely translated accounts of the wider world was the *Travels of Sir John Mandeville*. This work, ostensibly a book telling pilgrims how to reach Jerusalem, digressed into descriptions of Asia and China and told tales of the weird and wonderful creatures to be found in remote parts of the world. It became a byword for the transmission of the unreliable and the fabulous. And yet of the stranger realities that lay beyond Europeans' ken *Mandeville* was, of course, entirely ignorant. And so it remained until the discoveries of the later fifteenth century. Not only that: Europeans huddled on the north-western extremity of the great land-mass of Europe–Asia–Africa, increasingly hemmed in by the Ottomans, were for the most part isolated from and quite unaware of the massive shifts of empires and cultures going on out of their sight in South and East Asia.

The problem on the very eve of the discoveries of the West Indies and the American continents was not so much that these places and their peoples were seen to be new and strange. It was rather that Europeans treated them, like anything apparently exotic and unfamiliar, within a framework of analogies with those things they already knew and understood. Moreover, it was nearly inconceivable that classical cosmologists and geographers, let alone inspired scripture, could have made assumptions about the world and Christian peoples' place in it that were massively lacking in vital information and therefore substantially wrong in their results. In a world where giants and monstrous human-like creatures were expected to be found and copiously described in the earlier literature, it was perfectly possible to question the full humanity of the new peoples met within the Americas. It is hard to imagine a people worse prepared intellectually, culturally, or morally for the role of colonial overlords over the rest of the world than late medieval Europeans.

Received ideas about the sixteenth century

Any historical period accrues around it a certain number of interpretative conventions, which can in turn become historical clichés. The sixteenth century supports an unusually large number of these, although the academic aspiration to debunk them means that few are nowadays advanced in exactly their traditional form. Nevertheless, there remain certain concepts or ideal-types that all historians, students, teachers, and authors, seem compelled to work with. The growth in population, the 'price revolution', the 'print revolution', the 'rise of capitalism', the Reformation and Counter-Reformation, the 'rise of the nation states', the growth of secular thought in philosophy, politics, and science: these concepts are all essential building blocks in the subject. However, these portmanteau terms carry with them certain assumptions. They tend to prioritize dynamic movements over continuing stability, which is a distinctly late modern rather than traditional way of thinking. They tend to prioritize large and powerful polities, especially in Western Europe, over smaller or more complex entities. They tend to privilege those trends and developments that *seem*—not always correctly—to foreshadow or somehow to generate later developments and the rise of 'modernity'.

To some extent interpretative concepts are indispensable. The alternative is to abandon the search for overall trends altogether, to study only the microhistories of small areas and small issues. There is no shortage of histories that abdicate from the task of macro-interpretation in this way; the returns in terms of scholarly accuracy and exactitude may be considerable. However, the real challenge to scholarly history is to incorporate the microscopic detail, with as many of its nuances as can be grasped, into the overall picture. The big themes need to be tested, refined, contextualized, and where necessary modified or even discarded and replaced by something truer to the available evidence and insights.

Distinctive themes of this book

Accordingly the contributors to this volume have each in their own distinct ways sought to test and where necessary to modify our images of the sixteenth century in the light of the newest research. In Tom Scott's chapter on the economy, the emphasis falls convincingly on Europe's geographical diversity. Neither Eastern Europe nor the Mediterranean followed the same trajectory as the north-western regions of France and the Empire. Social structures were different, and therefore the patterns of economic development were necessarily different also. Secondly, Scott questions whether the old assumptions about whether this or that mode of agricultural or industrial production was 'backward' or 'inefficient' actually hold up. Here the relentless teleological emphasis of the older history may have misled us. Apparently outmoded methods of economic organization may in fact have been more rational responses to their context than others which appear with hindsight to be more 'modern'. Scott also warns us against reducing economic progress solely to ideal-type concepts such as the 'rise of capitalism'. He points out that a particular means of production may become popular for a whole host of reasons, some of which have little to do with economic motivation and more to do with cultural conventions. Finally, we are warned not to assume that the economic cycles (then or now!) observed the same chronology in one region as in another. The phase of expansion in the European economy lasted far longer in the Mediterranean south than it did in the maritime north.

Mark Greengrass similarly refocuses our attention on aspects of political and military development that a single-minded quest for the 'roots of the modern' would prefer to disregard. He concludes that the most powerful political entities of the sixteenth century were dynastic monarchies. Dynastic monarchies grew by marriage alliances, convenient inheritances, and conquest; they shrank by the partition of inheritances (where permitted by law), the endowing of brides, the extinction of hereditary lines, or military defeat. The accidents and cultural peculiarities of human pairing, reproduction, and survival determined the political arrangements of the greatest regimes in Europe. The relentless evidence of the dynastic principle leads Greengrass to argue that 'nowhere could we find a "nation state" in the sixteenth century'. In other words, no state had 'natural' frontiers, or a unique and indefeasible identity that could guard it against being accumulated into a dynastic composite or multiple monarchy.

Even one monarchy that appeared to have a long and robust history of institutional cohesiveness, the English, changed dramatically through the sixteenth century. The English crown absorbed its Welsh possessions fully into the central system of rule, then raised Ireland into a co-monarchy of sorts in the 1540s. For just over two years in the 1550s, the ruling house became part of the sprawling Western Habsburg complex of Flanders–Spain–Milan–Naples–America. Then, in 1603, the reigning dynasty died out and was replaced by the Stuart monarchy of Scotland, despite that dynasty having been formally excluded from a claim to the sucession. However, the vicissitudes of England fade before the extraordinary history of the Habsburg monarchy. This bizarre conglomerate, chiefly comprising Austria, Hungary, Bohemia, Flanders, Castile, Aragon and parts of Italy, came into being between 1516–19 and 1556 through a combination of dynastic accidents, premature mortality, and fortunate inheritance. This process clearly served the interests of none of the territories that it doomed either to part-time government by the constantly distracted Charles V, or to a succession of regencies.

Within the structures of Renaissance monarchy, however, the style of nobility required to serve the monarch changed. With the ever-increasing role of written documents and government by committee, there was a place for territorial aristocrats who were willing to become deskbound administrators, and even more for administrators who aspired to the attributes of nobility for which their skills now qualified them. Yet the counselling of princes also included a vital cultural component. The social airs and graces required of a courtier-administrator included besides professional skills, rhetorical, artistic, and even military techniques still deemed suitable for a monarch's attendant, as well as the more indefinable and constantly evolving qualities of civility and good manners. The impression is of a Europe stumbling backwards into modern systems of ruling, still maintaining the illusion that a royal court was merely an augmented aristocratic household, and that courtiers were the personal retainers of the monarch as much as, or more than, the administrators of a government.

Christopher Black confronts us immediately with the dilemmas of the history of early modern society: is 'society' to be analysed in terms of the supposedly eternal socio-economic struggle of one class against another? Or is it to be envisaged as a basically harmonious organism in which the 'orders' of society worked together in a system that both understood? Put this way, it seems that the preference for one or another of these interpretative schemes tells us more about the political affiliations of the historian than about the period studied. Nonetheless, evidence for both of these attitudes can be found at various times within the sixteenth century. At various critical moments, during the Reformation struggles or the various agrarian disturbances that broke out across Europe, the rhetoric of social rivalry and class conflict could be heard albeit in forms—sometimes cloaked either in legalistic conservatism or religious radicalism and apocalyptic—distinctive to the age.

Incipient or potential class conflict notwithstanding, this was still an age in which people were bound one to another by a vast diversity of social and ethical ties. It was taken for granted that each individual formed part of an array of face-to-face networks, including but not confined to family and kin groups, parish communities and confraternities, and trade or craft guilds. Black's specialist interest in southern Europe refocuses a perspective that is too often dominated by French or German models at the expense of the rest of Europe. Here as in the economic chapter, we are warned against too facile a characterization of the whole continent. In the south the rich diversity of confraternal life subsisted, despite the doubts of clergy and secular rulers alike, much longer than in many parts of Northern Europe. Moreover, the degree of subtle social differentiation varied greatly: some regions had relatively flat social structures with an extremely narrowly based aristocracy and official class; more typical was a delicately shaded and infinitely complex hierarchy of status, both in rural and urban society, with marked gradations of rank even within a given activity or trade.

Christopher Black's chapter also opens up for us the surprising diversity of life-choices that might (or might not) become available to women in the age of the Renaissance and Reformation. Against the general pattern of women's structural exclusion from positions of power and influence (except for princesses and queens) and their much more limited opportunities for education and training, some exceptional artistic or creative women acquired individual reputations with a lustre denied to the majority of their contemporaries. Here again the Italian perspective is illuminating: perhaps only in Italy could the literate 'courtesan' become an international celebrity and a figure of some cultural power and control. In general, as the sixteenth century progressed, the degree of freedom to challenge social and ethical norms diminished. This had mixed effects. On one hand some freedoms previously allowed to women to live and work with some measure of independence were constrained or reduced. On the other hand society was 'disciplined' through both police measures and welfare policies. Nothing better illustrates the distance between the sixteenth century and the modern era than the ambivalent responses that the former's policies of social control and regulation commonly evoke. Paternalistic and yet protective, moralizing but aspiring to some level of benignity, sixteenth-century social regulators saw it as their role to oversee the moral standards as well as the physical welfare of the poor, the vulnerable, and the dependent. It is perhaps as well that, as Christopher Black demonstrates, such social discipline rarely functioned as efficiently or as remorselessly as its theories dictated.

The sixteenth century is the age of the Northern Renaissance, but also of the end of the Renaissance. There is a cruel irony in the way in which humanism was taken up north of the Alps. A dubious cliché has depicted Italian humanism as secular and northern humanism as religious. The cliché needs significant revision: there were secular humanists north of the Alps before 1500, and for that matter there were religious humanists in Italy as well. Nevertheless, the most distinctive contribution of Northern Europe to Renaissance thought, as Charles Nauert describes it, was the programme of patristic and scripturally based ethical spirituality advocated by Erasmus of Rotterdam. And yet Erasmus's programme hardly had time to make a significant impact on the literate peoples of Europe before it became caught up in the debates around the beginning of the Reformation. One could even argue that Erasmus's programme only gained the fame and attention that it did because the debates of the Reformation had raised the profile of religious writing to such a level of prominence. So the Northern Renaissance, and Erasmus in particular, offered Europe a distinctive approach to the Christian life just too late for it to acquire whole-hearted adherents.

Consequently, any account of the Northern Renaissance in the sixteenth century has to explain how it became diversified and specialized, as the religious terrain was increasingly taken over by militant dogmatic camps. Accordingly Charles Nauert's chapter reviews much of the thematic diversity of the thought-world of the sixteenth century, including literary, legal, mathematical, and what would now be called 'scientific' subjects, as well as the more obvious humanist curriculum in moral and political philosophy. The Renaissance 'ended' with the dispersal of the approaches and attitudes learnt in the first wave of enthusiasm for the classics into a broader reformed architecture of European thought. The grandiose claims to make a better human being through 'humane letters' were scaled down somewhat; what remained was a superior set of techniques for literary and textual criticism, a better understanding of antique history, culture, and philosophy, and a restructured sense of the curriculum of learning and education. The fracturing of the religious world-view may in some modest but significant way have helped to make the other intellectual disciplines more autonomous and independent of each other. Thinkers from different religious persuasions could interact, correspond, and debate in such areas as mathematics, cosmology, or the 'life sciences' without needing to bring questions of the ultimate into their conversations. However, the fragmentation of areas of knowledge—an inevitable consequence when knowledge expands and develops at rapid but uneven speeds—must inevitably have generated a degree of uncertainty. Nauert's chapter concludes with an exploration of the trends in sceptical thought and rational doubt that emerged at the end of the century. Systematic uncertainty about how one might attain to absolute truth seemed, to a few independent-minded thinkers at least, the only reasonable response to an age of brutal adjustment to unthinkable realities.

The sixteenth century was also, pre-eminently, the era of the Reformation. In a previous generation, it was quite normal to argue that the religious upheavals of the century ought best to be explained in terms of something else: something concerned with economics or social class struggles, something more supposedly 'real' than religious belief. It would clearly be a mistake to go to the opposite extreme, and to depict every decision made in religious affairs as the product of deeply felt spiritual inquiry at one end of the scale or ideologically motivated fanaticism at the other. There were spiritual people, and fanatics, but also secular-minded calculators as well, in the era of Reformation and Counter-Reformation. The course of religious history was determined by a whole series of complex and unpredictable interactions between sincere belief, half-informed prejudice, and cynical evaluations of personal or group advantage.

What is clear, nevertheless, is that the Reformation ultimately inaugurated a fundamentally new concept of the role of religion in human life and destiny. Before the Reformation, Christian worship took place in order to transfer the collective righteousness and purity of Christ, held in trust by the Church that Christ founded, so that they became the individual righteousness and purity of the believer. God's acceptance of that transferred purity as the Christian's own would ensure the salvation of that soul. After the Reformation (in those countries where its core message was accepted) the Christian faith consisted in the believer's trusting acceptance that the favour and forgiveness of God was poured out to cover (rather than remove) the impurities and imperfections of his or her intrinsically sinful and impure soul. The role of the Church was to teach believers about that favour and forgiveness through word and sacrament, to bind up the community in acts of gratitude and goodwill in response to it, and to maintain the moral and social discipline that even the saints required. Purification by ritual, in short, was replaced by forgiveness through understanding.

Once one has grasped the core principle around which the Reformation mainstream movements agreed, much of the rest of its programme can be unfolded by logical deduction: where it cannot, one can expect to find controversies and divisions. What cannot be deduced from ideas alone, however, is the extraordinarily complex process that turned reforming teachings into reformed social and political realities. Each narrative forms a complex tissue of overlapping motives and encounters: so the best that the historian can do, within the confines of a short narrative, is to try to extract a series of more or less typical trajectories or 'paradigms' of how Reformation happened. None of these 'paradigms', the south-western German free city paradigm, the Baltic-Hanseatic paradigm, the Scandinavian monarchical paradigm, or the 'refugee paradigm' associated with those influenced by John Calvin, should be regarded as more than broad guidelines or generalizations.

And yet even when all due allowance has been made for historical contingency and accident, one must still accept that present-day Christianity, not just in Europe and the Americas but wherever in the world the divisions of Latin Christendom have been replicated, bears the marks of its sixteenth-century heritage. That remark is particularly true of Roman Catholicism, the faith that was on the face of it the least profoundly affected by the events of the century. In the case of Catholicism it was not so much the content of the Church's teachings that changed—though even there a degree of selection and narrowing of options was evident—but rather the way that those teachings were administered and purveyed to the population. Roman Catholicism absorbed from the sixteenth-century context the hieratic authoritarianism of an age of 'social discipline', the confidence that confessional verbal formulae could encapsulate the transcendent, the desire to instruct through rigorous standardized catechizing. Protestantism absorbed many of these traits from the surrounding culture also. The difference was that in Catholicism they persisted for far longer.

The transition between the 'discoveries' of the rest of the world and the establishment of overseas colonial empires has often been taken for granted, as though the natural European response to finding more territories should be to colonize them and expropriate, subjugate, or assimilate their peoples. That, of course, was never a necessary consequence in any way. D. A. Brading's analysis of the rise of the Iberian empires rightly throws light on the interaction between maritime discovery and the determination of Western rulers to extend their power and influence in the name of trade, territory, or Christianization. Discovery turned into empire because the rulers of the maritime powers were able to organize the ships, the personnel, the equipment, and the lines of financial credit to make these far-flung acquisitions first attainable, and then worth the trouble to defend and exploit. Perhaps due weight should be given to the power of bureaucracy and finance in extending European influence, along-side the audacity and aggression of the entrepreneurs who created these European societies across the ocean.

One of the striking ironies of the Iberian colonial story is the ambiguous role played by the Catholic Church in the establishment and maintenance of the European hegemony in the conquered lands. On one hand Catholic priests and friars saw in the indigenous peoples souls to be saved. The Church therefore sought somehow to mitigate the harshest and most brutal features of the colonial exploitation practised by the European colonizers, at least to prevent the utter brutalization of the new underclass. A strong strand in Catholic thought of this period emphasized the basic humanity and spiritual needs of the peoples of the New World (though a similar discourse was startlingly absent in the case of those plundered from the coasts of Africa). However, that same desire to win souls for the Christian God also entailed an unqualified commitment to the superiority of the European way, and not just in respect of religious observances and ethical norms. For some time historians have documented the evolving European reactions to the peoples of Central and Southern America. Initial praise for the age-of-gold simplicity of the people of the Caribbean was later replaced by suspicion of the authoritarian nature of their regimes and appalled dismay at their religious rites. In such circumstances ethical and economic needs could coincide to make the 'Europeanization' of New World society appear as an absolute imperative.

A critically honest and scholarly account of the continent of Europe in the sixteenth century must not be simplistic, but it does not have to be confusing or overlong. Nor does it need to abdicate all responsibility for discerning overall patterns, at least provisionally. The contributors to this volume have approached their task with sensitivity to the enormous complexity and subtlety of human affairs in a continent of nearly a hundred million people at a time of rapid and often painful change. They remain convinced that the pattern-seeking and model-building work traditionally performed by the historian offer valuable insights and explanations for the evolving shape of European society. How far the following chapters will appear, in due course, to be products of their own age will become manifest as one wave of cultural and social development succeeds another.

1

The economy

Tom Scott

Traditional accounts of the economy of Europe in the sixteenth century have emphasized three features. First, the lands at the western end of the Mediterranean—Italy and Iberia—which had been the power-house of the medieval economy succumbed to sclerosis and involution, as the centre of economic gravity shifted decisively north-westwards to the Atlantic seaboard in an age of overseas exploration, followed by economic exploitation and colonial settlement. Secondly, in economic terms the sixteenth century should have its chronological boundaries shifted backwards to around 1470 and forwards (in some, though not all, instances) to the 1650s. For during what is called the 'long sixteenth century' an upswing in the cycle of economic development occurred, observable in (though not necessarily caused by) the recovery of population, until the point where pressure on resources—land and the food it provided—led once again to famine, dearth, and economic downturn. That was accompanied by an unprecedented rise in prices (once called a 'price revolution')—though not in wages—which was marked by inflation, debasement, and the immiseration of large sections of the population. Thirdly, the 'long sixteenth century' is held to have been stamped by the beginnings of capitalism, that is, it marks the birth of the modern economy in terms of growth, innovation, and accumulation; indeed, in Immanuel Wallerstein's analysis, an early capitalist 'world-economy' is discernible, in which emergent core areas consigned hitherto thriving centres to a semi-periphery and came to dominate the economies of a new periphery, both within Europe itself and overseas, in an exploitative colonial relationship.

At numerous points this narrative has come under attack in recent years and can—at least for the period before 1600—no longer be sustained in its entirety. To put the matter in a nutshell: the impact of the New World on the economy of Europe, in terms of the allegedly inflationary and destabilizing impact of bullion imports, was barely perceptible before the 1580s, while the decisive shift from the Mediterranean to the Atlantic, the launching-pad of New World ventures, is supposed to have occurred (in the scathing verdict of one recent historian) in a span of no more than thirty years, from 1590 to 1620. Furthermore, the imbalance between people, land, and resources was already visible in many parts of Europe before 1600. More serious still, this approach entirely overlooks (except in Wallerstein's highly problematic analysis) the role of the East European lands, whose economies during the sixteenth century were for the first time integrated (whether beneficially or exploitatively) into the European economy as a whole. By contrast, the contribution of the New World to the gross domestic product of the European economy in the sixteenth century (if we were able to measure it in a pre-statistical age) is likely to have been marginal.

Populations, prices, and wages

To examine these issues, the chapter analyses the economy of Europe in three broad regional sweeps, the East, the Mediterranean, and the Atlantic, before offering some concluding remarks on commercial linkages and the manifestations of early capitalism. It should be understood that these 'regions' possess no intrinsic or distinct identity, and the boundaries between them are obviously fluid. They reflect, nonetheless, the divisions within which historians have customarily treated Europe's economic development (or retardation). At the outset, however, we must set out the fundamental changes in population, prices, and wages. On the most reliable recent estimate (that of Jan de Vries) the population of Europe increased from 60.9 million in 1500 to 68.9 million in 1550 and 77.9 million in 1600, a rise over the century of 27.9 per cent. The rate of increase chimes well with earlier calculations (such as Peter Kriedte's) which put the rise at 26 per cent for a wider span of countries including European Russia (west of the Urals), Hungary, Romania, and the Balkans, giving totals of 80.9 million for 1500 and 102.1 million for 1600. These pan-

European figures conceal, predictably, substantial regional variations, and it is the latter on to which historians, eager to find evidence of differential economic performance, have been quick to latch, pointing to a population increase in Northern and Western Europe of 44.7 per cent. Within that area, for instance, England's population between 1500 and 1600 is reckoned to have risen from 2.3 million to 4.2 million, by far and away the fastest rate of growth of any European country at 82.6 per cent, with only the northern Netherlands (the Dutch Republic) coming anywhere close at 57.8 per cent. Yet in the same period the population of Scotland and Ireland rose by no more than 25 per cent. Nevertheless, these figures for the 'Atlantic' palpably outstripped growth in the Mediterranean, at a mere 21.8 per cent, or Eastern Europe at 28.3 per cent. For west-central Europe, however, reckoned by de Vries to have grown by 27.2 per cent overall, the figures raise worrying questions. Germany's population in 1500 is given as 12 million, rising to 16 million in 1600 (an increase of 33 per cent), but more recent estimates by Christian Pfister put the population in 1500 at no more than 9–10 million, though in 1600 at 16–17 million, giving a rise over the century of 60 per cent at worst and 88.8 per cent at best, the latter figure even higher than England's! The parting of the ways came in the seventeenth century, with much of Germany devastated by the Thirty Years War, while England's population continued on a brisk upward trajectory until 1650, more than doubling to 5.5 million from its 1500 level.

Although any increase in population must, in broad terms, have swelled the demand for goods and services, it is often argued that the performance of the economy was chiefly influenced by the balance of population between town and country, with the former the principal centres of manufacturing and consumption. Here the figures at first glance tell a sobering story, albeit one which casts the Mediterranean in a more benign light. Rates of urbanization throughout Europe— never high to begin with—remained low, and often static, throughout the sixteenth century. In Switzerland, the urban quotient declined from 6.8 per cent to 5.5 per cent (a 20 per cent fall), even though its total population is supposed to have increased by 50 per cent. The highest rates of urbanization were in Italy (static at just over 22 per cent), Flanders (likewise more or less constant between 28 and 29.3 per cent in the period), and the northern Netherlands, whose urban ratio rose, on one calculation, from 29.5 per cent to 34.7 per cent (an increase of 17.6 per cent), but may in fact have risen more sharply (though perhaps only after 1580), since by 1650 42 per cent of the population lived in towns of 2,500 inhabitants or over, with Holland alone (distorted by Amsterdam's exceptional growth) reaching 61 per cent. Parts of the eastern Netherlands, it should be noted in contrast, remained quite sparsely populated, let alone urbanized. England's experience in some ways mirrored that of Holland. Although the initial rate was much lower in 1500, at a mere 7.9 per cent, that had risen by 1600 to 10.8 per cent (up 36.7 per cent), and kept on rising thereafter, with London's unique expansion (40,000 inhabitants in 1500, 400,000 in 1650!) making a disproportionate impact.

But what do these figures tell us? The weak correlation between rates of urbanization and economic vitality in the sixteenth century, with only the Dutch Republic offering a seemingly straightforward connection, suggests that urbanization was scarcely a reliable guide *in the long run* to economic performance—not to mention the sixteenth-century phenomenon *par excellence* of the hypertrophic gateway/capital city, thronging with beggars and casual labourers, such as Seville, Lisbon, or Naples (with populations of 90,000, 100,000, and 281,000 respectively by the end of the sixteenth century), which were an economic drain on their hinterlands.

The point at issue can be illustrated if we look at Castile, where the number of towns with populations of 5,000 to 10,000 (not small by contemporary standards) shot up from thirty to nearly eighty by 1600. Yet the bulk of these new towns remained economically isolated, poorly integrated with the larger regional centres, none of which, barring Toledo, exceeded 15,000 in the whole of Old Castile or Andalusia. Or take the more *outré* example of Red Ruthenia (the region north of the Carpathians south-east of L'viv (Lvov/Lemberg) in present-day Ukraine, but formerly in Poland), where a veritable explosion of urban foundations occurred up to 1600, whose economic impact, however, was nugatory, not least because they had been established by the local nobility as administrative, rather than commercial, centres.

That prices were on the rise in the sixteenth century no one disputes (and as contemporaries themselves lamented), but how far this was the first age of rampant inflation in Europe is open to question. For one thing, there were substantial fluctuations between countries or regions, and between commodities. In general, the cost of foodstuffs, especially the staple of grain, rose more quickly than that of artisan goods. Taking 1500 as the base-line, cereal prices shot up six-and-a-half times in France, more or less quadrupled in England, the southern Netherlands, parts of Spain (Valencia and New Castile), and Poland, but rose only two-and-a-half times in Germany and the Austrian lands. It should be immediately obvious that these rates of increase correlate very poorly with the figures for population growth in the various countries of Europe. Historians have focused—quite understandably—on cereal prices, for bread is the staff of life, except for those parts of southern Europe where it was replaced by rice, but it is clear that the price of other comestibles rose much more slowly. Figures for Basel (a Swiss city after 1501) show, from the same basis, the index for beef rising to 262, wine and butter to 290 and 293 respectively, and (dried) herrings to 350 by 1600; only eggs matched grain (in this case spelt, the low-grade variety of wheat planted in much of south-west Germany) at 400 and 408 respectively. How reliable these figures are remains a matter for conjecture: was Basel exceptional in finding its cereal prices quadruple while in the rest of the German lands the index reached a mere 255?

Various explanations have been advanced to account for the sixteenth-century price rise. The most venerable, and least plausible, stresses the impact of bullion imports from the New World. Not only did bullion not begin to flow from the Americas in any quantity until late in the century, but its inflationary effects are not self-evident if the economy were growing. Even in Spain, where some inflationary pressure is undeniable, most silver was immediately re-exported to repay German and Genoese bankers: Spain suffered a shortage, not a surplus, of gold and silver. Such arguments may apply less to Portugal, however, which had imported vast quantities of gold from North Africa long before the influx of American silver, amounting perhaps to as much as 40,000 kg, the equivalent of 520,000 kg of silver. By contrast, the central European mining boom of the early part of the century was flooding the market with around 50,000 kg of silver per annum (possibly rather more), a figure not matched by the Americas until the 1560s. In certain instances—England in the 1540s and 1550s is the *locus classicus*—debasement of the coinage by the state contributed to inflation, but it needs to be remembered that the sixteenth century was an age in which the fineness of struck coin remained by and large intact, quite unlike the preceding century. Much greater weight should be accorded to credit, as opposed to currency, inflation, with the pioneering of new forms of funded public debt, or the establishment of joint-stock banks and bourses. A veritable explosion of credit expanded the money supply and accelerated income velocities, and hence conduced to inflation. Of course, population growth played its part, too, provided that we account for differential elasticities. In plain terms, that means that disposable income would, in the face of rising prices, be diverted from luxuries or utilities to essentials, primarily food, and especially grain, demand for which is held to have been relatively inelastic. This seems to be confirmed by the faster rise of cereal prices than other foodstuffs, or craft goods, but a note of caution must be sounded. Figures compiled from a range of German towns in the last quarter of the century reveal that the daily wage of a mason's or carpenter's apprentice would buy 8.9 kg of rye, 6.8 kg of peas, but only 3 kg of beef, 2.4 kg of pork, and a mere 0.95 kg of butter. The argument for a switch back to cereals—or pulses—seems incontrovertible. From the perspective of modern nutritional theory, which regards a balanced diet as consisting of 12 per cent proteins, 27 per cent fats, and 61 per cent carbohydrates, cereals and pulses score very highly, since they are the only foodstuffs, apart from sugar and rice, to have a significant carbohydrate content, the main source of energy and heat. But fats contribute here, too, with butter, cheese, dripping, or bacon all providing useful nourishment. Proteins, essential for the development of body tissue, were by contrast only obtainable in any quantity from meat, eggs, and fish. Some dietary substitution, therefore, may have been possible between carbohydrates and fats, or between carbohydrates and proteins—and historians are often surprised at the amount of meat in early modern diets. In southern Italy no such return to wheat-growing occurred, though in Lombardy the cultivation of maize was observable from mid-century, but it only gathered pace after 1600. In comparison, manufactured or craft goods everywhere broadly doubled in price, except for the Austrian lands, where they went up a mere 10 per cent, and England, where they recorded a 50 per cent increase.

Throughout Europe in the sixteenth century wages failed to keep pace with prices. The figures available for Northern Europe show the wages index rising by 50 per cent at best, in the case of France no more than 10 per cent, while in Austria they dipped below the 1500 base-line by 10 per cent. Only in the southern Netherlands did the index rise to 300, more than for craft goods, but still less than that for cereals. In real terms, therefore, the wage-worker faced progressive immiseration as the century wore on. For Basel (to complement the data given above) the index of daily wages rose from 100 in 1500 to 168 in 1600, but measured against the food price index the purchasing power of wages had already declined from 100 to 47 by mid-century, and remained in that trough thereafter. Why wages should have lagged behind prices cannot be explained by the economic laws of supply and demand alone. In many towns magistrates intervened to set a cap on wage-rates, not least because they could count on the tacit approval of those master craftsmen who employed wage-labour. Similarly, even where wages began to catch up with prices, as in Antwerp after mid-century, the estates of Brabant quickly intervened to demand that they be limited by statute. At the same time, it is clear that wages continued to be paid at least partly in kind, and for rural labourers and hired hands their employment often entailed free board and lodging in the farmer's household. That helped to shield the poor and landless from the worst effect of price inflation of foodstuffs. Nevertheless, the numbers of those described in municipal records as propertyless or destitute was certainly growing.

Eastern Europe

The lands of Eastern Europe have frequently been regarded as the victims of economic retardation in the early modern period, in comparison with Western Europe. This view rests largely upon an assessment of intensified cereal production, and tends to ignore the thriving cattle-trade and the boom in mining precious and base metals. Mining is in any case held to have been dominated by out-siders, producing little benefit for the local economy. The emergence during the sixteenth century in Eastern Europe, or more precisely the lands flanking the Baltic east of the River Elbe—Mecklenburg, Pomerania, Brandenburg, Poland, Prussia, and Lithuania—of special-ized cereal agriculture on large commercial estates (latifundia) under the control of the nobility has customarily been taken as evidence for the colonial dependence of Eastern Europe on the markets of the west and as the explanation for the rise of an intensified seigneurial regime, under which the peasantry was degraded to the status of personal or bodily serfdom, forced to perform often unpaid labour-services, and latterly driven off its farms by expropriation. This view is misleading. Grain exports from east Elbia did indeed rise substantially in the course of the century. Statistics for the port of Gdańsk (Danzig), the principal outlet for Polish grain (as well as from Volhynia and Ruthenia), show exports of rye, the grain of everyday bread, in the late fifteenth century at a mere 2,300 łast (around 4,600 tonnes):[1] from 1490 onwards the figures rise gradually, from 10,000 łast in 1500 to 14,000 łast in 1530. Although there were periodic dips, not least during the years after the death of the last Jagiełłon king in 1572, which unleashed an international struggle for control of the Polish crown, exports thereafter regularly exceeded 20,000 łast, and in the 1590s 30,000 łast, though the figures after 1600 were of a different order altogether, averaging between 70,000 and 90,000 łast. Total exports to the west were, of course, higher, since grain was also shipped from Szczecin (Stettin), Elbląg (Elbing), Königsberg, Tallinn (Reval), and Riga. Toll registers of shipping through the Sound record around 50,000 łast of grain in 1550, dipping in the 1570s, but recovering to their former level by 1600. These latter figures include hard grains other than rye, chiefly wheat, which may have made up as much as a third of rye exports in the seventeenth century.

What drove the intensified cultivation of cereals, however, was not overseas, but local or regional, demand. Total Polish grain production in the 1560s amounted to 600,000 tonnes (after deducting the tithe and retained seedcorn), of which a good two-thirds, 415,000 tonnes, was consumed domestically. Of the remaining third, 60 per cent was offered on the open market in Poland itself, and only 40 per cent, 74,000 tonnes, was exported, around 12 per cent of total production. This low figure need occasion no surprise. Poland's population density was higher than often supposed: in 1580 it amounted to 21.3 persons per square kilometre, a figure not matched by England until 1650. Gdańsk itself was a major consumer, its population growing from 26,000 in 1500 to over 40,000 after mid-century (with a further

---

[1] The łast was a measure of a ship's capacity, not of weight. Its weight, therefore, varied according to the commodity carried. In the case of rye, it approximated to two metric tonnes (other grains were less bulky).

spurt to 70,000 in the seventeenth century).[2] But even what was exported often went to markets in the Baltic region. Especially in Mecklenburg and Pomerania, rye was sent to the Baltic ports and to the fast-growing city of Hamburg. Where soft grains, such as oats or barley, were grown, they supplied a different market. Barley, above all, fed the burgeoning brewing industry in Lübeck, Hamburg, Rostock, and Gdańsk itself. That applied in turn to Bohemia, the one East European territory to be highly urbanized in this period and hence with a large internal market for agricultural produce, where the famous breweries in Plzen (Pilsen) and České Budějovice (Budweis) none the less created a stronger demand for barley than for hard grains.

If we view the trade from the other end of the telescope, it rapidly becomes apparent that the northern Netherlands were not nearly as dependent upon Baltic grain as once thought. Older estimates of 25 per cent of the annual Dutch grain requirement coming from the Baltic have been scaled back to between 13 and 14 per cent, but even that proportion now seems too high, not least since grain was imported from western Germany down the Rivers Elbe, Weser, Rhine, and Maas, as well as from England (especially soft grains) and northern France. More tellingly, one recent calculation extrapolates that, if one last of grain could feed ten people per annum, Baltic exports in the second half of the century would have fed up to 600,000 mouths— at a time when the Dutch population did not approach that total! The answer is that a sizeable amount of Baltic grain was re-exported, with perhaps only one-quarter being consumed in Amsterdam. Much went to Portugal and Spain (even during the Dutch Revolt!), some to England, and latterly to Italy, where in the space of ten years from 1592 the number of ships (not all grain-carrying, of course) arriving at Livorno, the newly founded free-port of the Grand Duchy of Tuscany, went up from 200 to 2,500. Moreover, Dutch merchants were speculators in their home market, with Amsterdam contractors advancing money to Gdańsk merchants for long-term deliveries, so that they could hoard grain until times of famine drove prices up. Far from the east Elbian grain trade displaying the classical symptoms of

[2] These figures, taken from Edmund Cieślak and Czesław Biernat, *History of Gdańsk* (Gdańsk, 1995), 103, slightly modify those given in Jan de Vries, *European Urbanization 1500–1800* (London, 1984), 272.

colonial dependence, the terms of trade with the west remained favourable, with the cost of grain exports exceeding the cost of manu-factured imports, such as textiles.

That point is underscored if we turn to trade in other agrarian products, notably cattle and wine. Areas of Poland unsuitable for grain-growing, such as parts of Mazovia, and Podlasia, were signifi-cant exporters of cattle, amounting to between 20,000 and 40,000 head before mid-century. But with the Polish annexation of the Ukraine in 1569, exports shot up to 60,000 head and a peak of 80,000 head in 1584, to a point where Polish cattle were threatening other East European exporters. These cattle reached markets in all parts of western Germany, though exports seem to have tailed off after 1600. By far and away the main exporter to the west, however, was Hungary, with an estimated 100,000 head being sent abroad by 1500, amount-ing to between 50 and 60 per cent of all Hungarian exports by value. The full impact of the Hungarian cattle-trade was only felt from the 1560s onwards, when a new and heavier breed of white-grey steppe cattle, weighing up to 500 kg, began to displace the smaller peasant cattle (of around 200 kg) in international markets, though the latter were still traded regionally. Hungarian exports went not only to Austria and Upper Germany but also to Venice, and if one adds cattle reared in Transylvania (in present-day Romania) total annual exports were regularly topping 150,000 head by the 1570s and may have reached 200,000 head by 1600, a trade largely in the hands of the nobility and gentry.

Parts of Scandinavia, too, became major players in the inter-national cattle trade to the west. Although exports from Denmark and Scania (southern Sweden) made up a modest 20,000 head around 1500, a century later that total had reached 50,000 to 60,000 head; these were store cattle, not lean steers, shipped in the spring to the lush pasturelands of the Weser and Elbe marshes for further fattening, and then driven south for sale in the metropolises of Upper Germany. Around 1570, Ian Blanchard has calculated, as many as a million beasts were handled at international marts, whose value, estimated at the equivalent of 150,000 kg of silver, outstripped that of Baltic grain three times over.

Hungary was also a major producer of wine. In the western districts around Sopron (Ödenburg) more than 40 per cent of the harvest went for export, though total exports for the whole of Hungary amounted to no more than one-tenth of annual production. Aside from primary products such as furs and wax, which had been exported throughout the Middle Ages, other commodities from eastern Europe now began to find ready markets in the west: Livonian flax and hemp shipped through Riga and Tallinn, for instance, at a time when many areas of western Europe were already seeing an expansion of linen manufacturing in the sixteenth century; or timber, especially planks of straight-growing oak trees from forests in Lithuania and southern Poland, which were used for picture panels.

Yet the most substantial economic investment in early modern Eastern Europe was channelled into the mining industry, and it yielded spectacular returns. Silver was the main prize, with deposits in northern Bohemia, Slovakia, Carinthia, and Tirol. Hitherto, silver had been found principally in lead ores, but with the technological breakthrough of liquation, which supplanted cupellation after the mid-fifteenth century, silver could be extracted from argentiferous raw copper through the admixture of lead. As a result, a secondary market developed both in lead (from Slovakia and Poland, though most came from much further afield) and copper itself, whose refining and alloying with zinc to make brass supplied a demand for household goods and armaments which flourished even after the silver reserves became exhausted. It has been pointed out that precious metals were far less important to the European economy than iron. That is true, but Poland, Bohemia, and especially Slovakia also had iron ore deposits, while in eastern Austria a cluster of iron foundries, at Steyr on the Enns in the duchy of Upper Austria, and at Judenburg, Leoben, and Bruck on the Mur in Styria, which produced a range of specialized craft goods such as scythes, had already achieved international renown in the fourteenth century, though the peak of production was not reached until 1550. Other metals were found in smaller quantities: gold in Lower Silesia and Hungary; tin, zinc, and cobalt in the Erzgebirge, the mountain range straddling the border between Saxony and Bohemia. Austria, moreover, was a major source of rock salt, mined in a belt stretching from north Tirol eastwards to Styria—in Hall, Schwaz, Reichenhall, Hallein, and Aussee—which was exported to the cities of Upper Germany. Slovakia and Little Poland also had salt-mines, producing essentially for regional demand in Silesia, Bohemia, and Hungary.

The mining industry of east–central Europe was opened up chiefly by investment from the trading and finance companies of the Upper German cities, drawing upon the expertise of local pioneers. The most famous of these was Johann Thurzo, a Carpathian German from Levoča (Leutschau) in the Zips[3] who as a Kraków councillor had established the first large copper foundry in Poland near Kraków, deploying the technology of liquation. In 1494 Thurzo entered into partnership with Jakob Fugger of Augsburg, and together they poured money into Slovakian copper and silver mining at Banská Bistřica (Neusohl) in a venture called the 'Common Hungarian Company' (Der gemeine ungarische Handel). Up to 1526 the Fuggers may have been making yearly profits three times their investment from total sales of around 40,000 tonnes of argentiferous copper, much helped by generous customs and transit dues exemptions from the Hungarian crown. After the Fuggers had bought out Thurzo's heirs, they continued the enterprise single-handed, marketing a total of 60,000 tonnes of copper and nearly 120,000 kg of silver up to 1596.

The Bohemian silver-mining boom around Jáchymov (Joachimsthal) likewise began as a local initiative on the part of the noble family von Schlick (Šlik), later stimulated by investment from the Fuggers and other Augsburg houses such as the Welsers and Höchstetters. Until the late 1520s production rose steadily, in line with other mining regions, but, taken together with the Erzgebirge to the north, output then shot up dramatically in the 1530s to a peak of around 48,000 kg, representing between 40 and 50 per cent of central European production, though a steep decline thereafter levelled out to bring it back in line with other areas up to 1570.

In Tirol, a somewhat similar story unfolded. The silver mines in Schwaz, and the lead glance (galena) deposits south of the Brenner in Vipiteno (Sterzing) had been controlled at the outset by a welter of petty-capitalist stakeholders, but in the recession around 1500 had passed into the hands of a clutch of north Tirolean entrepreneurs. Within a decade, however, Augsburg merchant houses—the Höchstetters, Baumgartners, and Pimmels, all trailing behind the Fuggers—had penetrated Tirolean mining and by the 1520s had gained complete ascendancy, driving the native companies out of business. The one local firm to survive, the Stöckl, did so largely

---

[3] The Zips (Hungarian: Spiš) was the long-settled German colony in northern Slovakia on the Polish border, formerly in the kingdom of Hungary.

because it threw in its lot with the Fuggers. Schwaz's output shot up to an annual total of around 6,800 kg in 1522, and 12,000 kg the following year, the highest in Europe, though it soon to be eclipsed by northern Bohemia and the Erzgebirge. What marked out Tirolean mining was the very high proportion of silver retrieved in relation to argentiferous copper, at around 80:20. In comparison, Slovakia had achieved only 50:50 at its height, and Thuringia 60:40. In the course of the sixteenth century the percentages were everywhere reversed (except in Tirol), but new fortunes could be made in copper (or tin). German investment—Upper German 'high finance' (in Wolfgang von Stromer's phrase)—had by the 1520s succeeded in replacing the previously separate trading networks of central European silver production by an integrated international system of production and distribution in the hands of a few major oligopolies.

The boom in east–central European mining, however, was not to last. The reasons were both structural and conjunctural. The output of argentiferous copper declined rapidly in the 1540s, from around 45,000 to 30,000 kg per annum, held steady until the 1560s, but then slumped further to 20,000 kg at the end of that decade. Already in 1546 Anton Fugger had quit Slovakian mining, though the firm continued in business and sought to diversify, not very successfully, into iron-mining (it faced stiff competition from Styria). At the same time, the German merchant houses which had traded precious and base metals (and other commodities) through Antwerp in return for spices, in close commercial alliance with the Portuguese, were hit hard when the Portuguese crown withdrew its spice monopoly from Antwerp in 1549 and transferred it to Lisbon, at the very moment when rising production costs in east–central European mining were beginning to make its silver uncompetitive in the face of imports from the Americas.

That did not spell the sudden end of silver-mining in Europe. For a time, a new technology, amalgamation, whereby non-plumberifous ores were treated with mercury to extract the silver, allowed the range of ores which could be profitably worked to expand. But it was only a reprieve. By the 1570s, cheap silver from Peru began to flood the market, and although the price of mercury declined, the death-knell of European silver-mining had finally been sounded. Those entrepreneurs who were fleet of foot switched to other metals; some Italian investors turned to copper and iron, but in the case of the Fuggers (and other late-comers from Augsburg such as the Haug and Manlich companies) they preferred to play the copper market rather than engage in direct production, which passed in many cases to state-run enterprises.

It would thus be easy to concur with the older Marxist verdict (echoed by Wallerstein) which viewed the commercial capitalism of Augsburg's and Nuremberg's merchant houses as responsible for the economic ravaging of Eastern Europe, and hence for the social and economic backwardness of these regions in the early modern period, cut off from the outside world and forced to communicate through intermediaries. But this judgement is too sweeping and too facile. By the sixteenth century there is every sign that Eastern Europe was stamped by trade between the different countries and regions of the east as much as it was by exports to the west. One telling example: the customs registers of Bratislava (Preßburg), the Slovakian capital, in 1542 showed foreign textiles making up 70 per cent of all imports—but they came from Bohemia, Moravia, and Silesia, not from the west. That applies by the same token to linen and hemp manufacturing in Poland and Silesia, whose cloths found their way eastwards to Lithuania, the Ukraine, and Russia. And all this before we recall the regionally driven demand for Baltic grain.

Accordingly, another culprit must be found—the nobility, whose aversion to improvement and investment, coupled with a lifestyle of representation and luxury, precluded it from engaging in the economy in a 'rational bourgeois' (i.e. capitalist accumulative) manner. It is certainly the case that the nobility not only controlled the commercial cereal agriculture of the Baltic, but also manufacturing and mining in Silesia and Bohemia, as well as the Hungarian cattle- and wine-trade. Perhaps that is why, by extension, they preferred to manage their estates, mines, and manufactories 'feudally', that is, by recourse to serfdom and labour-services, rather than by resorting to capitalist leases, higher rents, and free-market wage-labour.

This argument is convincing only if formulated in entirely different terms, and if the areas of commercialized agriculture in east Elbia are distinguished from other sectors of the east European economy. It used to be thought that the grain-producing latifundia were obliged to introduce servile dependence, in a region where the peasantry as colonists had originally been free, in order to secure an adequate work-force. But this view is quite untenable. For the rise of intensified feudal lordship (known in German as *Gutsherrschaft*) preceded, in some cases by as much as two centuries, the emergence of labour-intensive cereal agriculture on large domains (the system known as *Gutswirtschaft*). *Gutsherrschaft* had its origins in the aftermath of the fourteenth-century plague and agrarian crisis, when grain prices slumped; it cannot, therefore, have had any connection with the need for a pool of labour in the face of overseas cereal demand. Rather, feudal lords in a region of already sparse population, where many farms had been deserted, had a unique opportunity to consolidate their scattered estates by fusing rights of landlordship and feudal jurisdiction in one hand. What is vital to understand is that this intensified seigneurialism in the fifteenth century was intended to underpin the *tenurial* dependence of the peasantry, that is, its obligation to remain on the lords' farms; personal hereditary serfdom, the imposition of labour-services, the expropriation of peasant farms (*Bauernlegen*), and the compulsion of peasants' children to work for fixed terms on the lord's demesne (*Gesindezwangdienst*) were essentially phenomena of the *seventeenth* century (and then only patchily), when overseas demand for grain was indeed at its peak, and when the local labour force had been depleted by warfare (the ravages of the Thirty Years War and the Northern War of 1655 to 1660 between Sweden and Poland).

That the feudal nobility was able to practise such coercion (*Gutsherrschaft*) to a unique extent in east Elbia derived from the structure of social and political power, as it had developed under weak monarchs and princes from the fourteenth century onwards, compounded by the disruptions of warfare and civil strife, notably the Teutonic Order's struggle to maintain its territorial integrity in the face of aggression by the Polish crown. As a result, the nobility acquired an unusual degree of influence over the crown or territorial ruler—the Polish monarchy as prisoner of its noble Estates in what amounted to an aristocratic republic being latterly the most famous example— with such towns or bourgeois that did exist relegated to the sidelines and unable to offer a credible counterweight.

Why, in contrast, the feudal lords should have taken up cereal agriculture on such a scale can be explained by natural endowment and opportunity costs. The lighter sandy soils of the Baltic littoral were uniquely suitable for grain-growing; at the same time, it is unclear what alternative forms of profitable investment might have offered themselves. The sheer size of the latifundia and the continued availability of uncultivated land—even in 1500 between 30 and 40 per cent of land in Brandenburg was described as 'waste'—also encouraged cereal agriculture, since profits could be made without huge expenditure on machinery or an increase in crop yields. Yet we are still left with the puzzle of why lords resorted to direct exploitation (*Gutswirtschaft*), rather than leasing out farms to tenants at commercial rates, or by rack-renting. This is a question which exercised the great Polish historian, Jan Rutkowski. His answer focused on the nature of seigneurial power. It was easier to make a profit by reducing the peasants' standard of living (by consigning them to servitude) than by seeking a greater income-stream through cash rents (which they might well have found it difficult to pay), while resorting to hired wage-labour would only have made landlords uncompetitive in international markets. Hence exports could be profitable even with lower grain yields than in the west. In other words, the seigneurial regime and the resources available to it favoured 'inefficient' agriculture and discouraged 'improvement'. But it also seems likely that, where as much as three-quarters of the harvest (on noble estates) was marketed, the most 'efficient' and indeed lucrative way to organize production was by direct labour: the parallels with the later plantation economy of the New World spring to mind.

Yet there were areas east of the Elbe where *Gutsherrschaft* did not lead inexorably to a domanial economy (*Gutswirtschaft*), Silesia and Upper Lusatia being two immediate examples. Many of the peasants there were personally free and enjoyed good tenure, in what was a region of partible inheritance where rural by-employment and specialized crops were commonplace. Silesia was famed for its linen industry, with dyestuffs such as madder grown around Wrocław, while Upper Lusatia was an area of wool-production. In these circumstances, *Gutswirtschaft* was unlikely to develop, yet in the second half of the sixteenth century intensified seigneurial jurisdiction (*Gutsherrschaft*) was on the advance, as nobles used their concerted rights of lordship to batten onto existing economic activity by promoting crafts and textile production. Instead of expropriating tenants, they released demesne and common land for new settlement by cottagers, and lured linen manufacturing away from the towns to their country estates, where it was integrated into the system of feudal rents. Rather than seeking to control production, lords used their seigneurial power of extra-economic coercion (serfdom) to enforce monopsony (that is, to require their subjects to buy only the domain's produce) and to capitalize upon their banal rights, such as the monopoly on brewing. That can also be observed in the Austrian lands, where feudal lords used their jurisdictional rights to promote their own markets and to deflect trade from the chartered urban markets, which gave rise to repeated protests by towns in the Austrian duchies and in Styria in the early sixteenth century.

This pattern was echoed in neighbouring Bohemia. Here the rural economy revolved around animal husbandry, pisciculture, and brewing, none of which particularly lent themselves to a production regime based on servile labour. Where labour-services rather than wage-work were deployed, they were usually confined to a fixed yearly quota, rather than compulsory weekly *corvées*. The feudal lords were more concerned to use extra-economic coercion to enlist paid compulsory hired labour or to enforce domain monopolies. Nevertheless, intensified seigneurialism in the broader sense of concerted jurisdictional rights can be traced back to the fifteenth century in the wake of the collapse of the Hussite Revolution, when power in the localities devolved upon the nobility, whether Hussite or Catholic, in the system of administrative districts known as landfrids, while after 1500 the first signs of hereditary subjection, restriction on movement, and even compulsory labour by serfs' children can be observed—well before the battle of the White Mountain in 1620, the traditional watershed of Bohemian social development. In Hungary, too, serfdom was used to underpin the nobles' banalities and control of distribution, rather than as the instrument of a domanial economy.

The issue of 'backwardness' in the economy of Eastern Europe has been tied too closely to the revival of serfdom, the dominance of the nobility, and the character of production. None of these three factors in itself contains any inherent explanatory capacity—though bundled together they may. Rather, issues of investment and credit, and the institutional framework of the economy, deserve more attention than they have hitherto received.

The Mediterranean lands

The stigma of 'backwardness' so often applied to the economy of Eastern Europe in the early modern period has also been attached to the once-thriving Mediterranean—Italy, Iberia, and southern France. This verdict is no more plausible for the south than it is for the east, though in Wallerstein's typology the Mediterranean became a semi-periphery, rather than a colonial dependency, of the Atlantic core-economies. Most parts of the Mediterranean—both northern and southern Italy, southern Spain and Catalonia, and the French Midi—not only maintained their medieval legacy of urbanization; their larger cities continued to grow in the sixteenth century (albeit some hypertrophically), with the result that 17 per cent of the population of Italy and Iberia lived in towns of 5,000 or more inhabitants, compared with a mere 8 per cent north of the Alps in 1600. The Mezzogiorno, for instance, often superficially regarded as a 'backward' region of Italy, had forty towns with populations of 10,000 or more in the sixteenth century. This does at least suggest a sustained consumer demand for goods and services—and, above all, for food, with a corresponding impact on the agriculture of the cities' hinterlands. Urban elites invested heavily in the surrounding countryside, often acting as agronomic improvers, for instance, the Venetian patricians who began to buy up estates on the *terraferma* after 1500. Much of the cities' grain requirement, none the less, could only be covered by imports, both regional (from Apulia and Sicily in the case of Italy) and overseas, especially from the eastern Mediterranean—Egypt, Greece, and Bulgaria.

Cereal crop yields varied considerably. In Castile yields of 1:8, and in the Romagna of at least 1:7, have been posited for wheat, but elsewhere the seed/yield ratio was much lower, or else declined appreciably over time. Cereal yields in Castile may have fallen to a mere 1:4 by 1600, though the reasons remain controversial. Over against older views that the *tasa*, the government-imposed price ceiling, made grain-cultivation unattractive and that the transhumance of large flocks owned by the Mesta, the sheep-farmers' guild, caused soil erosion, it now appears that tax increases, especially of the sales tax, the *alcabala*, which rose two-and-a-half times between 1560 and 1590 (and by the same again to 1620), coupled with the sale of communal lands—the *baldíos*—on which the peasants relied for pasture and manure, by urban elites eager to recoup their own tax assessments, made arable agriculture barely profitable. In the Romagna, where yields in the 1590s sank to no more than 1:5, no such obstacles presented themselves; rather, the decline presumably occurred as a consequence of bringing less fertile land under the plough to feed a swelling population. One sign of the renewed emphasis on cereal cultivation was the retreat of viticulture, attested for the Languedoc as for many other parts of Europe. The fall in output must not, however, be equated with a crisis for those peasants reliant upon a cash crop, if what was at stake was the abandonment of low-lying vineyards on poorly drained soil, which rarely produced wines of quality. A retreat to the better slopes and sites, therefore, may well have been an altogether healthy contraction. In several parts of France the 'strong-farmers'—those possessed of sufficient assets to accept the risks of commercial production—in the villages actually added to the size of their holdings in order to take advantage of the market for specialized crops, be they maize or silk in the south-west or viticulture in the Languedoc and Aquitaine.

But for the bulk of the peasantry the strategy for survival remained diversification, not specialization. Common to many parts of the Mediterranean was the practice known as intercropping or particulture (often called by its Italian name *coltura mista* or *promiscua*), whereby vines, olives, and cereals were grown intermingled, in order to spread risk and ensure subsistence rather than to respond to changing market opportunities. The evidence from Sicily after 1450, however, suggests that given certain preconditions—access to overseas markets, good rights of tenure, and foodstuffs readily available for purchase—peasants successfully engaged in a form of *seasonal* diversification, quite distinct from subsistence agriculture, whereby flax was grown and processed in high summer and winter, silk between May and August, wine in the spring and autumn, and latterly olive oil (in the early spring and mid-winter), which created a vibrant economy. True specialization, by contrast, can be observed—again under specific conditions, in this case the use of irrigation—in the plains of central Lombardy, where high rates of productivity were achieved on large farms leased out on market-driven cash rents to rural entrepreneurs deploying seasonal wage labour; here the fallow was abolished and cereal production integrated with grazing on water meadows.

Throughout the Mediterranean, though, peasants commonly farmed their holdings on sharecropping contracts (in French *métayage*, in Italian *mezzadria*), whereby the owner of the land extended credit to the cultivator, in the form of seed, tools, capital, or the land itself, in return for a share of the harvest (usually one-half). Sharecropping has been seen as inefficient and backward: it gave no encouragement to investment or improvement by lord or tenant. Wallerstein regards it, indeed, as the characteristic agrarian regime of the semi-periphery, for it allowed the urban elite to acquire rural estates as a pathway to social status and as a protection against famine, without engaging directly in agriculture. For southern and western France recourse to *métayage* has been identified as the reason why its agriculture remained relatively backward in comparison with England, even if its social impact might be beneficial (inasmuch as it enabled younger peasants without capital to gain a foothold in farming). Faced with the overwhelmingly negative verdict on sharecropping by most commentators, some qualifications are necessary. It is not clear, in the first place, that sharecropping *in itself* inhibited agricultural advance. The large landowners, almost always nobles, who dominated the rural economy of Andalusia began by investing in commercially oriented farming; only towards the end of the century did they drift into sharecropping and become *rentiers*, as the income from state bonds outweighed the riskier returns of direct farming. In central Italy and southern France, moreover, lords used sharecropping to promote labour-intensive crops (vines, fruit trees, mulberry trees for silk) which yielded higher profits than cereals; the question therefore is, what did they do with those profits? Sharecropping, as Robert DuPlessis has argued, may well have begun by directing capital to the countryside and only subsequently became the cause of stultifying involution. There is no doubt that sharecropping areas were characterized by peasants with little or no land of their own: the attraction for the lords was that such peasants received for their labour a 'wage' costed at less than the market rate, so that labour-markets were rudimentary and any incentive on the part of the peasants to embrace commercialization or specialization was severely dampened. Yet sharecropping flourished where the natural endowment encouraged landowners and investors for their part to switch in and out of commercial crops and where a sizeable local market (in the towns) existed. In that sense, sharecropping may have been functionally efficient while structurally inefficient, and it was certainly not incompatible with proto-industrialization in later centuries, as in the case of the Lombard silk-industry.

Pastoral agriculture faced no such constraints, and during much of the sixteenth century wool-production and exports in both Italy and Spain were booming. Sales of sheep and wool in the kingdom of Naples, organized by the pastoralists' guild, the Dogana (the equivalent of the Mesta in Castile), increased fourfold after 1550. Earlier, in Castile exports of wool to the staple at Bruges, which had amounted to a mere 13,000 sacks per annum in the 1510s, reached 70,000 sacks by 1550, though they halved in the century to come. The decline in wool exports was closely linked to disruptions in overseas markets (the Dutch Revolt), a switch to lesser quality wool in preference to Merino fleeces, and the increasing self-sufficiency of the New World. But there was another side to this coin. Bruges's loss was Florence's gain, as new flows of Castilian wool reached the Tuscan capital.

In any case, most Castilian wool was destined for domestic textile producers. In an access of mercantilism, the Spanish crown gave the native industry first option on one-third of the wool crop, while banning foreign imports, and also imposed strict quality controls on the finished cloths. Two regions of production in Castile had emerged by 1500: the one north of Madrid, centred on Segovia and Ávila, producing bulk textiles of medium quality, the other south and east of the capital, around Cuenca, Toledo, Ciudad Real, and stretching down to Murcia, Córdoba, and Jaén, weaving high-quality broadcloths from Merino wool. Over time, the smaller textile centres were brought into dependence on the merchant capital of the larger cities, partly in response to the growing institutional clout of the craft guilds (as in Toledo), which may have encouraged the industry to relocate to the countryside. To a degree, Castilian manufacturing was also the inadvertent beneficiary of others' misfortunes, since the textile industry of France and the Low Countries was disrupted by the Wars of Religion and the Dutch Revolt. The sixteenth century has indeed been hailed as the golden age of Castilian textiles (with Segovia making a successful turn to quality cloths), but once the 'artificial protection' (in J. K. J. Thompson's phrase) of foreign wars had been removed, and the crown had reversed its policy by throwing domestic markets open to foreign competition, the Spanish woollen industry went into rapid decline (though some merchants were shrewd enough to change horses by becoming importers of foreign cloth and exporters of wool).

All the same, the Castilian textile industry never matched that of France for size. Here, too, much of the production was organized by the putting-out system, with the countryside subsisting in symbiosis with the mercantile cities. Yet for symbiosis read dependence, for the perils of putting out were manifest whenever a downturn in the economic cycle beckoned, as merchants drew in their horns to concentrate on urban manufacturing, leaving the countryside to its own devices. In Italy, putting out seems to have been less common, though there were sharp regional variations. Competition might be tolerated, as in the case of Venice, whose cities on the *terraferma* became major woollen producers in the sixteenth century, with the Republic content to safeguard its own luxury cloths and to give the mainland free rein. Or it might be suppressed, as with Florence, which jealously asserted its manufacturing monopoly at the expense of the economy of the cities of its *contado*, and in the long run at the price of its own economic vitality.

Broadly speaking, most areas of the Mediterranean flourished during the sixteenth century, though there were structural shifts within particular sectors of the economy—the trend of woollen, linen, and silk manufacturing to move from the cities to the smaller towns and countryside, whether by putting out or not—and difficulties in specific regions—the decline of the Basque iron industry, for instance. Commerce with the Mediterranean's traditional trading partners in North Africa and the Levant continued unabated, whatever befell exports to Northern Europe. The Portuguese crown's decision to transfer its spice monopoly from Antwerp to Lisbon in mid-century could not conceal that it had already been undermined by Venetian and Genoese merchants. Over the span of the century spice imports from the east increased fourfold, with the two Italian cities claiming the lion's share as Portuguese imports stagnated. The resilience of these twin mainstays of medieval Mediterranean commerce, despite periodic downturns, is quite remarkable. Venice remained not only the principal entrepôt for the carrying trade to the east but a major centre of manufacturing and processing as well—in glass, soap, sugar, wax, and ship-building—underpinned by government monopoly.

Their joint-stock banks continued to prosper; Genoa, indeed, was able to capitalize on the ruin of the Antwerp and Lyon exchanges, seizing the initiative by having the Besançon fairs, set up in the 1530s, moved to Piacenza in Lombardy in 1579, where they remained under Genoese mercantile control well into the next century.

That the Mediterranean economy (in common with other parts of Europe) was coming under strain as the century drew to a close cannot be denied, but where the blame should be laid is open to dispute. Frequently, the burden of state taxation and the public debt is adduced as the chief cause of economic sclerosis, but this argument needs to be treated with caution. In France, royal taxation to meet the debt rose sharply, but did it keep pace with inflation? Between 1547 and 1574 royal income may have risen by 33 per cent, but the *livre tournois*, the official money of account, lost 50 per cent of its value. Similarly, in Spain the burden of the sales tax, the *alcabala*, was no higher in real terms in 1600 than it had been in 1500, even if it had shot up dramatically in the latter decades of the century, while the real totals of all crown tax revenues increased only 10 per cent over the century. For the mass of the population, those who worked the land, the story was rather different. Much land in southern France, in Spain, and in southern Italy fell into the hands of the Church and the aristocracy, or was acquired by bourgeois landowners, who were either exempt from taxes, or else contrived to pass the burden on to their peasants. The issue, therefore, was not so much the burden of taxation as on whom it fell. Landowners' incomes, moreover, were predominantly channelled towards conspicuous consumption, or into titles and offices, and, above all, into state bonds, rarely into agricultural investment. Meanwhile, as wages fell, prices rose, and famine and dearth became more frequent, the ranks of the landless, jobless, and impoverished swelled—in human terms a misery, in economic terms a drag, for underconsumption (as Adam Smith recognized) was the ultimate barrier to economic growth.

North-western Europe

The 'Atlantic economy' is a catch-all concept which embraces regions as diverse as western Germany, northern France, and the southern

Low Countries, on the one hand, and the (northern) Netherlands and England, on the other, not to mention those areas which remained partially or resolutely underdeveloped (the Scandinavian periphery, or Scotland and Ireland). Within the Atlantic region, the economy of north-western continental Europe in the sixteenth century has often been contrasted unfavourably with the dynamic growth which occurred in England and the Dutch United Provinces. In a recent polemic, Peter Musgrave has contended that it was the least successful medieval economies on the Atlantic periphery (England and the northern Netherlands) which first 'modernized' rather than the already mature ones (echoing Wallerstein's view that 'backwardness' was a precondition of growth), because they were more unstable (and hence contained the potential for rapid transformation).

For the agrarian economy this argument would offer a funda-mental challenge to the assumptions underlying the recent debate on agricultural development in late medieval and early modern Northern Europe, initiated by Robert Brenner. He originally contrasted the advance towards agrarian capitalism in England with the subsistence agriculture of the traditional peasant-proprietorial regime in France, which led inexorably to involution. More recently, he has extended his argument to the maritime provinces of the Dutch Republic. The 'Brenner debate', which has been couched largely in terms of social structure (class relations), property rights, and legal or institutional frameworks, cannot be pursued in any detail here; in essence, it turns on whether one is prepared to allow that peasant proprietors may, given the incentive, act as agrarian entrepreneurs. In much of north-ern France—an area of champaign agriculture with large arable farms—the same concentration of land in the hands of the 'strong-farmers' with a concomitant pauperization of the smaller peasants as wage-dependent labourers that occurred in England can be observed. For the region around Paris, however, under demographic pressure towards mid-century the share of the crop reaching market declined, as peasants abandoned other commercial crops or pastoralism to grow more grain for their own households, and divided up their holdings to provide land for their numerous children. But where impartible inheritance prevailed, as in much of north-western Germany, that option was not available; the cereal farms remained intact, extruding surplus family labour, and continued to produce for the market, while in the coastal regions peasants turned increasingly to profitable pastoralism. In terms of productivity, the differential between 'peasant' and proto-capitalist agriculture was not foreordained. Crop yields in Scandinavia, given the climate and poor soil, were predictably poor, 1:4 at most, in western Germany slightly better at 1:5—still lower than the supposedly proto-capitalist England or the Dutch provinces at 1:7 or more—yet yields in Flanders (including those districts now in France) perhaps reached 1:9 or 1:10. These figures prompt several comments. English yields began to decline around 1630, precisely at the time when capitalist agriculture is supposed to have been in full swing, while the Dutch figures are in a sense irrelevant, since the economy became a net importer of grain after 1500. The yields for the southern Low Countries and parts of the Rhineland had already been boosted by the deployment of catch-crops, such as nitrogenous legumes, and by more extensive use of manure from stock-rearing, foreshadowing the 'up-and-down' husbandry of early modern England, whose agricultural growth is held to have depended upon the complementary integration of arable and pasture. Yet the agricultural regime of the southern Low Countries rarely made the transition to agrarian capitalism on the English model. This suggests that the issues which Robert Brenner originally raised have still to be fully resolved.

The 'Brenner debate', in any case, has until recently paid culpably little attention to the transformation which was already under way in the rural economy of much of north-western continental Europe in the fifteenth century, and which reached its peak in the sixteenth: the spread of rural textile manufacturing—linen, fustian (a linen-cotton blend), and wool—often promoted by urban merchants through the putting-out system. In western Germany, the linen and fustian industries of the south had chiefly been located in the larger cities, but by 1500 production had long since spread to the countryside, as entrepreneurs sought to circumvent guild restrictions and civic regulation; there they latched on to an already flourishing cottage industry, harnessing it to manufacturing for regional and international markets. But the role of the merchant companies in the middling cities, such as Ulm, Konstanz, Nördlingen, or Memmingen, was progressively undermined not only by the emergence of cartels in the leading metropolises—Augsburg succeeded in throttling the mercantile initiative of smaller centres within a 70 km radius—but also by competition from northern Germany, in Westphalia and in Saxony, where Chemnitz became the headquarters of a linen industry embracing town and country in the mid-1500s. In response, some Nuremberg textile firms began to shift their attentions north-eastwards to Silesia and Lusatia, where they helped to build up new centres of manufacturing. Yet rural linen production was less exposed to the penetration of urban capital than fustian-weaving, for supplies of cotton had to be imported from the Mediterranean to the cooler and wetter lands north of the Alps by merchants with the necessary organizational skills and capital resources. It would be unwise, none the less, to view the commercialization of the west German rural economy too readily as the prelude to capitalist transformation, whatever role putting out may have played, since in an age of population growth the peasants of south-western Germany, as a region of largely partible inheritance, regarded by-employment and outwork as indispensable safety-valves which allowed a primarily subsistence economy to survive.

Linen and fustian were cheap cloths; with fine woollens, not to mention luxury textiles such as silk or satin and their role in the manufacture of ribbons, brocades, carpets, or tapestries, the situation was rather different. As we have already noted in Spain, the sixteenth century was marked by the spread of both cheap and high-quality textiles, destined for markets at home or abroad. That was true also of northern France, where cheap woollens were produced in Picardy, Normandy, and Champagne, alongside luxury wares such as the silks of Tours or Lyon, or the tapestries of Paris and Orléans, which were sold throughout the Mediterranean, North Africa, and the Levant. In Flanders, by contrast, the success of the three leading cities, Ghent, Bruges, and Ypres, in reserving to their own urban weavers the right to manufacture high-quality woollens had encouraged a switch from wool- to linen-weaving in the countryside, which could be carried out independently of urban capital as a cottage industry. After a slump in the 1400s, production revived, as Flanders and Brabant turned to lighter cloths. By 1565 sales of linen cloths at Eeklo, the main Flemish outlet, had risen tenfold from the early part of the century, and Bruges emerged as the centre of a new fustian industry. Where wool-weaving continued, it was organized as small commodity production (the so-called *Kaufsystem*), in which the initiative rested largely with the producers, rather than depending on putting out.

The ability of the southern Netherlands to adapt rapidly to new fashions in textiles can be attributed to a thoroughly commercialized economy, in which the cities' jurisdictional rights over their hinterlands enabled them to control a labour-market rendered especially flexible by the fact that peasant holdings were usually too small to sustain subsistence agriculture. This adaptability was evident in the sixteenth century above all in the rise of the so-called 'new draperies'. These did not depend on any new technology, but on the straightforward imitation of the high-quality 'old draperies', but using cheaper wools, simplifying the finishing process to leave the cloths mostly unfulled and unsheared, and by admixing wool with other fabrics, such as linen ('linsey-woolsey') or cotton. These new cloths, known as says or serges, revived the fortunes of the Flemish textile industry after 1500, nowhere more spectacularly than in Lille, where production of the new draperies soared tenfold from the 1530s to the 1550s; the manufacture of cheap cloths with a silk sheen, known as *changéants*, alone went up from around 2,000 pieces in the 1540s to 175,000 pieces in 1619. In parts of western Germany (and England), however, the new draperies had a different connotation. Here the cloths were not short-staple woollens, but either worsted (long-staple) cloths, or blends with a worsted warp and a woollen weft. Lighter than the traditional broadcloths, these textiles served a new quality market; they were produced by domestic industry, notably in the Black Forest, where dyers in the sheep-rearing region around Calw had by the turn of the century begun to organize pastoralists and country weavers in a system of vertical integration, leading to the foundation of the famous Calw Worsted Company in 1650.

The rural economy of north-western continental Europe in the sixteenth century was therefore deeply implicated in the secondary sector (manufacturing), and in a web of town–country relations, so that distinct economic landscapes began to emerge. Underpinning these developments lay the cultivation of industrial crops ancillary to textiles, principally dyestuffs. The region around Erfurt in Thuringia (western Saxony) became famed for its woad, whose production involved sizeable capital investment on account of the time-lag between planting, harvesting, crushing, and maturing; it supplied the woollen industries of Hesse and Lusatia, the latter also benefiting from the availability of the red dye madder grown in the district west of Wrocław. The only sector of the commercialized rural economy in north-western Europe to suffer a decisive retreat was viticulture, but here the downturn should be seen as a structural transformation, not as a crisis, for the abandonment of less-favoured sites and concentration on production from better slopes and soils went hand-in-hand with the rise of brewing. What had hitherto been a beverage produced for immediate consumption to satisfy local demand became, through the addition of yet another industrial crop, namely hops, a commodity which improved with storage and could be exported to regional markets. The fortunes of the Franconian brewing industry (Kulmbach, Bamberg, Nuremberg) or the Lower Saxon (Braunschweig, Einbeck, Goslar), alongside that of the Hanseatic coastal cities already mentioned, were all laid in the sixteenth century.

Against the background of a continental Atlantic European economy whose hallmark was rural diversification into manufacturing and processing, it is not immediately evident that England or the northern Netherlands should be regarded as special cases. The agricultural history of the northern Low Countries has customarily been written as a narrative of weak seigneurial control, vestigial serfdom (if it had ever existed), extensive peasant ownership of the land, held under impartible inheritance, and a brisk land-market. The preconditions for the emergence of a 'strong-farmer' society, rather than the expropriation or disappearance of a traditional peasantry, seemed in place. Under the pressure of population growth and strong urban demand, however, the core Dutch provinces (Holland, Zeeland, Friesland, and Utrecht) followed a different path, in which *both* configurations existed side by side, with only the eastern provinces (Drenthe, Overijssel, and Gelderland) continuing to display many of the features of a feudal regime. Some peasants in the maritime provinces devoted themselves full-time to producing for the market on large capital-intensive farms—principally cattle and dairy products—whilst the surplus rural population, rather than emigrating, turned to new employments in the countryside—road- and canal-building, brick-making, peat-cutting, ironmongery, or petty dealing.

There has been endless argument (which need not detain us here) whether these specialist farmers still counted as peasants, or whether the rural non-agriculturalists constituted a proto-proletariat. Of immediate importance is why peasants with good property rights should, uniquely in the northern Netherlands, it seems, have pursued economic strategies which were potentially capitalist. Here ecology played a decisive role. The sinking of the peat-bogs in the later Middle Ages led first to their drying out and then to their flooding: the result was agricultural degradation. Although the rural population remained for the most part owners of their land, they had thus in effect been deprived of their means of subsistence (though not of their means of production), so that strategies which elsewhere reinforced subsistence (division of holdings, by-employments) had to be rejected in favour of riskier specialization, in which peasants were driven by the market to invest and accumulate, for they had no viable alternative to fall back on, or else to quit agriculture altogether. One test of this argument is to consider what happened in the agricultural depression which hit the northern Netherlands after 1660, when the capitalist dynamic remained in place, even in the face of collapsing prices and rent arrears. Then, failing tenants were simply expelled by their lords in favour of incomers who had the resources to survive; there was no division of farms or any attempt to restore the peasants as subsistence farmers, unlike the southern Low Countries. The key issue in the transformation of Dutch agriculture from the sixteenth century onwards was, therefore, as Jan de Vries has concluded, not whether peasants owned the land as such and hence what their motivation or rationality might have been, but rather, in his phrase, the 'quality of assets' at their disposal—in the context or an urbanized society with advanced market integration, good communications, extensive credit facilities, and a burgeoning export trade.

In salient respects the growth of the English rural economy after 1500 was a mirror-image of developments in the northern Netherlands. A traditional peasantry holding land on customary tenure was supposedly expropriated, as landlords extended their property rights, buttressed by the courts and parliamentary sanction, to convert copyhold to leasehold, letting out land on competitive leases at market-determined rents, and jacking up entry-fines. Between 1450 and 1700, it has been reckoned, the gentry came to own half the land in England, though perhaps one-quarter to one-third of farmland was in the hands of yeomen. By the same token, land once farmed in open fields was enclosed or 'put in severalty' (that is, assigned to individual farmers), and often turned over from arable to pasture in order to raise sheep to supply a woollen-textile industry responding to buoyant domestic demand in an age of surging population growth. This was the high road to agrarian capitalism which distinguished early modern England from its continental neighbours and which formed the starting-point of Robert Brenner's comparative analysis of agricultural transformation.

This assessment of the English rural economy (Scotland and Ireland stand apart) has come under attack from many directions in recent years. Most historians, even if they share the basic assumptions, accept that the changes were altogether slower and patchier than hitherto believed; the erosion of copyholders' rights, for instance, is barely detectable before 1650. Likewise, the extent and pace of enclosure or engrossment (the combining of farms into larger units) have been questioned. A fairly typical Midland county such as Leicestershire had only 10 per cent of its farmland enclosed before 1600, though in the course of the next century the figure reached 50 per cent. In general, it was the Midland counties, supplying the vast London market, which witnessed the bulk of enclosures. Nevertheless, there had already been substantial enclosure before 1500, at a time when the economy was languishing, which elicited protests from politicians and churchmen alike (most famously Sir Thomas More, whose tract *Utopia* complained of sheep that had 'become so great devourers, and so wild, that they eat up and swallow down the very men themselves'), but the enclosures were mostly confined to the north-western counties where pastoralism had always predominated. If Parliament did intervene over enclosures, it was usually to protect the customary tenants, not the enclosing landlords. In any case, land held under freehold—perhaps one-quarter of all farmland—could not be enclosed at all.

It is over the legal rights of tenants, however, that recent arguments have begun to retouch the familiar picture. The rise of copyhold tenure did not erode peasant proprietory rights; on the contrary, by 1600 it had all but been enshrined in law as the equivalent of fee simple (absolute possession). As a result, those who had formerly been customary tenants—manorial villeins—became, in R. C. Allen's verdict, peasant proprietors, and it was from their ranks that a class of 'strong-farmers' emerged just as much as from among the leaseholders. No parliamentary legislation of the sixteenth century promoted leasehold at the expense of copyhold; for historians such as Richard Smith these copyholding yeomen remained therefore indubitably peasants. That landlords and yeomen both embraced capitalist agriculture was the outcome of a particular political and socio-legal evolution in England, whereby a precociously unified realm had through the courts come to recognize individual property rights at the expense of private seigneurial jurisdiction, and where feudal appropriation was not replaced (as in France and elsewhere) by onerous state taxation. The emergence, moreover, of a national market, driven by London and sustained by a network of regional fairs established in the late Middle Ages, encouraged agricultural investment and specialization.

One consequence was that the English wool industry underwent a significant reorientation. Exports of wool as a raw material were abandoned in favour of domestic cloth production, which was abetted by a ready pool of largely unregulated rural wage-labour, no longer tied to a subsistence agricultural regime. The geographical heartland of the woollen industry, previously located in the south-west (especially in the Cotswolds), began to switch to East Anglia, Lincolnshire, and Yorkshire, convenient for exports to the continent. Before 1550 only woollen broadcloths and kerseys (ribbed narrow cloths) had been exported, but after mid-century a range of textiles, including new draperies, was sent overseas. These exports were facilitated by crown charters to the merchant companies involved: in 1555 to the Muscovy Company, marketing woollens in Russia and as far afield as Persia; in 1579 the Eastland Company, trading in the Baltic from its base at Elbląg; and in 1581 to the Levant Company, which sold Suffolk broadcloths and later East Anglian new draperies in the eastern Mediterranean.

Yet the engine of English growth remained essentially the domestic market, whereas the Dutch economy was more geared to exports, and was to suffer setbacks when international markets were disrupted in the seventeenth century. Despite somewhat different trajectories, their rural economies and the textile industry built thereon shared institutional features which set them apart to some degree from the rest of north-western Europe. That was much less true, however, of other branches of manufacturing and of the mining industry. The sixteenth century was scarcely an age of technological innovation in Europe (apart, perhaps, from the rapid diffusion of the printing-press using moveable type), but those extractive and processing industries which consumed copious quantities of fuel were able to draw upon the first supplies of mineral coal, rather than relying upon charcoal or timber, to fire furnaces and forges. In Germany the first seams of bituminous coal, as opposed to the more widely available but poorer quality brown coal (lignite), which was obtained by open-cast mining, were being worked before 1500 in those regions already engaged in mining and metallurgy, such as the Ruhr, the Aachen basin, or southern Saxony, but they made up only a fraction of the total fuel requirement. Further west, by contrast, the Liège coalfields were producing 48,000 tonnes per annum in 1545 (when records begin) but 90,000 tonnes by 1562, which fed the blast-furnaces of the Ardennes iron industry. Here the number of furnaces and forges shot up from ninety in 1500 to 220 in 1565. But after the Dutch Revolt the reimposition of Catholicism on the southern Low Countries led many craftsmen to emigrate and plunged the industry into a decline from which it did not recover until the early years of the seventeenth century. The English coal industry was spared such disruptions. The fields in Northumberland and Durham were located in the vicinity of clusters of population and thriving local industries dependent on fuel—brewing, glass-making, and salt-boiling. But coal was also exported in large quantities by the coastal trade, not least to southern England, where it was used both for industrial power and as domestic fuel for heating: exports of around 45,000 tonnes in 1510 had risen to 500,000 tonnes by the middle of the next century.

With iron, the balance of advantage tilted back towards the continent. Although production in England increased sharply from around 5,000 tonnes in the 1550s to 24,000 tonnes a century later, these figures are a fraction of the total output in Northern and Central Europe of around 70,000 tonnes per annum in 1500, and double that amount by 1600, with two major centres of production in Germany, in the Süderland east of Cologne, and in the Upper Palatinate north of Nuremberg. The Süderland had achieved fame even before 1500 for wire-drawing, tools, and cutlery; so specialized was production, using blast-furnaces and hydraulic power, in the principal centres— Solingen, Altena, Iserlohn, and Lüdenscheid—that they abandoned iron-ore refining and instead imported pig-iron from the Siegerland further south. In the Upper Palatinate a veritable industrial landscape around Amberg and Sulzbach grew up, in which 20 per cent of the population were employed in the iron industry. Its production fed the advanced metallurgical trades of Nuremberg, where the techniques of tin-plating and wire-drawing were being deployed in the fifteenth century. The city became the centre of a range of specialized metalwares, ranging from blades, knives, needles, and compasses to armour and weaponry. Initially, the Upper Palatinate produced more iron than the whole of France (whose 460 forges in 1542 were mostly of recent foundation), but as the century wore on the number of forges declined, until by 1609 production had sunk to a mere 9,500 tonnes from 182 forges, with two-thirds of those closing down over the next decade. But if the Upper Palatinate was declining— producing only one-third of German iron in 1600—other regions continued to flourish: iron-making spread outwards from the Süderland to the eastern stretches of the Sauerland into northern Hesse and southern Westphalia, while new centres sprang up in Saxony and the Harz mountains in the later sixteenth century, not to mention the extensive open-cast iron-ore mining of the Saar valley.

Saxony and Thuringia were also important centres of silver production, attracting investors ranging from local petty-capitalist stakeholders (Martin Luther's father, for instance) to international merchant houses such as the Fuggers. The latter even shipped copper-ore overland from their Slovakian mines to be refined alongside the production of the copper-shale districts around Mansfeld in their smelteries at Hohenkirchen in the Thuringian forest. Even when silver production fell away towards mid-century, the copper which remained was used to manufacture household goods, or else exported to the burgeoning metal centres of the Rhineland around Aachen, where it was processed with local deposits of zinc and calamine to make brass, the linch-pin of the growing armaments industry of the sixteenth century. The decline of copper-mining in any case spelt no disaster for Saxony for its place was taken by tin-mining. From an annual yield of a mere 10 tonnes in 1470 output in southern Saxony had reached 200 tonnes by 1600. The only mineral essential to the refining of silver from copper-ore in which Saxony was deficient was lead, which had to be imported from the Harz, or from the Eifel and Vosges mountains in the west, or indeed from overseas (English lead from the north-east, Derbyshire, or Devon).

Emphasis on the fundamentals of production in analysing economic growth in early modern Europe has recently come under attack from those who draw attention to the role of consumption, especially in those economies which are held to have been in the vanguard of capitalist development. That the rise of a broadly based consumer society was indeed a hallmark of both England and the northern Netherlands is not in question, and it undoubtedly contributed over time to their economic exceptionalism. But whether such a society emerged before the mid-seventeenth century is a moot point. In the sixteenth century conspicuous consumption of material goods—or, for that matter, cultural goods—originally regarded as luxuries and confined to the wealthy remained the preserve of those cities and their elites which had been the centres of Renaissance patronage (Venice, Milan, or Florence in Italy), or which were emerging as the capitals of monarchies and principalities whose rulers understood the ideological import of public display and courtly culture (Madrid, Naples, Lisbon, Brussels, Vienna), as well as of the cities which served as their entrepôts or outlets (Seville, Antwerp). While the quotidian economy of the southern Low Countries was disrupted by the impact of warfare and religious persecution, their luxury trades survived relatively unscathed: embroidery and diamond-cutting in Antwerp; majolica, jewellery, furniture, tapestries, glassware, mirrors in Brussels and Antwerp. Over time, indeed, those tastes, albeit with less ostentation, came to be shared by the burgher culture of the northern Netherlands, where the ceramics of Delft or the tapestries and carpets of Leiden adorn the canvases of Dutch genre artists, alongside tableware and glass containing, latterly, the enticements of sugar, tobacco, coffee, and fine wines. In certain instances, luxury trades can be regarded as a compensation for the decline in demand for mass consumer goods. As Augsburg's fustian industry gradually lost ground after 1600, the city carved out for itself a new reputation in the decorative and applied arts, its workshops bustling with gold- and silversmiths, engravers, printers, cabinetmakers, ivory-carvers, makers of musical and scientific instruments, and, not least, armourers.

Conclusion

The differing economic trajectories which manifested themselves in Atlantic Europe should encourage us, in conclusion, to reflect more broadly on the underlying patterns of economic change in the early modern period, especially on the alleged rise of capitalism and the place of the so-called 'long sixteenth century' in the development of the European economy. The emergence of agricultural capitalism, in the first instance, raises several contentious issues. Was the commercialized export-driven agrarian economy of north-eastern Europe, based on latifundia under noble ownership (*Gutswirtschaft*), in any way comparable with the expansion of aristocratic landholding in England on farms which were leased out at market-determined rents to yeomen who employed landless wage-labour? Because of its role in the emergence of a capitalist world-economy, Wallerstein has argued for the essentially capitalist character of *Gutswirtschaft*. Others have pointed to the obvious similarities between the estates of east Elbia worked by serfs and the plantation economies of the New World worked by indentured slave labour. Yet the agrarian economy of east Elbia was not in any strict sense capitalist, since lords had few money costs of production and hence were barely sensitive to price or market indicators; in these circumstances a fall in prices would not necessarily lead to a cutback in production, for the availability of coerced labour might trigger an increase in output by way of compensation. It would be better to describe the agrarian regime in Eastern Europe as 'market-oriented feudalism' (in the words of Robert DuPlessis), a description which would fit equally well those nobles' domains which were geared towards rural crafts, industrial crops, or textiles, and where coercion was applied at the point of distribution rather than production.

In the case of England, recent historical writing, as we have seen, has suggested that the road to agrarian capitalism could be traversed by traditional peasants as readily as by leaseholding yeoman tenants. For the northern Netherlands the revisionism has been even more severe: farm enlargement (and the spread of commercial leases) represented only one of several pathways to agrarian capitalism, and where the latter did emerge, it did so at some geographical remove from the areas of merchant capitalism. For Holland itself, Peter Hoppenbrouwers has posited four separate configurations of agrarian capitalism, with only the last—a fully three-tiered system with landowners as the providers of land and capital, farmers as tenants (leaseholders), and hired labourers—corresponding to the English model. In any case, he adds, small peasant proprietorship was still widespread. This argument has been taken further by Bas van Bavel in a recent study of the Dutch river area in the south of the country, which displayed both the emergence of rural tenant-entrepreneurs and the survival of peasants with good property rights; yet the former acted on their own initiative, not at the prompting of merchants or noble landowners, or in response to the penetration of urban capital, while the latter in the face of population pressure and land shortage did not subdivide their holdings or revert to subsistence, and so failed to conform to Brenner's pattern of peasant involution. It will not do, therefore, to advance England and the northern Netherlands as straightforward pioneers of agrarian capitalism in contradistinction to the rest of Europe: the differences between *and within* them are too great to be accommodated in such a starkly bipartite model.

Similar caution should be exercised in assessing the role of putting out (*Verlag*) as a bridge between medieval merchant capitalism and modern industrial capitalism. Its prevalence throughout those parts of Europe—Spain, France, western Germany—which did not experience an early turn towards industralization, together with the increasing switch from the fifteenth century onwards to putting out in the countryside as the basis of rural textile manufacturing, thereby helping to underpin a peasant economy and society, should make us sceptical about its capacity *autonomously* to effect decisive economic transformation. Putting out rarely drew the capital-providers and entrepreneurs fully into the production process, and it is questionable whether the dispersion of production in the countryside, rather than its concentration in urban centres, conduced to institutional efficiency by lowering transition and transaction costs. In that sense, *Verlag* was indeed an *early* capitalist phenomenon, and as such contained no teleology of economic growth. That remains true even where putting out was deployed in genuine proto-industries: the metallurgical firms of Nuremberg, for instance, had established 'proto-factories' before 1500, but for centuries to come they remained just that: they did not evolve into industrial plant.

Even the occasional instances of vertical integration betokened no decisive shift. The worsted enterprise founded by Heinrich Cramer at Altenburg in the Siegerland in the late sixteenth century may have employed immigrant Dutch weavers using the latest yarn-spinning-wheels in one hundred weaving sheds, complete with fulling-mill and dyeing-plant, and drew its wool from the extensive sheep-farms in which Cramer had invested in the surrounding countryside, but it never became the prelude to the full-scale industrialization of the district. Likewise in Spain, one textile firm in Segovia employed more than a hundred workers in the 1570s, engaged in all stages of manufacturing, with recourse to rural spinners as outworkers, but by 1600 it had folded. A similar fate befell the building firm founded in the 1540s in Antwerp by Gilbert van Schoonbeke, which had its own brick-kilns, chalk-burning ovens, as well as dormitories for over a hundred peat-diggers, but with the completion of new fortifications round the city its *raison d'être* disappeared and the business was abandoned. Even the Fuggers, who had deployed vertical integration in their Slovakian copper-mines, withdrew, as we have noted, from manufacturing and distribution to concentrate upon playing the copper market.

On the other hand, the rise of joint-stock companies in the sixteenth century heralded modern methods of raising venture capital. Of course, the Italian *commenda* partnerships of the Middle Ages had foreshadowed joint-stock companies; but whereas in the former the risks were shared equally with all partners doing business on their own account, the latter comprised new partnerships called *rederijen*, in which many more investors, both large and small, could take shares as sleeping partners. These were first established in the northern Netherlands in the fifteenth century as a result of the need to raise capital for ship-building and commerce in a land still underdeveloped. By the later sixteenth century, such joint-stock companies had seized control of England's overseas trade, with the Muscovy Company regarded as the first true enterprise of this kind: they were the forerunners of the subsequent East India and West Indies Companies.

What marks out the economy of sixteenth-century Europe is indeed the explosion of credit and credit instruments. The rise of Antwerp as a centre of finance as well as commerce (until the disruptions of mid-century) is a story often told; less well-known is the emergence of Basel as the financial capital of the Swiss Confederation in this period, providing over half of all public credit and attracting investors from abroad, including south German princes and prelates. The key to this financial revolution was negotiability: strikingly, England had led the way with negotiable credit instruments as early as 1437. At the turn of the fifteenth century, the Hanseatic capital Lübeck recognized bearer bills, followed by Antwerp in 1507, and the entire Spanish Habsburg Netherlands by 1541. In that same year the Habsburgs legalized interest-payments on loans up to 12 per cent (brushing aside the canonical provisions on 'usury'), thereby removing a major obstacle to discounting negotiable bills. Promissory notes for short-term loans also became fully negotiable, as did government bonds (*rentes*), which created a huge credit market, especially with the foundation of the Antwerp Bourse in 1531. Though the city—and the southern Netherlands in general—fell victim to Habsburg intransigence in the Dutch Revolt, the financial instruments developed in the south were adopted lock, stock, and barrel in the north: Amsterdam supplanted Antwerp, with its Exchange Bank opening its doors in 1609. Of course, such a rapid expansion of credit created its own problems: the bubble burst in the 1560s with the first in a string of international bank crashes, as overstretched lenders to the Spanish and French crowns were left high and dry when the monarchs defaulted by converting debt into state bonds, leaving the financiers with effectively worthless paper. Even the Dutch government had difficulty in meeting interest-payments on its *rentes*, which hit small investors hard. Nevertheless, the search for the origins of Dutch exceptionalism, the path to mercantile greatness in the Golden Age of the Dutch economy between 1580 and 1700, should perhaps start with its institutional advantage in credit and finance, provided that we remember that its origins lay as much in the south (with negotiable bills) as in the north (with *rederij*).

The Dutch United Provinces were also the beneficiaries of what in modern parlance would be called technology transfer, as religious refugees fleeing Catholic persecution brought their skills and expertise with them. The Flemings who fled to Holland in the wake of the Dutch Revolt, for instance, helped revive the ailing Leiden textile industry. Such dispersion, of course, was not confined to the Low Countries—the flight of Calvinists from France and Italy to Geneva in mid-century springs to mind—and it was to reach its extraordinary climax in the expulsion of the Moriscos (who had already been forcibly dispersed throughout Castile in the wake of their rebellion from 1568 to 1570) early in the seventeenth century. Yet the main economic diaspora was from the southern provinces of the Habsburg Netherlands, with craftsmen, entrepreneurs, and financiers scattering far afield, not only to Holland but to England (and Scotland), and western Germany, where several new towns were specifically founded as refugee settlements to harness the skills of worsted weavers (Frankenthal), hosiers (Hanau), or cabinet-makers (Neuwied).

If England and the Dutch Republic are to be seen as exceptional, then the ability of both countries to ride out the economic difficulties which beset Europe from the 1560s onwards is testimony to that fact. These difficulties manifested themselves in what is loosely termed a Malthusian crisis, in which a swelling population could no longer adequately feed itself from the land under cultivation, and hence succumbed to famine and disease, exacerbated by a series of protracted harvest failures in the early 1570s, mid-1580s, and late 1590s. Rather than simply attributing the crisis to the inelasticities of an overstretched agrarian economy or peasant conservatism, historians have recently emphasized the role of climate change. From around 1560 much of Europe was seized by a 'little ice-age', which lasted until 1630. The period was characterized by a general fall in annual temperatures, a shortened growing season, and cold polar airstreams. This climate deterioration, however, was more pronounced inland than in coastal regions (thereby putting England and Holland at some advantage), and seems to have affected cooler Northern Europe, where the growing of bread-grains and vines as Mediterranean crops always ran the risk of harvest failure, more than the sunnier and warmer south. Those who have written of the 'long sixteenth century' up to 1650—Fernand Braudel and others—had the Mediterranean firmly in their sights; they argued that the epoch only drew to a close with the so-called 'seventeenth-century crisis'. But north of the Alps it is the decades after 1560 which mark the gradual end of the economic cycle which had begun in the 1470s.

Braudel also pointed to the sapping of entrepreneurial vitality in continental Europe as a cause of economic sclerosis in the later sixteenth century. Merchants and financiers, *parvenus* in a world of feudal-aristocratic values, aspired to noble titles and landed estates. A classic instance of this 'refeudalizing' tendency—Braudel dubbed it the 'treason of the bourgeoisie'—is supposed to have been the retreat of the Fuggers of Augsburg into landlordship, where by 1600 they had acquired estates worth two million florins, the same amount as they were to lose in the bankruptcy of the Spanish crown in 1607! That bourgeois desired to become seigneurs is not in doubt; but the argument misses the point. What mattered in the long run was whether institutional factors promoted investment and risk-taking. If the state—be it a monarchy, city-state, or republic—guaranteed property rights, protected market outlets, and eliminated corporate obstacles to trade, then the risks of investment were diminished. Yet in much of continental Europe rent-seeking opportunities by 1600 were beginning to outweigh the rewards of entrepreneurial investment—and in this regard England and the Dutch Republic were indeed the exception which proves the rule.

2

Politics and warfare

Mark Greengrass

On 7 May 1511, the Consejo Réal (Royal Council) of the Spanish monarchy met in Seville. Its assembled judges heard a royal secretary read out a petition addressed to 'my most powerful lady' Queen Joanna of Castile by Don Diego Colon, Admiral of the Indies. The dossier that accompanied the petition was a hefty one as befitted the bold privileges it pursued. In six articles, Diego (son of Christopher Columbus) laid claim to huge 'rights', a substantial percentage of the profits of the trade with the Indies, which his father said he had been granted in various 'capitulations' by the Castilian monarchy in return for his remarkable New World discoveries. The great explorer had found that it was easier to be shipwrecked in the sea of sixteenth-century politics than in the Atlantic. He had returned to Seville after his final voyage, encumbered by debts and determined to press his claims to a just reward for his efforts. He sent repeated letters to Queen Isabel (1474–1504) and King Ferdinand (1452–1516). 'It is a sure thing that I have served Their Majesties with as much diligence and love as I might have used to win the gates of Paradise and more. If I have failed in other matters it was beyond my knowledge and my strength', he pleaded in November 1504. He used family, relatives, and friends to press his case: his brother the *Adelantado*, his son Diego, the royal secretary Juan de Coloma, and a Florentine banker to whom he owed money, Amerigo Vespucci (1454–1512). The latter went to court at Segovia on Columbus's account in February 1505, carrying in his pocket his recently printed letter to a Medici prince, soon to be retitled 'The New World', that implied the 'New World' was his, Vespucci's, discovery. It was this book which influenced a map-maker in 1507, working for the duke of Lorraine far away in Northern Europe, to imprint the legend 'America' on his map and our consciousness thereafter: a monument to Florentine political shrewdness. Dissatisfied with endless delay, Columbus eventually went to court in person. This was despite terrible gout, which had led him to investigate whether he could not borrow the wheeled catafalque owned by the archbishop of Seville. But Columbus was shrewd enough to realize that it would do his cause no good to arrive at court in a hearse. Honour, reputation, standing was everything in his endeavour. So he made it by mule to Medina del Campo, and then to Valladolid, where he died on 20 May 1506, his case still pending. It was left to his son—and his heirs thereafter (the case being still actively pursued by the Columbus family in the eighteenth century)—to claim justice. In 1511, the judges viewed things differently. In their ruling, signed off on 11 June, they rejected the petition on the grounds that it infringed the inalienable sovereign rights of the Spanish monarchy. And this despite the fact that Don Diego had married a cousin of the king and been appointed 'Admiral of the Indies'— a power in the land and a significant figure at the Spanish court.

This petition takes us to the heart of the political process in sixteenth-century Europe. On the one hand, there were formal political structures—royal councils, senior judicial courts, thrones and chambers, laws and ordinances. But alongside these formal elements lay informal power networks; favour and influence, promises and rewards, individual and family honour, privilege and status. Both formal and informal political structures had their own rules of engagement. The one depended on historical precedents, juridical claims and the guardianship of the *res publica*. The other relied upon friendship and personal contacts. Politics in the sixteenth century lay at the intersection of these two structures since it was their interplay which made its political systems work.

Unified spaces

From the central Middle Ages onwards, Europe's polities were, in character and background, highly variegated. By the sixteenth century, they included republics with some claims to be maritime empires (Venice, Genoa), city states shorn of a hinterland (Geneva, Dubrovnik, Gdańsk) and an emerging provincial republic that, by 1600, had something of a statelike structure about it (the Dutch

Republic). There was an old empire that was in the process of acquiring the trappings of a dynastic state in its Habsburg heartlands (the Holy Roman Empire), alongside a new condominium that called itself a republic (*Rzeczpospolita*) which tried to avoid that route (Poland–Lithuania, merged in the Union of Lublin, 1569). Self-governing rural oligarchies (the Grey Leagues—*Grisons/Graubünden* which ruled the valleys on the southern flanks of the Swiss Alps towards Italy) coexisted alongside a loose confederation of often city-dominated republics (the Swiss Confederation). Numerous small principalities—more than we generally imagine, since the Italian peninsula, bits of the Pyrenees, northern Germany, and the Netherlands had political entities like this—governed themselves for most practical purposes, though often owing loose allegiances to bigger neighbours. Some of them were the decaying volcanic craters of what retrospectively we might regard as older, 'failed' states (Burgundy, Navarre). There was still plenty of free space in Europe's politics too, especially at its margins—places by and large exempt from a formal political dominion of any measurable character. Cossack bands of Poles and Muscovites dominated the steppe margins of Europe, the Gaelic lords of Ireland ruled beyond the English Pale, and the Uzkok pirates held sway off the Dalmatian coast in the Adriatic. Then there were the elective monarchies of the east and north (Bohemia, Hungary, Poland, Denmark, Sweden) and a unique elective monarchy governing the largest state in central Italy (the Papal States). Finally there were the states that we now remember most, and tend to make the pattern for the rest: the hereditary monarchies. Some of these depended on old foundations, even if their ruling dynasties were recent (the Valois on the French throne from 1328, the cadet branch of Valois-Angoulême from 1515; the Tudors on the English throne from 1485; the Habsburgs in Spain from 1516).

Nowhere could we find a 'nation state' in the sixteenth century. That is a conceptual framework of the nineteenth century, which historians of that period imposed upon these hereditary monarchies. They do not fit since they were essentially dynastic enterprises—more responsive to the vagaries of family fortune than the claims of national identity. Dynastic mishap had reconfigured the political map of the lower Rhineland in 1477 with the death of Charles the Rash in battle, the last male duke of Burgundy. It would do the same in the Spanish peninsula in 1580, when the young King Sebastian of

Portugal died aged 24, having refused to marry (apparently because he feared impotence). Dynastic opportunity would unite the English and Scottish thrones in 1603 to create, for the first time, a conjoint British monarchy. It was not merely political artfulness that brought Charles of Burgundy to unite the rulership of the Netherlands with the recently conjoined monarchies of Castile, Aragon, and Naples but the unexpected death of Don Juan, heir to the Castilian throne, back in 1497 (he died aged 19 of, so it was said, an excess of 'copula', i.e. sex), then that of his father Philip the Fair in 1506, and finally the demise of Ferdinand, king of Aragon, a decade later in 1516. This laid the basis for what would become the largest dynastic confederation that Europe would ever see: the Habsburg dynastic empire, a dominant super-power in sixteenth-century Europe. Even in western Europe, state boundaries were often uncertain, reflective of dynastic claims and counter-claims rather than culture, language, or institutions. The kingdom of France grew spectacularly by about a third in the century after the Hundred Years War, mainly on the basis of realizing canny dynastic alliances in Brittany, Burgundy, and elsewhere. In Eastern Europe frontiers were even more uncertain, especially after the partition of Hungary with the Turks in the wake of the battle of Mohács (1526).

What was the secret of a successful dynastic state? The Habsburgs knew it, if anyone did. 'No family has ever attained such greatness and power by means of kinship and matrimonial alliances as the House of Austria', wrote Giovanni Botero in his *Reason of State* (1589). Some speculated that Habsburg success was, in part, the result of Germanic inheritance customs which allowed inheritance in the female line. This was in contrast to the French royal inheritance custom, governed by the 'Salic law' (in reality an invention of later medieval lawyers to exclude the English claim to the French throne) which forbad it. But inheritance customs were always convenient in certain circumstances, inconvenient in others, there to be conformed to, not changed. Those same German inheritance customs encouraged partible inheritance which continued to subdivide the principalities of northern Germany. The important point is that a dynasty represented more than a family. It was a collectivity of inherited rights and titles that transcended individuals. Charles V and Francis I justified their military interventions in Milan, Naples, and the Low Countries by claims that went back, in some instances, to the thirteenth century.

Ancestral traditions lay at the heart of dynastic politics. In his famous speech condemning Martin Luther at the diet of Worms in 1521, Charles V began with an explicit allusion to 'my ancestors . . . most Christian emperors, archdukes of Austria and dukes of Burgundy' who had all defended the faith and 'handed on these holy catholic rites after their death by natural right of succession'. Dynastic rule was therefore inherently conservative—tiresomely so to the historians of the nineteenth-century nation state who often sought in vain for some kind of dynamic state-building rationality in the behaviour of its rulers. A legitimate ruler was one who did not merely have a claim to rule but also one that preserved the 'rights' and 'privileges' of his peoples—these being complementary and coterminous with those of the dynasty itself. So the politics of the sixteenth century was dominated not by state-building rationalities but by the dynastic facts of life: marriages, births, and deaths.

Of the three, marriage was the most susceptible to political arrangement. Dynastic alliances were, as Erasmus remarked in his treatise on the *Institution of a Christian Prince* 'called the greatest of human affairs' and 'generally considered as the unbreakable chains of general peace'. Princely promises of marriage, carefully deliberated upon in princely councils, underpinned military and diplomatic alliances. The archbishop of Capua wrote to Charles V: 'In time of war, the English made use of their princesses as they did of an owl, as a decoy for alluring smaller birds'. And Charles himself noted that 'the best way to hold your kingdom together is to make use of your children'. The main plank of the victorious settlement dictated by Charles to Francis I in 1526 was the wedding of the French king to the emperor's sister Eleanor. The famous treaty of Cateau-Cambrésis (1559) was sealed by no less than three proposed royal nuptials. But the terms of these treaties remained flexible. They recognized different levels of engagement in which a good deal could happen between a betrothal, a marriage, and its consummation, especially since the parties in question were often under the canonical age of majority (12 years). In general, it was accepted that the greater the degree of affiliation between one dynasty and another, the more binding the arrangement was likely to be. Princely marriages were political events: an occasion for dynasties to renew their sense of destiny and moments of political reconciliation. Catherine de Médicis invested so much in the latter that she spent months carefully negotiating the marriage of her daughter Marguerite ('Margot') to the emerging Protestant leader in France, Henri de Navarre. The eventual marriage in Paris in August 1572 was planned as a triumph of courtly and Neoplatonic love over the destructive forces of religious controversy, although, within ten days, it turned into the greatest political disaster of the century: the massacre of St Bartholomew (24 August 1572). In England, Elizabeth I's well-advertised reluctance to marry became the greatest bone of contention between herself, her councillors, and the Parliament. There was no doubt among contemporaries that dynastic marriage conveyed honour, status, wealth, and inheritance. It was a means to establish an overlordship without the necessity for annexation although (and this was Erasmus's main point) through over-complex intermarriage it also became a source of conflict by causing rival dynastic claims. In reality, the dynastic principle made the world go around in the sixteenth century.

Dynasties functioned as clans. They were at once corporatist and hierarchical. The elderly emperor Maximilian thought of himself, his daughter Marguerite of Austria, and his grandson and probable inheritor, Charles V, in the same breath, being 'one and the same, corresponding to the same desire and affection'. Later, Charles V would offer aid to his brother Ferdinand in 1526 'whom I love and esteem as an alter ego (*comme ung aultre moymesmes*)'. To Ferdinand, he counselled that Habsburg enemies would seek to 'disunite us, divide us the more easily in order to break our common power and bring down our house'. That fear was common to all dynasties although, in reality, their divisions generally came from within, and when they did so, they were highly destructive. Philip II's son Carlos was the first person to challenge his rule directly and, in the mid-1560s, sought to create his own party at court and send out feelers to the rebels in the Low Countries. The results led to Carlos's death in tragic circumstances. The scarcely concealed enmity between the last Valois king of France, Henri III and his younger brother, François-Hercules duke of Alençon, later duke of Anjou, was evident from 1576 until the latter's death in 1584. It helped to bring disaster upon one of the major dynasties of Europe. That fear was why all Europe's ruling dynasties evolved an informal hierarchy of gradations within the clan, stretching outwards to include its male and female, legitimate and illegitimate members, and reflected in the numerous dynastic histories of the period. For the most part, the junior branches of a clan accepted the need for allegiance to the head of the dynasty and their role in advancing its common destiny in return for a real protection of their personal interests.

Births were political events in dynastic states. Sex was the stuff of court politics. Wedding nights were public. Castilian law was not alone in requiring the presence of notaries at the royal bedside on the wedding night. Francis I and Pope Clement VII both watched the 14-year-old Henri II and Catherine de Médicis 'joust in bed' on their wedding night. Difficulties were rapidly reported, and sometimes a source of satire and humour. Brantôme claimed to have seen Francis II of France 'fail a number of times' in bed with Mary Stuart—the poor boy's testicles had not descended from his pelvis. Joyeuse and Epernon, *mignons* at the court of Francis's younger brother Henri III became widely presented in France as 'the princes of Sodom' to a homosexual king who had failed to produce an heir. Royal lyings-in were the subject of intense political speculation. 'In this country, the queen's lying-in is the foundation of everything' wrote the imperial ambassador Simon Renard from the Tudor court in 1536. Rituals left no doubt as to the magnitude of the occasion. Tapestries recalling the illustrious history of the dynasty lined the walls of the Tudor 'lying-in' chamber. The expectant mother wore robes of historical significance to the dynasty, and auspicious relics were deployed to assist in the outcome. This is readily understandable. Over half the Habsburg queens in the sixteenth century died in childbed. The wife of King John III of Portugal gave birth nine times, but only one child lived to the age of 20. Henry VIII's first two marriages resulted in fourteen recorded conceptions, but only two daughters survived. Dynastic states were dependent on the biological fact that, in the sixteenth century, it was not conception, but the difficulty of bringing a pregnancy to term that most constrained dynastic continuity.

The death of the head of a dynasty was a moment of extraordinary political transition. Funerals were occasions to express personal and family solidarities in conformity with inherited laws, traditions, and customs, elaborately prepared and recorded. At the same time, however, they were moments of rupture. Councillors of state found themselves out of favour. Pensions accorded by one prince were not transferable automatically to the next. In the French tradition, the master of the royal household solemnly broke his staff of office on the death of a monarch to indicate that his service, like that of all the court, was at an end. In France and England, the royal funeral traditions went to great pains to express the continuities, expressed in the phrase recorded as commonplace by the political philosopher Jean Bodin: 'The king never dies'. This was embodied in France by the construction of a lifelike effigy in wax to represent the dead king, which was placed on ceremonial display (*lit de parade*), offered meals at regular intervals, and reverenced as the king in name and fact until the completion of the royal funeral and accession of his successor. These effigies would, along with portraits, sculptures, trophies, and relics, in due course serve to educate the younger scions of the clan. Erasmus, whose treatise emphasized the importance of princely education, stressed the significance of such 'exempla' to the Romans. 'How thy father's nobility shines in thy face' (*Quantus in ore pater radiat*—the text came from Claudian) was the emblem for a medal commemorating the accession of Eric XIV, king of Sweden in 1560. Portraiture was a significant part of sixteenth-century political culture because it was a medium for these educative continuities, creating an absent presence which captured not merely a physical likeness but also the associated inner virtues. Across Europe, sixteenth-century dynasties constructed galleries where such painted portraits and other memorabilia could be displayed. The funerary counterpart was the mausoleum, such as the Lorenzo chapel for the Medici in Florence. The latter inspired the Valois monument at St Denis, commissioned by Catherine de Médicis. The elaborate Spanish Habsburg equivalent at the Escorial was designed by Juan de Herrera to include a cell for Philip II where he could come and commune with his ancestors, represented there by Leoni's statues.

Charles V's imperial abdication in 1555 was the most extraordinary political transition of the century. A 'political' death had no precedent and ceremony had to be invented for it. It began on 22 October in Brussels with the emperor's formal resignation as Grand Master of the Order of the Golden Fleece in favour of his son Philip. The assembled Knights of the Order were instructed by the emperor to renew their oaths of loyalty to Philip personally in his presence. Three days later, the abdication itself took place. The emperor sat on a dais in the great hall of the palace in Brussels, his son Philip to his right and his sister Mary of Hungary, regent in the Netherlands, to his left, before an assembled body of over a thousand dignitaries. When he made his abdication speech, he leant on the Prince of Orange's shoulder, had difficulty reading his notes with his spectacles, and wept. At the end, he spoke to his son in Spanish who knelt before him. The emperor solemnly invested him with his authority, urging him to defend the laws and true faith, and govern his people in justice and peace. The following day, Charles signed the formal act of abdication in private whilst Philip received the oaths of obedience from the delegates of the estates general of the Low Countries and, in turn, swore to maintain their laws and privileges. Continuities had been preserved in a formal act; and, informally, the loyalty of the political elites had been transferred from one generation to the next.

Political elites

It is considerably easier to present sixteenth-century Europe's dynasties than its political elites. From the central Middle Ages onwards Europe's polities had become multifaceted in their character, background and institutional context. This is evident from their central institutions. These consisted of councils and courts—formal and informal power structures working together coextensively and collaboratively for the most part. Government by council was an established reality even in monarchies with the most absolutist of pretensions. In the elective monarchies of Northern, Eastern, and Central Europe, the royal council enshrined the aristocracy's continued participation in power, sometimes embodying the claims of the estates or parliaments to represent the realm as a whole. In the emerging United Provinces of the Netherlands the twelve members of its Council of State, historically a descendant from its distant Burgundian namesake, became an executive committee of the States-General. Elsewhere, especially if a monarchy was composed of different, quasi-autonomous territories, the royal council was divided into separate territorial entities. The Spanish Habsburgs had different councils for Castile, Aragon, Portugal, and the Low Countries, as well as their possessions in Italy and the Indies. The Tudors had separate, subordinate councils for the north of England and for Wales. Everywhere, the increasing number of councillors led to the establishment of smaller inner, 'privy' councils with exensive political responsibilities, specializing in the 'great affairs' of state, for which confidentiality was essential. Membership of such councils was often predetermined by rank and status. In France, the royal family and princes of the blood regarded themselves as members of the royal council by right. In some Catholic countries, prelates managed to acquire the same status. In Poland, the chancellor, treasurer, commander of the army, and the bishops were members of the council *ex officio*. To attempt to exclude such individuals with a claim to a presence at the table was to risk the charge of being autocratic, or the prisoner of favourites, prey to one voice of counsel to the exclusion of others. To include everyone meant having an unwieldy governing elite. 'Good counsel' was a central political problem for elective and dynastic princes in the sixteenth century.

One way of approaching the problem was to allow everyday administrative business to become institutionally routinized and pass it on to 'professionals' to carry it out. The administration of justice at its highest level, originally handled by the king in his council, was increasingly delegated to separate councils or sections of the royal council. In the Councils of Castile and Aragon, there were already judicial and governmental branches by 1500. In France, the *conseil d'état privé* (handling judicial business that was evoked to the royal council) and the *conseil d'état et des finances* (to deal with royal financial affairs) gradually emerged as separate entities in the second half of the sixteenth century. In the German empire and most of its princely territories, the general court council of the king or prince (Hofrat) became judicial courts (Hofgerichte) in the course of the sixteenth century, often modelled on the Reichskammergericht of the empire, founded in 1495. Similar organizations, often called 'chambers' (which reflected their origins in princely domain administration) supervised the increasingly complex financial affairs of states. In the German empire, the Hofkammer of the Habsburgs, founded in 1527, was the model followed by other territorial states in due course such as Bavaria. In Naples, the Camera della Sommaria acted as both an auditing and tax-raising body. Arcane, but politically important, questions of coinage tended increasingly to be dealt with by separate cameral administrations of one sort or another. These trends were by no means universal. The senate of Milan remained a judicial and governing body and the English Privy Council, too, continued to have no specialized components. But everywhere the impression is that the raising of revenue, the handling of indirect taxes, the management of debt, domain administration, coinage, the payment of servants, the nomination of clergy, the handling of diplomatic traffic were all becoming more complex and more difficult to handle. It is not surprising that princely councils adapted their membership to include those with professional competence in their ranks. The degree to which they did so, however, varied in proportion to the specialization that had been adopted and the political culture they related to. So, by the sixteenth century, almost all the members of the council of Castile were university graduates. In France, by contrast, legally trained 'masters of requests' prepared dossiers for consideration by a council of state which was dominated by crown notables from a variety of backgrounds, legal and otherwise.

Everywhere, there was a tendency towards collective decision-making wherever possible in order to prevent the damaging political consequences of division and the fostering of dangerous faction-fighting. In Spain, this resulted in the greater elaboration of government by council, a model that was followed by the papacy where the College of Cardinals was subdivided by Pope Sixtus V in 1588 into fifteen 'congregations' (i.e. councils), each delegated an area of responsibility for the Papal States or the Universal Church. On the other hand, the growing complexity of government business and proliferation of councils made the establishment of some kind of co-ordinator a necessity, especially when the prince, for personal or institutional reasons, could not perform that function himself. Such individuals functioned at an uneasy interstice between the formal and informal power structures, dependent on personal favour and their position at court for their power, exercising their authority without any commensurate office. In Rome, the role became more formalized than anywhere else in the course of the sixteenth century through the evolution of the post of the cardinal-nephew (*cardinal nipote*), a figure with extensive, albeit defined, powers. In other instances, such co-ordination grew out of the traditional military and judicial offices of the crown. In France, the first of the great 'favourites' at the Valois court was the Constable Anne de Montmorency, rising to high favour with Francis I after 1529. At the court of the Austrian Habsburgs, the equivalent figure was the high steward (Obersthofmeister) or court marshal (Obersthofmareschall). Elsewhere, it was sometimes provided by the chancellor (or the equivalent 'keeper' of the Great Seal of State), titular head of the judiciary but often responsible for government and administration too. In England, the chancellorships of Cardinal Wolsey and Thomas More demonstrated the power of the position, although they had no direct successors in the sixteenth century. In Denmark, the king's chancellor (Kansler) had something of a similar role at various stages in the sixteenth century. The favourites of Henri III, the last Valois king of France, owed their influence to nothing more than the eye of a king who wanted individuals who were free of the aristocratic factionalism that was tearing his kingdom apart, and who would act as models of a 'reformed' aristocracy serving the king's majesty with absolute fidelity.

The most remarkable change in the co-ordination of government at the centre in the sixteenth century was, however, the rise of the secretary of state. Originally the notaries who attended the prince, the secretaries of state had begun to play a significant political role in the Italian states towards the end of the fifteenth century. By 1500, the dukes of Milan had four secretaries, each dealing with a separate kind of business (political, judicial, ecclesiastical, financial). The dukes of Savoy had three (foreign, home, war). The secretary of state became of central significance in England after 1530 with Thomas Cromwell. His successors—William Cecil, Francis Walsingham, and then Robert Cecil (later to be earl of Salisbury) under Elizabeth I—were the leading political figures at her court. The secretaries of state in Spain and Portugal used their positions as secretaries to the councils of state to reinforce their equally notable influence. In France, the secretaries of state evolved from the royal notaries within the chancellery to become, first, secretaries of finance then, from 1547 onwards, to have responsibilities for the expedition of 'affairs of state'. In due course (from at least 1561 onwards), they became members of the council of state and cemented their position as crown notables through intermarriage, office succession, and the acquisition of noble titles. The family de l'Aubespine rose from being merchants and lawyers in the Loire valley to providing a succession of secretaries of state to the French monarchy. Claude II de l'Aubespine (1510–67), baron de Châteauneuf-sur-Loire, was a key negotiator of the treaty of Cateau-Cambrésis. Along with his uncle by marriage, Jean de Morvillier, bishop of Orléans and keeper of the seals from 1568–71, and his brothers-in-law, Jacques Bourdin, secretary of state from 1558, and Bernardin Bochetal, bishop of Rennes, he was one of a small hub of competent negotiators and administrators around Catherine de Médicis who helped steer the most difficult of paths towards peace in the early phases of the Wars of Religion. His son-in-law, Nicolas III de Neufville, seigneur de Villeroy, descended from a family of Parisian fish-merchants, would carry on the family tradition from 1567 to his death in 1619, with only a brief exile from the affairs of state during the League from 1588 to 1594.

The political significance of the secretaries of state in the sixteenth century underlined an important evolution in the political process: decisions were increasingly registered and conveyed at a distance in written and printed forms. Great matters of state, edicts, and solemn pacifications between one polity and another had always been, and continued to be, issued and registered under the Great Seal, or its equivalent. The change came in the most heavily governed parts of dynastic Europe through the use and predominance of documents issued under the privy, or personal, seals of princely rulers. These came in a bewildering variety of forms—letters of commission, certification, permission, nomination, verification, passport, etc., sometimes graced with the term 'ordinance' to indicate that, as was often the case, they applied to more than a specific instance or to a given moment in time. The letter lay at the heart of the exchange and bargaining process between Europe's political elites and its governing entities. Letters of nomination determined the rights and perquisites of their offices, letters of privilege delineated their tax exemptions, letters of nobility rewarded them with titles, letters of commission provided them with the delegated authority under which they could enforce princely will upon others. Seven thousand of the letters of Catherine de Médicis have survived. When she complained to the young Henri of Navarre about the burdensome paperwork, he retorted bluntly: 'you thrive on this work'. Philip II worked at his papers until late at night, reading dispatches and writing or dictating his replies, often complaining of his exhaustion, eye troubles, and headaches. In May 1571, for example, he received a total of 1,200 petitions. His secretary Mateo Vázquez de Leca reported the king complaining that he had to sign 400 letters in one day. Networks of couriers and postal services were as important as military garrisons in the governing structures of sixteenth-century Europe.

How, then, should we regard the courts of Europe? The memoirs of Europe's statesmen and soldiers in the sixteenth century, not to mention the dispatches of its ambassadors, remind us of the central significance of the court to the functioning dynamics of its politics, an essential informal complement to the formality of its governing institutions. Even when they affected to despise the time and money that it required of them, Europe's political elites flocked to court like moths round a naked flame. As Blaise de Monluc, a provincial noble with years of military experience behind him said, it was essential to show a face there from time to time 'to warm oneself as one does in the sun or before a fire'. The court was hardly an institution, however, and more a way of life. In its origins, it was a household of servants and retainers to guard, escort, feed, clothe, and protect a ruler and his or her family. By the sixteenth century, it required a small army to clean the stables, attend to the accounts, maintain the buildings, keep the libraries, stock the arsenal, and feed, house, and entertain the guests of even a relatively modest prince. Although scale is difficult to determine with precision and varied from year to year, even the court of the tiny dukedom of Mantua had some 800 individuals on the payroll in 1520. That same year, the papal court had something approaching 2,000, whereas the imperial court of Maximilian I has been estimated at the time of his death (1519) as no more than 350 persons, with a further 170 left behind in Innsbruck. All the signs are that the courts of Europe were under pressure to grow in size during the sixteenth century. As they did so, they became less itinerant. Charles V had been endlessly on the move or on the march. Francis I, too, restlessly moved from place to place in his kingdom, calling on something like 18,000 horses to transport the court's belongings in order to do so. Elizabeth I, too, often progressed around the south of her kingdom, entertained at her nobility's expense and seeking their support. But by the second half of the century, the governing capitals of Europe were definitely emerging: London, Paris, Madrid, Prague, Stockholm. There was a degree of political and social centralization at work. Even when Philip II was away from court—escaping from business to his various palaces of retreat at Valsaín, El Prado, and (from the 1580s onwards) the Escorial—government business continued to be conducted in his absence at the Alcázar palace in Madrid, with secretaries and influential nobles relaying to the king really important matters of business that could not wait.

The court was politically crucial because it was where informal influence upon formal decision-making could have a real effect.

Wherever government was personal, the location of rule was where the prince was, or in times of conscious absence, where he determined it to be. There lay the source of preferments, honours, gifts, favour, law, and its implementation. And favour lay at the heart of good government, just reward being the counterpart of fidelity. François de L'Alouette, writing in his *Treaty on Nobles and their Virtues* (*Traité des nobles et des vertus dont ils sont formés*) of 1577, painted an idealized picture of the well-governed realm in which the nobility was 'so loved and favoured by Kings and Princes that they had freedom of entry and familiarity in their houses as though they were servants'. A good prince was one, he added, who rewarded well-earned merit. L'Alouette was writing in a tradition of courtier conduct books, of which Baldassarre Castiglione's *Book of the Courtier*, first published in Venice in 1528, proved to be the pre-eminent and best-read example in the sixteenth century, with sixty-two Italian editions and sixty vernacular translations to 1619. Its greatest success was between 1528 and 1550, with fifty editions and translations alone and its popularity only began to wane in the 1590s. In Castiglione's discourses, the ideal courtier was intelligent, well-born (though not necessarily noble), handsome, skilled in the arts of war, a master in the arts of conversation, a respecter of women, and the calm master of his emotions. The implication of Castiglione's text was that, at least at the court of the (absent) duke of Urbino, where the discourses were taking place, such a courtier would 'speak frankly to his prince' and see his virtuous manners and unquestioning loyalty rewarded. The problem was that every service deserved reward in the eyes of a supplicant. Satisfying everyone was beyond the limits of the possible. When Morata, one of Philip II's court jesters, asked him why he did not give to all who asked for his favour, the king replied: 'If I were to grant all their requests, I would soon be begging myself'. The problem led to systemic rivalries in a world where honour and virtue were the cards to hold, and where they were gained competitively, by depriving and demeaning others. Where you were seated at the council table, whether your case was heard, whether your salary was actually paid, whether the prince looked favourably upon you became matters of signal importance. The politics of the sixteenth-century court was as much about the implied as the spoken: the promise as much as the performance. Its masters and mistresses were those who knew how to make the most of playing to the gallery; smiles, gifts, humour, and compliments were all ways of implying political favour; slights, silence, and exclusion the reverse.

Faction was therefore part of court life. How to keep it from being destructive was another question entirely, and one to which there was no satisfactory answer. Sixteenth-century politics was as much about the overmighty subject as the overmighty prince. When the former were brought down to size, it was with the kind of fanfare from the latter that greeted the 'treason' of the constable of Bourbon in France (1527), or the execution of Count Pepoli of Bologna by the papacy (1585). More often, however, feudal nobles surrendered their earlier ambitions to independence and threw in their lot with the princes themselves. The latter made it worth their while. So long as tax receipts were increasing and greatly expanded credit facilities were available to princes to fund the military expeditions in which the aristocratic elites were major stakeholders, there were rewards aplenty. But it was more difficult to sustain in the long term. Expenditures overran incomes, which in turn outpaced what we know of the underlying economic base. Princely credit became over-stretched. There are signs of this occurring in the 1550s, with the Habsburgs failing to meet their commitments to their Genoese and German bankers in 1557, followed two years later by the Valois defaulting on their 'grand parti' credit arrangement with a consortium of Lyon-based (mainly Italian) bankers. The result was a partial collapse of the consensual politics between prince and high nobility, and just at the moment when religious divisions were calling into question the simple ethos of loyalty and obedience to the powers that be.

There were those who knew how to exploit the situation. Antoine Perrenot, Cardinal Granvelle, was the senior counsellor to the newly appointed regent in the Netherlands, Margaret of Parma, following Philip II's departure for Spain in 1559. He saw his role as controlling royal patronage on behalf of a regent with little experience in matters of state. He did so by establishing a secret *consulta* or inner advisory committee consisting of himself and two others in order to bypass the established council of state. At the same time, he called in a few favours on his own behalf: 'Not for anything in the world would I be deemed importunate by Your Majesty, but no less would I wish that my relatives and friends should tax me with undue carelessness in my own case ... for it is so many years now that I have received any favour (*merced*).' He was rewarded with the archbishopric of

Mechlin, something of a poisoned chalice (as it turned out), since it gave out the message that he had rather more influence over Philip II than was the case. The leading lights of the old nobility in the Netherlands were Lamoral, count of Egmont (1522–68) and William of Nassau, prince of Orange (1533–84). The former had been a senior and respected military commander in the Habsburg empire. The latter had his own independent principality in Germany and an enclave at Orange in the Rhône valley. Initially they accepted the new status quo, so long as their recommendations and nominations went forward. When they did not, they complained bitterly about Granvelle's autocracy and set about building up their local power bases and turning them into a regional network of fidelities, beholden to them. And they were none too fussy about whom they promoted in order to do so. Duke Mansfeld in the tiny duchy of Luxembourg, for example, was reported to sell posts in the town council of his duchy for 10 gold florins, accept bribes, let off a murderer for 100 écus, appropriated the legal fines of the ducal court, and browbeat its attorney-general. By the spring of 1563, both Granvelle and his aristocratic opponents were at work behind the scenes, building up their parties, inviting likely supporters to dine with them and spreading innuendo about the other. Their success was, at least in the short term, mixed. Gentlemen, short of means and seeking employment, were readily won over to their cause. Granvelle found support among the banking community at Antwerp, whose investment in the empire and status quo was colossal. The burghers and councillors of the towns, however, played a waiting game, refusing to commit themselves to the grand seigneurs, and anxious not to be wrong-footed in their relationship with Brussels, Granvelle, and the council in Madrid. In the short term, the climate of faction was defused when Philip II took the familiar root of sacrificing an unpopular figure (it would happen to a succession of viceroys in Naples and elsewhere too) when he ran up against the opposition of the local elites. Dismissed in 1564, Granvelle discovered the Achilles heel of all executors of regional authority in sixteenth-century Europe: the impossibility of cultivating their power base at the centre whilst simultaneously being at the periphery. Faced with advice from his secretary and confessor, and growing opposition to Granvelle from the Eboli faction, Philip II triangulated the forces at court and decided accordingly. In the medium term, however, he had stored up noble resentments which would, in due course, determine the course of the Dutch Revolt. The script as it unfolded in the Netherlands could be written, albeit more dramatically and with many different nuances, for the Valois court after the unexpected death of Henri II, killed in a jousting tournament in July 1559. The underlying political developments were similar. They both depended critically on aristocratic affinities.

If we put too much emphasis upon the systemic problem of faction among sixteenth-century political elites, however, we cannot appreciate that clientelism (the politics of client networks) had its positive side. It provided an informal power structure to complement the formal ways in which centre and periphery related to one another. Affinities—loose networks of fidelities, often based around kinship—were inherently personal, flexible, and capable of moulding themselves within existing institutional, feudal, and local identities. They recognized the most common social dynamics of sixteenth-century society: kinship, honour, reward, friendship. Affinities brought potential benefits to both parties. To the client came hopes of advancement, a voice at high table, the protection of a privilege. To the patron came loyalty, service, and a regular supply of invaluable information. The hopes of advancement came in many forms; but so, too, did the service. Princes understood and exploited patron–client relationships themselves: it was the essence of 'personal' monarchy. That said, it required all their judicious personal skills to exploit the loyalty of their clients effectively. There were times, especially those of 'minority' rule, when it could not work effectively. And there was a recurrent pattern in sixteenth-century politics of yesterday's loyal client being today's dangerous political opponent. Aristocrats, for their part, exploited their positions at court and in the provinces to act as brokers between a ruler and their particular locality. Here, too, they were dependent on their political skills, vulnerable to being wrong-footed at court by their enemies and criticized by unsatisfied suitors. Even so, the overall role of affinities has to be seen as positive. They linked local elites to a wider polity and helped to overcome the great enfeeblers of political systems in the sixteenth century: distance and time.

Clientelism was not the preserve of the dynastic state. It was liable to occur in all oligarchies—which is to say, the overwhelming majority of the political systems in sixteenth-century Europe. We can watch affinities working at something like their most elaborate at the court of Rome in the later sixteenth century. In many ways, it is a rather curious case in the sense that an institution which embraced celibacy limited the kinship bond. Discreet friendship, however, determined the politics at Rome. The process is documented in the autobiography of a future cardinal, Domenico Cecchini (1588–1656). From a good Roman family, he studied law at Perugia, and cultivated his connections with the Aldobrandini Pope, Clement VIII. When the latter died in 1605, he delicately approached the new cardinal nephew (Scipione Caffarelli) after a few months and asked 'if he would be so kind as to receive me under his protection'. Fortunately, he was 'most affectionate', and, in due course, Cecchini became one of the new pope's 'familiars' (*familiares*). In this way, the College of Cardinals was organized into a number of overlapping client networks by which succeeding popes were elected. Although they were perpetually changing as old cardinals died and the new took their places, the overall arrangement was remarkably stable because, like most patronage systems in an oligarchy, it was self-sustaining. In the city republics, something of the same pattern can also be observed around their great families and surrounding kin, lawyers, and bankers. Religious fraternities and guilds linked to parochial side-chapels, besides performing charitable endeavours, also supported the clans whose great palaces clustered around Venice's Grand Canal, the families who dominated the city's inner governing councils (the Council of Ten, the Savii Grandii, and the Savii di Terra Ferma). Venice was not alone among the urban oligarchies in trying to prevent such pressures by making the voting system by lot, by restricting or prohibiting the number of times any individual could be re-elected to a particular post, and by cultivating a patrician myth of public-sprited political behaviour. The reality simply meant the distribution of power marginally more widely within the same gloriously self-perpetuating and dominant elites, such was the power of kinship when linked to clienteles.

Where should we draw the limits of the power elites of sixteenth-century Europe? We may ask the question in respect of its numerous and generally still active representative institutions. Did the members of the Polish Sejm, the Swedish riksdag, the Danish rigsdag, the German Reichstag or princely Landtag, the Swiss Tagsatzung, the various Cortes in the kingdoms of the Spanish peninsula, the Dutch States-General and the English Parliament (to mention only a selection) belong to the power elites? There is no simple response to the question. Some were born powerful: that is to say, they had their position within the elite assured for them by virtue of their privileged birth and status as part of the noble estate—members of the English House of Lords, or the senators of the Polish Republic, who had a right of entry to the Sejm. Others found power through representative institutions—the leading burgher representatives of Amsterdam on the States-General of the emerging United Provinces, for example, or Thomas Cromwell in the English 'Reformation Parliament' of 1529–36. Others had power thrust upon them by representative institutions—the numerous representatives of the third estates at the infrequently summoned Estates-General of the French kingdom or the representatives of the peasantry at the Parliaments of Norway and Sweden. The power at their disposal was generally of a rather limited kind. In only a few exceptional cases (e.g. Austria) did they have the right to meet or dissolve on their own initiative. Historically, their power resided in their role in giving assent to new taxation but, for various reasons, it often proved difficult to hang onto this in the sixteenth century. The estates of Catalonia and Aragon managed to do so under Charles V; but the estates of Castile gambled and lost it for two generations in 1520. Their powers as legislators remained very varied, too, dependent on whether they had the right to make laws or merely propose issues about which laws would subsequently be made by the prince or ruler. The latter was generally enshrined in the right to present complaints (*gravamina, doléances*)—part of the more general petitioning process. More often than not, in fact, members of the prince's council and those of the representative institution instituted measures that, after negotiation, became enshrined in 'Capitulations', 'Recesses', or 'Articles' that became regarded in some way as the law of the land. But in the Swiss confederation, no individual partner was bound to accept the conclusions of the Tagsatzungen. In the Polish Sejm (but also in Valencia and Aragon), deputies had a right of veto which impelled unanimity upon all decisions taken at the estates. And, from shortly after the Union of Lublin, the sovereign courts in Poland ceased to be staffed by judges appointed by the king and became tribunals elected by noble regional assemblies. Overall, we should be sceptical of an older historiography that sets out Europe's representative institutions as necessarily in opposition to ruling authority and at odds with the dominant power elites. Their members were much more often complicit in the designs of the latter, bit-players of course, but consenting in the processes of government, constructively engaged in the conception of the latter as 'common-wealths' in which there was an implied mutuality of responsibility between governor and governed.

War and finance

On 24 April 1547, Charles V won one of the big military victories of the century: the battle of Mühlberg against the forces led by the Protestant princes of the Schmalkaldic League. The Elector of Saxony himself, Johann Friedrich, was captured, and his companion Philipp of Hesse surrendered two months later. A year later, the emperor penned a memorandum to his son, Philip II. Among the words of wisdom were: 'Always aim for peace. Go to war only when it is forced on you. It exhausts the treasury and causes great misery.' His pessimistic prudence about the impact of war on the state was based on a lifetime of experience of its hazards. Only four years later, he would be embroiled in yet another military campaign against his Lutheran German princes, and this time most of his erstwhile allies and the fortunes of war turned against him. Whatever else war may have done in the longer term by way of strengthening Europe's emerging political entities, it emphatically raised the risks for their survival and well-being in the short term.

A decade before writing his memorandum, Charles V and his great Valois rival Francis I had a remarkable personal encounter at Aigues-Mortes on the Languedocian coast of France in July 1536. The meeting had been secretly arranged between the close confidants of the two sovereigns deliberately to exclude any interference from the papacy. The French king broke with precedent and launched out to meet the Emperor's galley without any escort and before he was expected. Together the two men ostentatiously exchanged the kiss of peace in public, the first of several encounters, public and private, between two princes each seeking to outdo the other in virtue. It is an important reminder that, for the political leaders of Europe, peace was the outcome of a mutual exchange of 'faith'. Procuring peace for the whole of Christendom was part and parcel of their sovereign identity, God at work in the souls of princes, inspiring their hearts. Peace was a 'sovereign virtue', part of the mystique of monarchy, above and beyond the diplomatic treaties that might try to embrace it.

That kind of peace was certainly not greatly in evidence in the sixteenth century. The reality was that the risks for conflict among Europe's political entities grew considerably in the sixteenth century. A fundamental instability arose from within the Italian peninsula where fierce rivalries between its varying sized states and statelets had gradually created power blocs of allies in the fifteenth century, each of which developed ties and interests outside the peninsula. The south (above all, Naples) became bound to a Spanish dynasty with Mediterranean interests in opposition to those of Venice and Genoa to the north. Meanwhile the regions bordering the Alps (notably Milan) looked towards France for their protection. Milan and Naples became the key bridgeheads in the resulting Italian wars that over-shadowed the whole of the first half of the century from 1494 onwards. A similar vortex of conflicts threatened to engulf a similar constellation of varying sized states and statelets in Germany in the 1540s and 1550s. The German and Italian conflicts became grafted onto a major dynastic confrontation between Habsburg and Valois after 1516, in which France's fears of encirclement were dramatically encapsulated by their perception of a 'Spanish road' which linked Flanders, via the Free County of Burgundy and the various Alpine gateways to the Mediterranean and the hispanic peninsula, a percep-tion that was embodied by the flow of Spanish military resources to maintain its army in Flanders in order to subdue the long-running sore of rebellion there from 1567. Forty-two years of scarcely inter-rupted conflict of one sort or another followed before there were the makings of a truce in 1609. Then there was a further struggle between Christendom and the Ottoman Turks. This was epic in the eyes of many of Europe's publicists, a crusade. How could one make 'sover-eign peace' with the Turk? For much of the century, Christendom appeared to be coming out worse. Belgrade surrendered on 29 August 1521; Rhodes on 24 June 1522, opening up the eastern Mediterranean to Turkish warships. The fateful battle of Mohács on 29 August 1526 laid bare the Hungarian Danube plain and the Turks took Buda and Pest a month later. The destabilizing effects of the Turkish threat were felt across all the polities of Europe's south-eastern fringe. The Christian triumph of the Knights of St John at Malta in 1565 and the victory over the Turkish fleet at Lepanto in 1571 were both celebrated with relief across Europe. But they did little to diminish the Turkish threat in the short term since they had no enduring legacy. There was a renewed Turkish conquest of Tunis in 1574 which ensured an enduring Muslim hegemony on the North African coast and a gruelling war with the Turks in Hungary thereafter (from 1593 to 1606). Finally, to these major international fissures, we should add the various, more localized conflicts in the Baltic (notably the Seven Years War, 1563–70) and the civil/religious wars provoked by the Protestant Reformation in the second half of the sixteenth century. Military conflict was a fact of political life in the sixteenth century.

Military changes therefore had profound political effects and those associated with the early-modern 'military revolution' identified by some historians were already observable in the sixteenth century. Military architects evolved elaborate fixed defences against gunfire. The resulting *traces italiennes* (as they are known to Anglo-Saxon historians) still mark the European landscape in impressive fortresses at (for example) Turin, Milan, Siena, Palmanova (for the Venetian state), Navarrenx (for the little Pyrenean principality of Béarn), Sabiote (Spain), Breda, Antwerp, and a string of fortresses along the frontier between Habsburg Flanders and Valois France. Muscovy, too, began to rebuild its kremlins in stone and brick—it took seven years to construct the fortress at Smolensk, for example, with an estimated 150 million bricks. Meanwhile, even more significantly, western Europe's armies grew in size, especially in the first half of the sixteenth century. Charles VIII had invaded Italy in 1494 with 18,000 men at arms. Francis I did the same in 1525 with 32,000. His son Henri II captured Metz in 1552 with 40,000. In 1532, perhaps 100,000 marched in the name of the Emperor Charles V against the Turks. At the time of the siege of Metz in 1552, he had a force of 150,000, a total not exceeded by any European state before the later seventeenth century. Military campaigns were longer and fought further afield. Practical experience counted for more as infantry formations of arquebuses and pikes required veteran troops in large numbers who knew what they were doing. At the battles of Bicocca (1522) and Pavia (1525) Spanish infantry, inspired by the tightly formed squares of Swiss pikemen, demonstrated their superiority and began to organize themselves in smaller, more mobile squares of pikemen and arquebusiers, known as *tercios*, the invincible fighting unit of the sixteenth-century battlefield. In the Muscovite state, the germ of a permanent infantry corps armed with hand-guns, the *streltsy*, drawn initially from the gentry class, was laid in the 1550s; by 1600, they were a force of about 20,000.

The political impact of these changes was considerable. The costs of fortifications were colossal. They required long-term commitments to planning, execution, and subsequent maintenance, refurbishment, and manning—a continuing organizational demand. The larger armies needed to be recruited, trained, fed, paid, cared for, and equipped. Military changes posed immense administrative, financial, and logistic challenges to sixteenth-century states. The division between major political decision-making on the one hand, and its distant execution on the other, was reinforced at every turn. And, because of the combination of formal and informal power structures upon which Europe's politics depended, management was its weakest hand. This was why there was a tendency to subcontract military organization wherever possible. Mercenary captains recruited troops from the poorer parts of rural Europe which could not hold their population; the Swiss, the *Landsknechte* from Swabia and the Rhine, Albanians, Dalmatians, Scots, and Irish in the French and Spanish armies. But mercenaries had little loyalty towards the sovereign or state that paid them. When they were not paid, they refused to fight or, worse, took negotiators hostage or threatened the civilian population. Rome was put to the sack in 1527 by Charles V's *Landsknechte* when their pay was delayed. Even in armies that were not, formally speaking, mercenary, there was little sense of political loyalty. Recruitment was heterogeneous, wastage rates high, and revolt frequent. The Spanish army in Flanders mutinied forty-five times between 1572 and 1609; but desertion and mutiny also afflicted the Elizabethan forces in Ireland and the Netherlands in the later sixteenth century and the armies fighting for Henri IV's succession to the French throne.

Military changes thus increased political complexity and risk. The military lessons of antiquity offered no unambiguous lessons in how to deal with either. The changes also mostly outstretched the resource portfolios of Europe's states. These portfolios were complex, consisting of differing mixtures of domain revenues, direct and indirect tax receipts, and casual revenues of one sort and another. State finance was governed to a very considerable extent by inherited considerations and established precedents. Revenues were fiscally inelastic, relatively unresponsive to the dynamic elements of the European economy and incapable of reflecting the inflationary pressures which were a phenomenon that contemporaries found difficult to explain and to come to terms with. There were no options for raising significant revenues quickly that were devoid of political consequences. Royal or princely domain could be alienated or sold where it had not already been disposed of. Monastic estates and revenues could also be appropriated under the aegis of the Protestant Reformation—as occurred in the dissolution of the English monasteries in the 1530s. But these were once-for-all operations which affected property rights. They had inevitable political fallout, not least in popular revolt reflected in the English Pilgrimage of Grace (1536) and in peasant revolts in Norway in the 1550s–1560s. Indirect taxes on goods and services could be mortgaged to tax-farmers (as occurred to the *gabelles*, the French tax on salt in the sixteenth century), but this led to vituperative popular criticism of the hated *traitants* and *gabelleurs*. They could be subcontracted to local communities to collect, as with the *encabazamientos* of the *alcabalas* or sales-tax in Castile, although that too became the proximate cause for the widespread revolt in 1520 there, known as the *Comuneros*. Widening the fiscal base through indirect taxes was mostly successfully undertaken without revolt in the sixteenth century by republics such as Venice, Genoa, and the emerging Dutch Republic but even there it resulted in widespread smuggling. Elsewhere it tended to be the prelude to popular revolts such as that in south-west France in 1548. Raising direct taxes often entailed elaborate negotiation with representative institutions. The latter were skilful in the deployment of arguments on the basis of historic precedent, regional, or local privilege against such measures, resisting blandishments, and doubting the evidence for the imperative necessity adduced for the particular proposition in question. In Castile, for example, in the immediate aftermath of the defeat of the Armada in 1588, Philip II summoned the normally placid Cortes to grant him an exceptional *servicio* (direct tax). He revealed to the assembled deputies that expenditure on the combined army and navy in Flanders and the Channel had reached over 10 million ducats and that he needed an additional 8–10 million to maintain the Flanders army in the field and replace the navy. Deputies were menaced, bribed, and threatened with imprisonment. Aristocrats were asked to bend the ear of local deputies

to get them to vote in favour of the measure without imposing conditions (*condiciones*). Even so, there were prominent street protests in
Madrid, pamphlets openly criticizing the king, and some local nobles
prosecuted for fomenting sedition. In the end, after months of hag-
gling, all but three of the eighteen cities represented in the Cortes
agreed to grant 8 million ducats, but only over a period of six years
and with conditions as to its collection. Meanwhile, in Valois France,
where direct taxes could be raised in the form of the *taille* on much of
the central part of the kingdom without recourse to a representative
institution, its yield was limited by the fact that the amounts
demanded from particular localities were fixed by a historically
determined pattern of repartition and constrained by privileges
which exempted those with wealth in walled towns and among the
nobility. The reality was that, in most of Europe, state revenues hardly
kept up with inflation in the sixteenth century, let alone matched the
growing demands of warfare. The most evident exception was the
fledgling Muscovite state, which finally overthrew over two centuries
of Mongol rule towards the end of the fifteenth century and annexed
smaller independent principalities around it. The resulting confiscated lands were turned into military service grants called *pomest'ia*,
creating landed estates to maintain a cavalry officer, his family, and
his household slaves. Through these grants, the Muscovite state
acquired a powerful cavalry class (the *oprichniki*) which, in return,
was permitted to enserf the peasants on their estates. This occurred
especially during the period of Ivan the Terrible's 'state within a state'
(the *Oprichnina*, 1565–72). In a related development, the Muscovite
Grand Prince developed remarkable autocratic pretensions in the
course of the sixteenth century which, relatively untramelled by law
and precedent, meant that there were more fiscal innovations in
sixteenth-century Muscovy and an expanding range of agencies to
collect them (*prikazy*) than almost anywhere else in sixteenth-century
Europe.

The widening gap between income and expenditure was mostly
met by borrowing, organized in both formal and informal ways. The
pattern appeared most clearly in the case of the Spanish Habsburg
empire, whose money-box was Castile. The secret of Charles V's
apparent financial success was to convert the ordinary revenues of
Castile into a fund from which to pay interest to his creditors by
organizing informal short-term loan contracts (*asientos*) with the

imperial bankers in Augsburg, Genoa, and elsewhere, generally repaid at a scheduled term, or through more formal rents (*juros*) secured on those revenues and attractive to investors both from Spain and abroad. The partial collapse of these credit arrangements was signalled in the declared bankruptcies of 1557, 1560, and 1575. By 1584, the ordinary revenues of Castile amounted to 1,636.6 million *maravedís* whilst the annual payment on the *juros* alone had reached 1,227.4 million—75 per cent of total ordinary revenues. Even an unexpected influx from the royal share of Spanish American treasure in the 1580s and 1590s could not prevent a fourth declared bankruptcy in 1596. According to a report prepared for Philip II's son on his accession to the Spanish crown in 1598, all the ordinary revenues of Castile had been committed to the debt, with the result that the only resources available to the ruler of the empire on which the sun never set were the treasure from the Indies, ecclesiastical subsidies subject to papal approval, and the direct taxes painfully negotiated every three years with its Cortes. The same underlying pattern of formal and informal borrowing developed elsewhere in Europe too. By 1600, over half the revenue of the papacy was taken up by payments to office-holders who had purchased their offices and interest charges on the *Monti* (bonds, guaranteed on specific revenues). By 1596 and towards the end of the French civil wars, the French monarchy's debts were reckoned to be at least 105 million *livres* or 135 million if alienated royal domain and royal jewels were included in the calculations. At the end of the sixteenth century, Europe's most powerful governing entities were also its most indebted. That meant that they were also the most powerful redistributors of income to those who invested in their political enterprise, and the biggest contractors of the period. But the strains of deficit finance placed exceptional burdens on the powers of persuasion of Europe's rulers and exposed the fragilities of power structures that depended on informality for their effectiveness.

Images of rule

Sixteenth-century rulers were no strangers to propaganda. Emblems, engravings, printed edicts, monuments, official histories, speeches all testify to the significance it was accorded. They made skilful political use of the new power of the printing press. But we should not ignore the ephemeral representations of rulership in pageants, processions, and rituals associated with the 'entries' of rulers to their term of office, embodied by a ceremonial, or 'joyous' entry into a city, town, or place of authority. Their purpose was to break down tensions and represent the harmony of an established order. They did so by appealing to an identity or ideal over and above the particular and local. When the young King Charles IX was taken on a prolonged 'tour' of France by his mother Catherine de Médicis in 1564–6, elaborate entries were organized in accordance with traditions going back to the fourteenth century. In inscriptions, banners, triumphal arches, pageants and speeches that owed a good deal to the cultural imagination of the French court, the message was conveyed that divisions between Protestants and Catholics, lawyers and merchants, towns and countryside, were set in the shade by the shared and natural love of the French for their monarchy. At his father's coronation, Henri II had added a clause stipulating that the king was marrying his kingdom, taking France as his bride. Classical and Christian antiquity were combed for appropriately universalist harmonious themes. One of the most prevalent in the sixteenth century was the mythological figure of Astraea, under whose aegis a golden age of peace, justice, and knowledge would ensue. Europe's sixteenth-century polities have been termed 'theatre-states', not because their rulers were the masters of illusion but because rulership was embodied in its representation. 'Joyous' entries, coronations, enthronements, formal judicial acts of government (such as the *lit de justice* in France or the monarch addressing Parliament in England) made direct emotional appeals to loyalty, embodied simple truths about the nature of politics, and made them memorable. In general, sixteenth-century rulers laid claim to cultural hegemony that was larger and more seductive than that of their predecessors.

Sixteenth-century political thought has acquired a reputation for being obsessed by issues of *realpolitik*, the pursuit and unfettered use of power. This is an unfortunate effect of one very famous book, *The Prince* (1513) by Niccolò Machiavelli (1469–1527) (see Chapter 4 below, section on 'Political thought'). The work acquired its modern reputation for disassociating power and morality in the course of the sixteenth century. It was a misreading of the book, itself only one of

Machiavelli's works, and this has led to a distortion of the general direction of political thought during the century. Writing about politics in the sixteenth century was dominated by bigger humanist agendas and their methodologies, and reflected the wider intellectual currents of the period. The agenda, evident in the most innovative political commentaries of the century, was that political authority and the exercise of power had to be explained in terms of the organization of the society which conditioned it. Republics, monarchies, empires and states needed to be understood through their history, social fabric, and particular rationales. The humanist methodology was that such an understanding could be arrived at through the empirical and comparative study of examples from the past and the present. The wider intellectual current was the dominant belief that political wisdom was a practical extension of moral philosophy, and that virtue and rule could not therefore be disassociated. How that virtue was conceived was therefore a central question of study, comment, and debate in the sixteenth century.

One central element of that debate in the sixteenth century was whether such wisdom should lead to detachment from the world of affairs or whether to do so was not an abdication of a fundamental moral obligation to pursue virtue through public endeavour. The latter was the key underlying Platonic and Ciceronian legacy of the Italian civic humanists in Renaissance Florence and Venice. The latter regarded engagement in political life as educative to civic virtue, a vehicle for developing morality in which actions for the common good would shape individual force of character (virtue implying both the quality of the man, *vir*, and his force, *vis*).

Civic humanist discourse was readily translatable in the sixteenth century from the republican environments of Florence and Venice to the monarchical courts of Europe, its debates reflected (for example) in the private reading of Elizabeth I's secretary of state, William Cecil, or in the Latin hexameters composed for his own amusement by the chancellor of Catherine de Médicis, Michel de l'Hospital. What increasingly changed the way people looked at politics was the Protestant Reformation. Martin Luther (1483–1546) approached politics from the perspective of his Augustinian theology. Human kind was sinful and it was only by faith in God's grace that we were saved. Political authority emanated from God's will, and the political duty of all good Christians was to submit to the powers that be, since they were ordained by God. But he and (more evidently) other Protestant reformers also argued that the only legitimate princes are those who manifest God's righteousness and that no obedience is due to a ruler who demonstrates his ungodliness by perpetuating idolatry and persecuting God's faithful people. There was an unavoidable tension here, and it helped to refocus political thought away from issues of educative virtue and towards the nature and extent of political obedience. Its methodology was determined more by theologians and its agenda was adjusted to the task of divining God's purposes and applying them in the world. At its most revolutionary, Protestant political thought could be used to justify tyrannicide, although (in the event) it was a Catholic (Jacques Clément) who would be inspired to assassination on such grounds when he murdered the French King Henri III on 1 August 1589. At its most sophisticated, Protestant political thought also absorbed some of the agenda, methodology, and focus of humanist political thinking. The power of the amalgam is most readily appreciated in the writings of the French Protestant jurist, François Hotman (1524–90), especially his *Francogallia* (1573) (see Chapter 4 below, section on 'Political thought').

By the last quarter of the sixteenth century, however, the dominant political images and ideas were shifting in different directions, reflecting no doubt the deeper impact of the religious crisis of the sixteenth century on its political fabric. If the shared assumptions about the legitimacy of rule seemed no longer accepted, especially among the political elites in religiously divided Europe, the 'theatre-state' lost its natural points of reference with the audience. Moreover, reflecting the theological impact of the Reformation, there was an increasing emphasis on the unconditional and unquestioned power of rulers as a reflection of God's will and the necessity of stoical obedience towards them. So Philip II declined to go on progress round his kingdom, on the grounds that it demeaned his majesty, and increasingly withdrew from the world. The late portrait of him by Pantojà de la Cruz, to be found in the gallery of the library at the Escorial, depicts a deathly pale figure in black and grey within an ethereal space: abstract power, devoid of context. His French contemporary, Henri III, declined most opportunities for royal entries. He was criticized by his contemporaries for his exaggerated emphasis on court ceremonial designed to emphasize the royal majesty. He also engaged in regular extended retreats from public life, on pilgrimages and retreats accompanied by Franciscan-inspired spiritual exercises. Meanwhile, the Emperor Rudolf II mostly retired from active participation in affairs, and moved his court from Vienna to Prague and then Graz, and kept company with his alchemists and clocks.

Political commentators also began to reflect a world in which power was detached from its social and institutional context. The Piedmontese Giovanni Botero (1544–1617) published his *Reason of State* in 1589, an influential work that sought to define the state as a dominion over people, and 'reason of state' as the statecraft of applying rules of political prudence to maintaining that dominion. The term 'state' was one which by then had acquired common currency among north Italian diplomats and political writers. It took some time to be exported and had different contexts in different places. Elizabeth I reportedly hated the word. But by the end of the century Europe's political theorists and practitioners were beginning to define the *res publica* (in whatever form it manifested itself locally) as a state, and to identify it with central government. Finally, and in response to the claims of confessional groups to a right of resistance to established authority, there was a counter-assertion of the necessity of the state's absolute power over its subjects. It was to be embodied in the power to tax and make laws, without any necessary consent on the part of those being governed or obligation to reflect the customs of the society in question. These were the directions that would determine the politics of Europe in the next century.

3

Society

Christopher F. Black

In British modern political mythology a prime minister notoriously denied the existence of 'society' facing derisive comments from those who misunderstood the context. She was trying to emphasize the need for individuals to assume responsibility for their own fortunes, and not to blame the collective 'other' or 'others': society. While it is presumably accepted that individuals interact with others, and so have a social relationship, describing that resulting society, and the relationships worked within it, is as difficult for the sixteenth as for Lady Thatcher's twentieth century. For much of the twentieth century historians were embattled when dealing with the sixteenth century over whether the main description of European society should be in terms of 'classes' or 'orders' and status. The former approach, influenced by Marxism but by no means just emphasized by Marxists, gave priority to economic factors that governed the relationships between people, primarily in terms of who, and who did not, control the means of production. Much emphasis was given to the social conflicts and violence of the period deriving from such economic struggles. The opposing camps argued that sixteenth- and seventeenth-century society was much more hierarchically structured in terms of status, orders, and 'estates', as supposedly in the feudal past. The estates or orders might be those of clergy, nobility, and the third estate—which could be divided between urban and rural 'estates' in some political representative systems (as in the Tirol or Sweden). In the second approach birth, prestigious roles in society, degree of dependence on the sovereign, honour, military prowess might all be more important than economic and financial relationships, and control of resources and work. Those emphasizing orders and estates were inclined to argue for a more static and harmonious society, with mutual interdependence between social strata. In recent years historians have tended to emphasize the complexity with which early modern Europeans viewed and described their own society. They also incorporate many more factors into the relationships between people, going far beyond simple power, legal, birth, or economic relationships, and borrowing socio-anthropological concepts and approaches.

An analysis of society could include a consideration of all the ways in which an individual and his or her immediate family related with others: the physical environment and space, economic relations of employer and employee, institutional frameworks, senses of common identity, or alienation, the mental attitudes towards each other, from respect or fear, or indeed the means of communication (gesture, spatial relationships as well as language). A number of questions need to be asked in dealing with the sixteenth century, and how aspects of these social relations may have changed. Debates are lively on many of them. Dealing with all 'Europe', we need to consider how far a major divide existed between Western (which usually includes the Mediterranean world of Iberia and Italy), and Eastern ('east of the Elbe') Europe; or a north–south divide (the Atlantic and Baltic areas versus the Mediterranean and south Germanic). Were the divisions between urban and rural society rigid or fluid? Did those divisions vary geographically? How much physical and social mobility was there? Did conditions for women, and attitudes to them, become more or less adverse? Were there increasing divides between rich and poor, with harsher treatment of the latter through the century? What impact on society more broadly came from major 'changes' of the century: the Reformation crisis, the wider contacts with the non-European world, and the impact of considerably expanded printing of words and images? A number of these issues overlap with what is discussed in other chapters, and are better highlighted there. A modern broad approach to 'Society' inevitably increases possible interconnections.

As a way into various issues it is worth considering a now well-known individual, brought to fame by a stimulating and controversial example of fashionable 'microhistory': Domenico Scandella, better known as Menocchio, a miller from Montereale in Friuli (north-eastern Italy), who was executed on the orders of the Holy Office of the Inquisition in Rome, in 1599. He has been made famous by the Italian historian Carlo Ginzburg, in a book entitled (in English translation), *The Cheese and the Worms*. The phrase arises because

Menocchio told the inquisitors that he conceived of the earth starting like fermenting cheese, with angels and men emerging like worms from it. He had many ideas critical of orthodox Catholicism. Though seen by Ginzburg as a 'peasant', in part representing old and new ideas, and a spirit of independence, Menocchio played various roles in his community, including being a mason, carpenter, abacus-teacher, and musical entertainer at feasts, but as a miller he was in some ways a man apart. Millers were often feared and distrusted, playing as they did a crucial role in the food economy, and in taxation, whether by a lord or a communal government. Menocchio was literate, with access to some strange books, perversely interpreted; and to a vernacular (elite Italian) Bible, which the Catholic Church was increasingly eradicating, denying the laity access to it. The area was both remote, in the foothills of the Dolomites, and also a part of ancient communication networks. The people spoke Friulano, a language different from Venetian and even more from the standardized printed Italian. But those who visit Montereale can note that tracks and tunnels, centuries old, survive where men and animals could move (except in winter) north into and over the Alps; and access to the Venetian Lagoon was not that difficult. Since the 1540s Friuli had shown various signs of interest in Protestant ideas, including radical Anabaptism. Menocchio abjured after a first trial in 1583–4, was fairly lightly punished, and was allowed back into the community. He was investigated and tried a second time in 1598, having fallen foul of a new parish priest and some of his neighbours for too freely and loudly proclaiming strange and heretical ideas. Rome insisted on his death, as a dangerous teacher of heresy, when the local inquisition officials trying him again wanted to spare him.

The Menocchio story, while unique, warns one against seeing rural society as entirely remote and homogeneous, divorced from high culture and new learning. It also points to the strengths and weaknesses of attempted socio-religious control.

The bonds of society

An individual might be bonded in sixteenth-century society in a number of different ways that he or she would have acknowledged:

through extended family, kinship, village or urban neighbourhood, parish, trade guild, or religious confraternity. In a less benign way the individual might be bonded to a master or lord. A strong sense of belonging to a state, monarchy, or large geographical area was probably less common. Some of these social relationships changed through the period, but much remains debatable. While there might have been some move in Western Europe towards the nuclear family household, of parents and children (as noted in northern France, the Netherlands, and England), many different configurations of family and household existed. These were dictated as much by mortality, and an economic need for productivity or survival, as by culture. Many family households would have three generations living together, especially a widow, with extra never-married uncles, aunts, brothers, and sisters of the middle generation. Between 10 and 15 per cent of Western Europeans reaching adulthood never married, largely for financial reasons. While in Western Europe it was normal for children to leave home on marriage (or marry as and when they could leave home and set up a new household), there were plenty of exceptions to this. Married brothers might live together in the same urban household, or in a complex of connected living units in town housing, and countryside complexes as in southern France or Lombardy. This might be more convenient for running artisan businesses, or farms, to ensure co-operative labouring. Italian urban elites might have many members of the family living together in great households. Venetian patricians from the later sixteenth century might arrange for just one brother to marry, to keep the patrimony together; but other brothers (and possibly mistresses), and unmarried sisters remained together in the same palace. In Eastern Europe and European Russia families were often living in multi-family households, and working in close proximity. Among lower status families in parts of Italy, Germany, and southern and central France, married children stayed on with their parents because they could not obtain a separate farm to own or run.

In contrast to large household family groupings, evidence from the later sixteenth century shows significant numbers of urban 'households' headed by single persons, often widows, though they might have lodgers, apprentices, or servants with them. Many young people in Western Europe left home in their teens for a while, whether from elite families to establish social contacts and clientage links, or from lesser families to work as servants or apprentices in towns, or extra 'hands' on farms. In north–central Italy girls from small towns or villages would work as servants in large cities, to earn a marriage dowry. Single servants were found in quite lowly house-holds, and Rome and Bologna parish registers note prostitutes with a girl servant in attendance (and not recorded as their daughter). For many the mobility and interconnection between families was important for economic reasons, social networking, widening of horizons, fostering of rural–urban connections, or the spreading of characteristically urban ideas or material culture. Other regions benefited less. In southern Italy fewer children moved away for this period. In Central and Eastern Europe domestic service was rare, other than on the few great estates or in palaces.

Much debate has arisen over the importance of, and changes in, kinship and clan as part of social networking at this period. Kinship ties were played upon through society, from creating support for popes and cardinals, to securing positions at an English or French court, to the arranging of suitable marriages even at lower social levels, to keep property and resources together. The more extended bonding of clans persisted in the sixteenth century in major areas of France, Scotland, Spain, Corsica, Piedmont, the Kingdom of Naples, and Friuli. Clans could be important in the tight political control of cities like Genoa, Brescia, or Valladolid, but rulers saw them as a danger to the control of rural areas, and they came under attack in state-formation policies of the mid-century onwards. Clan links could exacerbate vendettas, and be the networking system behind serious social conflict as in Friuli in the early century, or in the French 'Wars of Religion' in the 1560s–1590s. Much of the latter struggle was shaped by territorial control by the Guise, Condé, Montmorency clans, and the feudal clientele systems. The Guises, using clientele networks with their immediate noble inferiors of the Rohan and La Rochefoucauld, could control much of Normandy, Picardy, and Champagne, in the interests of the hard-core Catholic cause, whether against Protestants or against the crown when the latter sought compromise and toleration.

Different social loyalties might be formed by geographical loca-tions. About 90 per cent of people in Western, Southern, and Central Europe lived in rural communities, villages, or hamlets, rather than large towns or cities. Some villages were lively self-contained communities, with various economic activities and social levels, as in southern England or the Netherlands. Others, as in southern Italy, might be large communities of many thousands, but monocultural, exhibiting no social diversity, and possibly little sense of community. Most village or small town communities were very protective of rights and privileges granted by monarch, neighbouring city, or feudal lord, and would unite peasants, artisans, and professionals against an outside threat to them. In Western and Southern Europe even feudal villages and towns had their assemblies, local officials, and judges to conduct daily affairs, and to negotiate with the feudal lord. In Spain lords and crown might battle over fiefs and their ownership, but (according to James Casey) communal control and vitality may have increased through the period. Village communities in most of Germany may have been swamped by princely state power, but communities in Württemberg remained very much in control of their local affairs. Though Central and Eastern Europe is sometimes seen as more oppressively 'feudal', local officials, if not communal assemblies could have some socio-economic and even legal decision-making and leadership (as in the Danubian communities) without the lord being totally dominant. Local village loyalties might generate local antagonisms as well as healthy competition. Often pressures were exerted not to marry outside the community, leading to petitions to bishops to dispense from rules of consanguinity, as in post-Tridentine Piedmont.

Within larger communities, up to major cities, the social bonds and networks outside the family were more complex, and changing. In smaller communities the parish church and its immediate vicinity was a focal point, not just for religious services, but also for public meeting—whether for trading, getting a letter written or read, a contract agreed, or a lovers' tryst. The same could apply in towns and cities, though up to the Reformation the churches of the religious orders held competing attractions for worship, support, and meetings. With the Reformation struggle all institutional churches sought to reinforce parochial loyalty and control. Parishioners were encouraged, nearly forced, to spend more time in church, for lengthy Protestant sermons, or more elaborate Catholic masses. From the Council of Trent the Catholic Church claimed control over the sacrament and contract of marriage (where hitherto marriages had been very variedly negotiated and contracted), and wanted the ceremony to take place in church. The parish church became for Protestants and Catholics alike more a place for education, in Sunday schools and schools of Christian doctrine; but it became less of a place for secular socializing. The secular state was inclined to use the parish church, and the more enforced gathering of the community, for issuing orders and advice.

Important for social grouping and meetings were the lay religious societies, now variously called confraternities, brotherhoods, sodalities, or religious gilds (the preferred term for the English version). On the eve of the Reformation they played a vital role in parts of Italy, Spain, France, England, southern Scotland, the Netherlands, and Germany. At a basic level they might be a burial society, ensuring a decent funeral and saying prayers for the departed. Some ran hospices and hospitals, provided dowries for poor girls, organized pilgrimages. Others, as in England, southern France, Piedmont, and Germany, mainly organized an annual feast-day celebration, a village social highlight, from which the village poor might marginally benefit. Luther condemned the German brotherhoods for encouraging drunkenness without giving help to the poor. While the Protestant churches condemned and closed such confraternities, in Catholic areas the authorities fostered them, though they redirected them, and attempted to impose more rigid clerical supervision. Confraternities increased their philanthropic activities for the poor and needy; some helped with religious education; some returned to active flagellation (a practice derived from the medieval origins of many) and other penances. From a wider social perspective, the confraternities contributed to social welfare, moralizing and social control. They could represent a godly elite (and act as its offensive wing for the recovery of French Catholicism from the end of the century). For some laywomen, who could join some, and occasionally run them, they offered a path to activity as well as prayer outside the family. While some were socially exclusive (nobles or artisans only), most had a social mix. About a third of families in urban Italy and Spain might have been involved intermittently with confraternities in the later century. Rural involvement was more patchy.

Economic guilds (which in urban Italy, Spain, and the Netherlands might have a religious dimension as well) could form another important dimension of social organization for urban communities. In major towns and cities of Western Europe trade and artisan guilds had the major function of controlling conditions of work and trade, of apprenticeships, debt collection, and many other economic issues. They might also hold the key to local city politics, as in Italian cities like Milan or Perugia, or London and York. They could fulfil religious and philanthropic functions, as notably in Venice. Venetian guilds mixed leading masters and journeymen, rich and poor, and could be socially cohesive; but elsewhere, as in Florence, Milan, or London, they could foster social divisions, while protecting an interest group. In the sixteenth century the most prestigious, for instance those of merchants, woolmasters, bankers, and notaries, tended to become less economic and more dedicated to socio-political elitism; they could be seen as fostering a class or order division in society.

Social hierarchies: peasants, labourers, the middling sort, and elites

William Harrison in his *Descriptions of England* (1577), commenting on 'The Degrees of People', declared: 'We in England divide our people commonly into foure sorts', namely (1) gentlemen, which could be differentiated between nobles, knights, esquires, and 'lastly all they that are simplie called gentlemen'; (2) citizens and burghers, possessing the freedom of the city; (3) yeomen in the countryside, 'those which by our law are called *legales homines*, freemen born English'; freeholders worth 40 shillings a year; or farmers, gentlemen 'possessing a preheminence and mere estimation' among the common people; and (4) day labourers, husbandmen, artificers 'as tailors, shoemakers, carpenters, brickmakers, masons etc.', servants, and people who have 'neither voice for authorities in the commonwealth, but are to be ruled and not rule over'.

England by now treated all as freemen; it did not have the lowliest strata, of serfs as seen in Eastern Europe and Russia, or of slaves that could still be found in some Italian and Spanish cities (Seville recorded 6,327 in 1565), and on galleys. Non-Christian slaves might be as well, or badly, treated as 'free' servants, and be rewarded for conversion. An Andalusian nobleman in 1590 married his Moorish slave, who was also the mother of his children. Serfdom in Russia had its hierarchies, and household serfs could be well treated and respected.

Sixteenth-century society was hierarchical, but in most areas the various strata should not be seen as rigid, or too simply constructed, as Harrison indicated. The simplest structures were seen in areas like Poland, Prussia, Hungary, southern Italy, central Spain, where society comprised a large mass of barely differentiated peasants, nobles with a household staff, a few educated estate managers, and the odd town or city with a middling sort of limited variety. Words like 'peasant' (pejorative in English, where the French *paysan* or Italian *contadino* are less so) covered many types of occupation and status (as suggested in the discussion of Menocchio above). 'Peasants' might include landless labourers and serfs heavily dominated by a lord; sharecroppers under a whole range of contracts, good or bad, with the landowner; small or large tenant farmers; small-holders and free-holders with wealthy multi-crop land; shepherds and cattle-drovers. A peasant or *contadino* might be a smith, shoemaker, tailor, or miller; while a southern Italian priest might have to work on the land or as a petty trader. A single family might at the same time, or over a few years, own a little property, sharecrop a piece, rent another, and pro-vide day labourers for a bigger landowner. Peasants could be very poor and despised, or rich and men of honour. A community, Puebla Nueva, in New Castile in 1575 was reported to have 350 families; 70 were given as peasants (renting or owning land), with the rest as day labourers or artisans, except 'three or four peasants say they are gentlemen (*hidalgos*), because they have a patent of nobility'.

The major generalization about 'peasant' society might be that in Central and Eastern Europe conditions worsened for most of them in relation to lords; while in the west and south changes were more variable. In England the increasing rural population with some freedom might end up as part of a rural proletariat, the new poor in a city like London or Norwich, or move into an expanding yeoman and gentry population. But Central and Eastern Europe saw the power of the lords used to prevent peasant population movement, legally tying them to the land (as in laws in Hungary in 1514, Silesia, Brandenburg, and Prussia 1526–8, or parts of Russia in 1580). Eastern landowners, and occasionally the state, were developing an agricultural economy, depressing and socially narrowing their own peasantry, while feeding the rising populations of Western and (from the 1590s) Mediterranean Europe, increasing their socio-economic diversity. Laws also gave lords rights to dispossess peasants with land, and turn them into landless or near landless labourers, owing services to the lords' estates, as in Brandenburg-Prussia 1540–72. Whereas non-negotiable service obligations to secular or Church landlords diminished in England or much of Italy, in the Central–Eastern areas labour services grew considerably—the villages under the Cathedral of Havelberg (Brandenburg) had to provide ninety days work on its lands by the close of the century. Noble power could secure formal state law to standardize labour services, as in Braunschweig in 1597. Lords could have considerable control over marriages, or the transfer of property that the peasant might still have. However some Eastern–Central areas broke this pattern, and did preserve through the sixteenth and seventeenth century free peasant populations, as in Polish lands near Kraków, or Prussian Colmer. Danish and Swedish peasants maintained much security of land tenure and freedoms, but were to suffer from rising taxes and dues through the century, as did free peasants in other parts of Europe. In Saxony the electors extended the state lands directly controlled, and preferred to protect peasants against noble pressures, depredations, and increased services: but they did so at least partly to secure their own state revenues.

Rural society could be full of tensions, whatever the land control systems, and not just between labourer and landlord. In Spain, the Kingdom of Naples, and the Papal State considerable friction existed between those who ran the great sheep flocks from plains to hills and the arable farmers. In our period much social tension was created by the enclosure and expropriation of common land (which was often the salvation of the marginal peasant), as in parts of England, Spain, Brandenburg, or central Italy. This drove some peasants to cities like London, Seville, Rome, or Naples, and others into rural banditry. Most of Europe probably had a rural society more polarized between rich and poor; that is, between those who could have some control of land and animals, and those almost entirely reliant on others. Comparative social harmony depended on whether the latter could move on successfully to towns (as in the west and south), or not, as in the east.

The century did see severe rural riots and revolts, in Friuli in the years around 1511, Hungary in 1514, through much of Germany, the Tirol, and Hungary in the 1520s 'Peasants War', in the late 1580s in parts of France, the Netherlands, around Naples, in the 1590s with the notorious *Croquants* revolts in France, and in Upper Austria and

Hungary. Virtually none can be seen as exclusively class wars of peasants against lords or the monarchy, though protest against serfdom or serf-like conditions was a major factor. Often artisans from towns joined in, also local priests, and dissident nobles, who might prefer to back their tenants and labourers against government taxation, or use them to further other ends, including religious dissent. Social relations could break conventional hierarchies.

Towns and cities

Moving to urban society, we usually find a more complex set of relationships. As Chapter I indicates, our period witnessed an overall urbanization, but within that a shift towards the north-west in the proportion of large towns or cities became evident by the end of the century. Those living in urban communities of more than 40,000 rose from roughly 2 to 3.5 per cent of Europe's population through the century; those in communities of 10,000 or more, from 6 to 10 per cent. This can be misleading since many English towns of 600–800 people could have a greater economic, social, and cultural diversity than a Spanish city of 20,000. Some Spanish, Italian, and German cities were static or declined, as did Salisbury, for example, in England. To survive, given urban mortality rates, cities needed a net immigration, whether from small towns or real rural communities. So some urbanites were recent 'peasants'. Urban communities might simply be subdivided into labourers, the middling sort of lesser merchants, artisans, and professionals, and the elites of nobles and top merchants. But a city could have a very diverse profile, with many economic and social gradations. A complex description was provided by Tomaso Garzoni in his *The Universal Piazza of All the Professions in the World* (*La Piazza Universale*, Venice, 1585, and many later editions). Imagining a piazza with all the groups, the most noble and honourable at the centre, and the most lowly latrine cleaners at the edge, he described about 400 occupations, from butchers, bakers, and lawyers, to lovers, whores, spies, perpetual drunks, inquisitors, and heretics. In reality, major cities might represent a large number of these in up to a hundred guilds or associations, providing identity and solidarity.

Towns and cities had all sorts of physical configurations, and sub-divisions. In some rich and poor were segregated, where the nobles carved out select areas or streets, as in Genoa's Strada Nuova. Those involved in noxious activities such as tanning, butchery, or fulling were often kept separate. But in other cities townhouses and palaces might have shops, workshops and lodgings on the ground floor below them, as in parts of Venice, Florence, and Paris. Within cities there thus could be neighbourhood loyalties, and clientele systems uniting several levels in the hierarchy.

Through the century urban society generally became more profes-sional, educated, and consumerist, more so in the west and south than the east. Education was more widespread: this reflected the expansion of printing, the humanist campaigns for a more diverse spread of knowledge, and the religious debates and confrontations. It also derived from the institutional churches' desire to ensure a proper religious education, led by a better educated clergy, whether trained in universities or seminaries. State consolidation, and the need to raise more taxes for war, fostered bureaucracies of offices (whether really functional, or less effective venal offices created to raise money for the crown). Lawyers and doctors became more status-conscious, and competed with older merchant and noble elites. Increasingly in Elizabethan England lawyers and merchants challenged the gentle-men and gentry of the shires politically and socially, and also invested in land. Consumerism was encouraged by competitive spending on cultural display, or propagandist culture for political and religious needs. Catholic areas in the later sixteenth century generated more of this in terms of buildings and decorations; but Protestant towns could compete with more elaborate town houses, civic buildings, or funeral monuments. In north–central Italy, the Netherlands, northern France, and key German cities urban housing began to give more family privacy, more comfortable and showy living, with elaborate beds and bedding, chairs, tapestries, decorated fine pottery, and Venetian glassware. Venetian records suggest some of this consumer-ism was spreading down into middling artisan families by the end of the century. This anticipated the consumerist leadership of the Netherlands in the next century.

Elites and status

The quest to differentiate between the middling urban groups and urban elites (or Henry Kamen's 'middle élite') forms part of a lively discussion by many historians regarding elites in early modern Europe. Increasingly we stress the variety of elites, their interconnections, and the tensions between the rich and poor within them. Legally titled nobles provided one kind of elite, but we can identify other political and social elites that had no noble title or designation, though in the west they might be increasingly called 'gentleman', 'gentiluomo', 'gentilhomme'. Urban elites persisted, including untitled 'nobles' (sometimes called patricians, as in Venice), of merchants, office-holders, lawyers; sometimes they were in competition with the landed nobility (though less murderously so than in early Renaissance Italian struggles). Sometimes a composite 'nobility' and 'aristocracy' (rule of the best) might be based on birth (a good lineage), virtue (as in military valour), competence (as a counsellor), and education. The assumption was that nobility and its associated power was based on land ownership, and income from land; this was particularly so in Central and Eastern Europe and Scandinavia, but it was a major consideration in Britain, France, or Spain, and parts of Italy. Some of the urban elites (as in north–central Italian cities, Rhineland Germany, and France, the Netherlands, Seville), having based their power and money on trade, civic government, the law, or the court, increasingly invested in land, for safer investments or social status. In a reverse process, land-based nobles might take over from merchants in running commercial cities, like Córdoba. From later in the century landed nobles might show a preference for living all or part of the time in the city, for reasons of culture or court politics, such as the dukes of Sessa in Córdoba, the Chincon in Segovia, or the Carracciolo, Carafa, or Pignatelli in Naples.

Under the Medici grand dukes of Tuscany from the mid-century, the elite or elites in Florence and around became interestingly mixed, comprising old patrician families with banking and merchant origin, new bureaucratic families, new and old families developing land interests and being granted fiefs, literary figures and academicians educating, honouring, and amusing the Medici court. Lesser members of old elite families (such as Capponi, Guicciardini, and Corsini), were prepared to be involved in leading crafts, as in gold-work, as well as being active merchants. The Gondi family trading with Lyon secured a French barony.

The landed interest remained powerful through the century, whether under traditional noble families, or newer ones buying up in rural areas, sometimes being granted new fiefs. The great Spanish grandee nobles controlled huge tracts of land and people, such as the dukes of Alva, Medinaceli, or Medina Sidonia. Philip II, in planning for the duke of Medina Sidonia to lead an Armada invasion against England, reckoned to draw on his resources and have a feudal force to man the invasion. Whether he succeeded or failed in an invasion and occupation, the duke's resources would be depleted, and he would be a less powerful magnate compared with the crown. From about 1589 the Zamoyski family built up a major territorial state within a state in Poland-Lithuania, moving towards the ten towns, 220 villages, and 100,000 people they controlled by the eighteenth century. Much of this aggrandisement may be seen as of considerable economic, social, and cultural benefit, as solid towns were built, churches and schools established, and rural commerce promoted.

For the elite strata the pursuit of titles, fiefs, and honour were an increasing preoccupation through the century. Elite priorities were dominated by the recognition of their status, as noble and gentlemanly, with or without title. Much literature in Italy, then France and England was preoccupied with honour, virtue, and the allied courtly behaviour, overlaid with at least a veneer of cultural appreciation. Baldassarre Castiglione's *The Book of the Courtier* (first published in 1528), was the most famous and popular example. This complex dialogue combined a civilized cynical version of Machiavellism in courtly advice to a prince, debates on ideal love and beauty, the need to tame noble warriors, and to have women provide a cultural civilizing mission at courts. While set in a court context, some of its messages were to be passed down the social scale to gentlemen by the end of the century. The attitudes encouraged those wanting to be considered noble and gentlemanly by virtue, not just birth, to patronize literature and the arts. But it helped to have one's noble status socially recognized by title, and even the award of territorial fiefs, which might give local power, and profit to boot. For some it was enough to be addressed by a suitable prefix: the Honourable, Most Illustrious, the Most Eminent, and so forth. In Spain to be recognized as Don, implied a noble *hidalgo* status, but also being a good old Christian, uncontaminated by recent Jewish or Muslim blood, or a heretical charge. The 'honour' concept was not entirely an elitist concern; being respected in society was of considerable importance, along with being the 'right' kind of Christian after the division of the churches. English town dwellers of the middling sort were intent on being recognized as 'gentlemen'. Italians appearing before both secular and ecclesiastical courts tried to secure witnesses to attest that they could be counted as a man of good repute—'un'uomo da ben'.

The princes increasingly granted titles (duke, count, marquis), with or without territorial 'fiefs', hoping to buy support by such means. A territorial 'fief' could involve control over a significant town and surrounding territory, with major jurisdictional control, and little recourse by the vassals to royal authority. Such was the case in parts of Spain, and the Kingdom of Naples, Poland, Brandenburg, for example. But in some cases, as in Piedmont or other fiefs in the Kingdom of Naples, the fief-holder's power was limited, the area restricted, communal control was active, and what mattered to the noble was his title, in prestige terms.

A key consideration for the elites was 'privilege', meaning either a positive right to do something, or a special exemption. At the political level it might be the privilege to sit in a particular senior representative assembly: the House of Lords in England, the second chamber in the French Estates-General or local estates (where the clergy were the first estate), the upper house of the Swedish riksdag, the Great Council of Republican Venice. 'Privilege' might include the right to be tried in a special court, to be executed by the sword and not ignominiously hanged, to have a coat-of-arms as a badge of birth and virtue, to carry weapons openly, to be exempt from certain taxes. The fullest privileges accompanied the grant of a fief with virtually full jurisdictional control. Some privileges, especially the right to carry arms, could be granted to people far down the social scale. Tax exemption privileges could be bought by towns, or individual burghers and bourgeois; sales of these brought immediate cash for the crown, despite the long-term loss to a tax-base. Vassals of a fief were not necessarily unhappy being such; it might be better to be under a Spanish or Neapolitan duke or marquis—often absent or anxious to foster a local clientele network—because his taxes, or demands for work on the demesne estate, might be lighter than the taxes and dues imposed on those under direct royal control. In contrast, vassals could make murderous attacks on fief-holders who were too extortionate or tyrannical; quite a number so suffered in Neapolitan fiefs 1511–12. It was wise to exercise 'privilege' warily.

Claude de Seyssel, a counsellor to Louis XII and diplomat, argued in his *The Monarchy of France* that the privileged nobility was the key to social and political harmony, if they used their privileged position and a good humanist education to limit royal power by good laws and counsel, and helped to ensure harmony between the orders of society by recognizing the rights and roles of other orders, and serving state and society. Such ideals were held in the period, even if very dominant French noble families were soon disastrously to foster civil-religious unrest.

The increasing stress of elites on honour, respectability, and virtue, on military prowess, and prosperity through land, has led to the criticism that top elites of nobles and magnates were inhibitors of economic and social change. This is misleading. Venetian patrician families might from the mid-century withdraw from risky international trade, and invest in Palladian villas, with working farms (as with the Barbaros' splendid Villa Maser) on the mainland; but that activity, as carried out by the Barbaro or Michiel, was thoroughly entrepreneurial and was accompanied by investments in irrigation and canals. The results raised the living standards of the mainland areas. The Foscarini remained involved in the olive oil and timber businesses. In Austria, Hungary, and Bohemia great magnate families grew rich through involvement in mining (such as the Auerspergs controlling mercury mines in Idria in Carniola), fish raising in artificial ponds (by the Hradec family), and notably (for Hungarian families like the Zays, Dobós, and Zrinkis), the cattle-trade, which fed Venice among other places. Some of this expansion was achieved by expropriating the lesser gentry, or by taking advantage of the alienation of royal lands.

Rural and urban society: mobility

Sixteenth-century society was significantly mobile, both in geographical and social terms, whatever the emphasis on birth might imply for the latter. Urban communities needed a net inflow to sustain their populations; many young people spent time away from home, and locality, to be servants, apprentices, or farm helpers. The shift from arable to pasturage, or the enclosure of common lands drove considerable numbers of peasants to Elizabethan London, and Rome or Naples in the same period. Seasonal migrations could take males especially considerable distances, as they took advantage of labour needs for harvests, or moved flocks to pastures and back to winter housing or slaughter. Some might be trekking with cattle from the Hungarian plain to near Venice, from the Anglo-Scottish border to the London area; mountain peoples from the Alps moved to French vineyards, or from Piedmont to Sicilian fishing fleets. Much migration was longer term or permanent. The overseas expansion attracted large numbers of Europeans to the Americas, and fewer to the African coast and Far East, primarily from Portugal and Spain in our period. The wars of the period added to the mobility; the Italian wars, with their enlarged armies, had French and Spanish nobles and lowly foot-soldiers on the move, along with Germans and Swiss mercenaries. Later the French Wars of Religion, and the struggles over the Netherlands attracted people from Italy and the German states, as well as putting many locals on the move. The results are illustrated by the strange tale of the impostor Martin Guerre, made famous by the film version of another excellent microhistory—by Natalie Zemon Davis—that has many insights into French society at several levels. The division of the Netherlands led many families or individuals unwilling to remain under Spanish rule in the south, to relocate in the north, adding to the social diversity, and wealth, of the latter.

Such primarily male mobility could be very disruptive of family life, and might encourage or enforce female mobility, whether women were seeking lost husbands, or employment as camp followers. The Christian recovery in Iberia in the late fifteenth century sent those of Jewish and then Muslim faith who were unwilling to 'convert' further afield—to North Africa, the Netherlands, Venice, or to the Balkans and Middle East (to cities like Salonika, Alexandria, and Aleppo), where the Ottoman Empire was more tolerant of Jews. Heightened anti-Semitism in the century, for instance from some popes, added to the disruption, as did the increase in formal Ghetto areas (created first in Venice in 1516, where the local name gave rise to the generic term) where Jews were to be allowed, but segregated.

The social interchange between country and town was not one-way, as some points above might suggest. The major annual fairs and markets all over Europe attracted 'peasants' and intermediary traders from considerable distances, as well as the big merchants. The urban experience would have a cultural effect on those returning—with news, gossip, new artefacts, fashions, or a taste for them. It is now thought possible that a market in second-hand goods may have affected rural as well as urban consumerism. Pedlars increasingly roamed through Europe, with trinkets, pots, or medicines, but also news-sheets, cheap images of the Virgin or a potentially helpful saint, or scurrilous attacks on the pope or friars (according to the local religious market). For good or ill rural communities were increasingly exposed to urban visitors, in the forms of tax-collectors, lawyers, and agents of landowners, senior religious officials checking on the merits of priests or pastors in dealing with their parishioners, or hunting out alleged 'witches', or at least dubious local healers. Some rural areas not too far from the great cities might be beneficially affected by the trend of some nobility to spend conspicuously on retreats from the big city—for pleasure or agricultural supervision. These creations—new houses, hunting lodges and villas, or domesticized old castles—were produced in Elizabethan England, or hilly areas around Florence, Rome, or Madrid. Some economic and cultural aspects affected the local population.

In the cases of more select influential groups, long-distance mobility can be discovered among students and religious dissidents, as well as artists and musicians. While Italy tended to be the main magnet for many, for religious reasons Italian exiles were to be found in Geneva—where they proved more fickle and theologically undisciplined than the French, as Calvin complained—and in Poland or England. Scots looked for inspiration in Geneva or France, or in Rome if remaining Catholic. Italian universities still attracted non-Italians, and Philip II's attempts to keep Spanish scholars within Spain were not entirely successful. Foreigners in key cities like Bologna, Perugia, Rome, and

Venice, whether students, visiting clergy, merchants, or artisans might join or form 'nations' that gave them a social and linguistic base, socio-economic networks, and a confraternity religious base. The nations could be narrow or broad according to numbers; a Bergamo or Norcia nation in Rome on the one hand, or a German nation that included Bohemians, Hungarians, and some Netherlanders (while others linked with the Flemish-French) at Perugia university. Glasgow University, influenced by Bologna, had different student 'nations', groupings still active through to the twentieth century. The more arti-san-based nations were a major social asset for immigrants. The Spanish national confraternity in Rome (which after 1580 embraced Portuguese, as well as Catalans and Castilians), linked ambassadors, Spanish cardinals, lawyers, and artisans. It has recently been seen as a key aspect of Philip II's imperial Spanish policies, and as a step towards a more modern concept of nationalism.

Gender relations

Our period witnessed debates about the nature of women, and their roles in society, especially in northern Italy, France, and England. Historians have debated with much controversy whether attitudes became more or less misogynistic, and whether socio-economic opportunities for females worsened or improved. No simple patterns of change can be detected. The spread of printing in the sixteenth century contributed to our awareness of a debate on gender rela-tionships; modern historians can point to both misogynist diatribes, and proto-feminist writings by males and females, in the latter case especially from the Venetian presses from the end of the century. Females were undoubtedly legally and politically inferior to men, unless they happened to be rulers like Mary and Elizabeth of England, Mary of Scotland, Catherine de Médicis as regent and queen mother in France. Women were not members of representative assemblies, nor members of city councils, and if allowed to be members of guilds were rarely if ever officials; though Cologne and Nuremberg had some women-only guilds at least in the early century. There were major restrictions on what legal contracts women could sign in their own right, and they normally needed their husband's permission to buy and sell as retailers. For such legal reasons they often escape from official historical records. But recently social historians have found more subtle ways of detecting female social and economic roles, or influences, often through studying wills and testaments.

For many families the family and household was an integrated socio-economic unity, whatever the configurations of generations. Girls and women—whether as wives, daughters, or widowed relatives—could help with artisan production, or running farm activities, in between looking after younger children. Young girls and unmarried women might be away from home for a while, as servants or textile workers, and then be incorporated into a household working unit. Possibly increasing numbers of females, unmarried and married, might have independent economic existences, especially in the Netherlands, northern France, and northern Italy in textile work and lace-making, and more occasionally as apothecaries, inn-keepers (with equal status as guild 'brothers' in London from 1514), and even blacksmiths in the Venetian arsenal. But the family artisan units and farms persisted. The women's work might generally be the more menial and less skilled than the males', but their literacy and numeracy could also be encouraged so they could be the book-keepers. We know also that with the expansion of printing in Italy daughters and wives became valued as typesetters and as proof-readers; and widows in the Netherlands as well as Italy could take over running the presses, if not doing the hard physical labour of pulling the presses. Women as widows in general could come into greater social and economic influence or power, but variations were considerable between occupations and geographical areas, with guilds taking very different attitudes. Printers and bakers probably fared better than those involved in the textiles industries. Women in various German cities lost out, partly through Reformation attitudes, but widows in England, Augsburg, or northern Italy might gain more power and influence. In terms of widows' and wives' positions, historians of Tuscany tend to stress continuing rigid control by male relatives, while those dealing with Venice and Rome detect increased female roles in handling their dowries, family matters such as marriage alliances, and even landed property, as sanctioned by the wills of husbands. Artisan widows in England, who often lacked the protective dowries found in Italian society, might be far more vulnerable.

The impact of the religious debates and struggles on the position of women remains contentiously debated. Arguably Protestant biblical reading fostered an attitude that women suffered from the sin of Eve, and so were both inferior and dangerous, because of their sexual wiles. Circles around Luther and his supporters fostered misogynist writings and prints. The visual images of Hans Baldung Grien, in drawings, paintings, and prints made from them, have been judged as contributing to the pornographic image of the dangerously destructive female witch, participating in orgiastic sabats or enticing with her nudity. Such depictions supposedly encouraged the witch-craze in Germany, along with the Old Testament injunction that a witch should not be suffered to live. Other images and literature in Germany and England argued that women were too dominant, were on top of men, usurping male roles; with the implication that the new religious teaching should keep women in their place at home as obedient wives and dutiful mothers. It is a moot point whether the images, or the English ducking-stool used against allegedly bossy, gossipy, or sexually scandalous women should be used as evidence of male tyranny and misogyny, or of continuing female success in asserting a rightful position in society. Protestant fervour led to the closure of civic brothels and red-light districts in some German cities, whereas Catholic authorities tended to continue tolerating licensed prostitution as a lesser evil that made honourable women safer from predatory males. All religious denominations promoted marriage and marital values more assiduously, even if marriage was no longer a sacrament in Protestant eyes. This rendered bastardy less tolerable, contributing to the greater abandonment of illegitimate babies, and the expulsion of pregnant servants, where in the past such might have been retained within larger households.

If the reinforcement of religious values had some adverse effects for women, more positive effects might also be discerned by the end of the century, at least in middling Western urban society. The intent that the family should be more devout and better informed about Christian values implied that prayers should be said at home, and improving literature read. In Protestant households the Bible might be the chosen text (though one must be aware that it could also be an unread token, opened mainly to record the family genealogy), but while Catholic households were discouraged from having vernacular translations of the Bible, they were encouraged by some Catholic reformers to have other religious devotional texts for home reading. While the male head of household had the duty to lead a devout family, his wife or mother might well be the one to teach the next generation to read so as to continue religious devotion. Venetian presses from the mid-century led the way in producing books to help parents teach children to read. In Catholic areas girls from more prosperous families might be sent to nunneries for an education; they might end up as literate mothers and not nuns in their turn. Those remaining behind enclosed walls are now shown in some cases to include composers, painters, and writers—of devotional works, plays, or letters of spiritual guidance; and some enclosed women like Maddalena de'Pazzi might goad cardinals or secular rulers into religious and moral reform.

In the circles of high culture, the sixteenth century witnessed the acclaim of a few women as leading poets, painters, and musicians. Several benefited from having fathers or husbands to train and encourage them (like the painters Marietta Robusti Tintoretto and Lavinia Fontana, or musicians like Francesca Caccini). Sofonisba Anguissola, despite having no such background, could move from Italy to the Spanish court as a portrait painter for while; she then returned to Italy to train her younger sisters, and to support her father and brother financially. Some leading contributors were courtesans (like the poet Tullia d'Aragona in Rome and Florence), or risked being accused of winning notoriety by providing sexual favours to patrons, such as the Basile sisters as singers at the court of Mantua and in Rome at the end of the century. The most notable example was the very talented Venetian poet Veronica Franco, whom Henri III of France specifically requested to meet when he detoured through Venice on his way back from his brief spell as king of Poland to take up the newly vacant throne of France in 1573, on the death of his brother. They subsequently exchanged poetry. She campaigned for the charitable treatment of less fortunate prostitutes and their children, as opposed to the prison-like institutions where they were often housed. This 'feminine side' earned Henri III the disapproval of those who saw his court as dominated by a quest for effete Italianate aesthetic delights rather than military prowess and true religion.

Italy retained a reputation for sexual licence, for males and females, even though its leading reformers joined northern Protestants in calling for sexual restraint, adherence to the strict bonds of marriage, and chastity. Fornicators came to be hunted by the godly 'police' as much in parts of Italy as in Scotland, Geneva, or Catalonia; but much of the moral policing in most areas must have been haphazard. Despite episcopal rules and investigations, local society might well continue, after Tridentine reformers went into action, to accept their local priest having a comely woman as housekeeper (and even mother of children), rather than an ancient relative, provided she was discreet and not bossy. Northern Italy and France were seemingly more prone to produce writings defending the equality of women and their rights equally to enjoy culture and sexual relations: these attitudes can be seen in the erotic poetry of Gaspara Stampa and Louise Labé as well as Franco. Despite draconian city statutes against unnatural non-procreative sexual acts—'sodomy' defined in a wide sense—especially when committed by males, the humanist climate in the early sixteenth century was inclined to celebrate or tolerate male love and friendship, spiritual and sometimes physical, and bisexuality. The *Autobiography* of the rumbustious Florentine goldsmith and sculptor Benvenuto Cellini celebrates this, with whatever distortions. Heavy sentences, including death, were very rarely inflicted, except upon paedophile priests. Florence and Venice were attacked for tolerating homosexual activity, as much as female courtesanship. Though the changing mood from mid-century fought against this (as Cellini's book and experiences also indicate) Venice at least maintained a reputation for male sexual licence, and supposedly attracted Elizabethan gentlemen visitors as a result.

The poor and social control

Poverty, like beauty, can be in the eye of the beholder; it is defined relative to expectations, and to fashion. It was a topic debated throughout the sixteenth century, and enlivens modern historical debate. From the early sixteenth century the problem was analysed by religious and political figures and leading humanist writers, led by the Spaniard Juan Luis de Vives, who wrote his *De subventione pauperum* (1526, 'On the Relief of the Poor') in the Netherlands. It was claimed that the numbers of 'poor' were increasing; that they were becoming more dangerous, especially in urban areas (with recent immigrants moving from war threats or the dislocation of landholdings); that old charity (supposedly indiscriminate) encouraged idleness; and that it did not help the genuinely needy and deserving poor. Local governments, led in the 1520s by Nuremberg, Ypres, Mons, Bruges, and Venice, in various ways introduced legislative controls, and looked for remedies. Cities like Wittenberg, Lille, or Venice attempted more systematic poor relief or the organization of food supplies in the face of dearth, even though their policies were largely negative. Measures taken included punishment and expulsion from the city of vagabonds (as attempted in Paris as early as 1516), or idle beggars (especially if recent arrivals), and sometimes prostitutes. Begging was banned or severely controlled. The more deserving might be allowed to beg under licence, as in London from the 1520s. Enforcing controls was however very difficult; but the mentality developed that governments could and should control a potentially dangerous population of 'poor', and should directly or indirectly foster some help for the genuinely needy and 'deserving'. The latter were usually envisaged as vulnerable children, old women, and (sometimes) the severely disabled. Pressures were also placed on communities, parishes, and families to assist their poor.

During the century attitudes and policies evolved in complicated and diverse ways through Western Europe. The religious conflicts had various effects. The Protestant attacks on and closure of monasteries and confraternities removed traditional sources of some help for the poor. Initially the advocacy of salvation by faith alone and the attack on salvation through good works supposedly reduced charity in Protestant areas, but almost certainly fostered diverse philanthropic activity in response in Catholic areas—in north–central Italy, Spain, and parts of France. But by the end of the century the Catholic–Protestant division was less marked. Protestants might exclude 'good works' from the salvation process, but leading Calvinists in England, Scotland, or Geneva, might encourage some philanthropy as a sign of being saved; though they were more inclined to encourage educational charity than material donations. Almshouses for the deserving old could be provided in Protestant London, Salisbury, or York, or in Catholic Münster and Venice. Both Protestant and Catholic governments could attempt the rationalization of hospital systems, amalgamating small hospices and their funds to create larger institutions (as Milan and other Lombard cities had already done in the fifteenth century). Hospitals were for the poor, not the rich (who had doctors come to the home). Syphilis, allegedly imported from the Americas in the 1490s, was noted first in Italy during the French invasion to Naples, and hence was called the French or Neapolitan pox. It led to the foundation of hospitals for the 'incurables' in Rome, Naples, and then elsewhere. Especially from the mid-century new institutions were fostered, to house orphans and abandoned children, repentant prostitutes, even battered wives. There were also mendicant 'hospitals' (led by Bologna in the 1560s, or London's Bridewell in 1553, and subsequent houses of correction in Ipswich and Norwich in the 1560s), which gathered in the begging poor, for a mixture of shelter, punishment, street control, moral control, religious education, in-house work for the able, and medical care. This institutionalization and social control was to become more fashionable in the next century, especially in France. The English moved towards a poor law system (in reality unsystematic) that tried to get the parish to support its own poor—with the mobile (especially London or Norwich immigrants) to be sent back to the parish of origin. Some Italian and Spanish authorities also encouraged parochial home relief, but without a back-to-base corollary.

By the end of the century urban Western Europe had, on the one hand, a better controlled set of social welfare systems (mixing civic authority, Church, and private philanthropy), and more rigorous moral-social control. On the other, poverty on the streets or within churches, vagabondage, street gangs (as allegedly well organized in Seville or Rome) were not eradicated, and the European-wide food crises of the 1590s made them worse.

Fears and tensions

Much comment on European society in the sixteenth century suggests that fears and tensions grew through the period. It allegedly became a society more troubled by economic dislocation in the disruption of landholdings, leading to more landless peasants; and was more disturbed by warfare, conducted on a grander scale, with larger armies, using more lethal weapons. Diseases and famine were major scourges. The Reformation struggles threw much in doubt, and as

Church leaders reorganized many more people probably feared how their beliefs and practices might be challenged, whether by consistories or inquisitors. Some cultural historians stress a seeming shift from the intellectual optimism of the humanist-led Renaissance, to an anti-Renaissance, where scepticism, doubt, irrationality, a reliance on astronomy and magical sciences predominated.

The so-called witch-craze has been judged as symptomatic of the tensions of the period, produced by the combination of fears of social dislocation and of strangers in the wider society, and an irrationality in intellectual circles that led those judging 'witchcraft' to be so credulous of fanciful stories about the work of the Devil and his agents. Fear of 'the other', the different was clearly in evidence; whether it was the Jew, the gypsy, the Anabaptist, or the threatening woman outside male control (and protection). All these were persecuted by society. It should be stressed that witch-hunting was very variable over time and place. There were some horrendous but very localized persecutions in Lorraine, around Geneva, or in Scotland. Much hinged on the local legal system and court structure, on how well the magistrates and judges were trained, how much torture was used, and whether accusers stood to gain financially from the condemned. In Iberia and Italy, issues of sorcery, magic, and 'malefice' (with or without a supposed diabolic invocation or worship) came under the Inquisition's control. In these countries the mass witch-hunt was virtually non-existent; harsh punishments of individuals were rare, and were reserved more for male clergy and others misusing the sacraments than an old crone on the village margins. Inquisition officials were well-trained, used torture sparingly, and were centrally instructed to be sceptical about neighbours' malicious denunciations when attempts at healing or love magic went wrong, or when a child died unexpectedly. European society had plenty of people, more female than male (since men led official religion and medicine), attempting lay healing, alternative medicines, love magic, prognostications; they could be helpful and appreciated, or feared if they did not perform as expected. The casualty figures for 'witches' have often been exaggerated, and they are not compared with the more elusive figures—and similarly barbarous punishments—for 'normal' crimes. Nevertheless, the overall preponderance of women to men (70:30) in witchcraft and sorcery cases would not be matched in other categories of crime.

Europeans during the sixteenth century were increasingly affected by the popularization of print that spread information—and misinformation. More could know more about events far-afield—whether St Bartholomew's Massacre, the murder of Henri IV, plague scares, or a monstrous birth presaging disaster. These could add to fears and tensions in society; other 'news' and information—about a religious war success, or a cure for the pox—might raise hopes. Through pedlars and oral communication much could percolate down to the illiterate majority in Western Europe at least.

In considering sixteenth-century society generally, the modern pessimistic historian can stress social, political, and religious conflicts. The more optimistic can highlight what held society together, the bonds and social interdependence, advantageous social and physical mobility in the west, the attempted remedies for social ills (even when these included a punitive element), the medical improvements, Western urban consumerism pointing to rising standards of living—at least before the gloomy depression years of the 1590s–1610s.

4

The mind

Charles G. Nauert

At the beginning of the sixteenth century, the culture of Renaissance Italy had begun to exert a powerful influence on Europe north of the Alps. Italian humanism passed along to Northern Europe many achievements. One was linguistic: a more classical style of Latin and mastery of two languages, Greek and Hebrew, that had been almost unknown to medieval Western Christendom. Along with the languages came greater access to classical literature. By 1500, most of the major Latin authors had been made available in print. A century later, most of classical and patristic Greek literature had also been published; in addition, a considerable body of classical literature had been published in vernacular translations. Even more important than such tangible influence, however, was the concept of Renaissance (cultural rebirth) itself, for humanists from the time of Petrarch (1304–74) had developed a characteristic outlook on the history of Europe and their own place in it. That view of history dismissed the medieval centuries as 'barbarous' and professed a sublime if somewhat vague confidence that ancient civilization could be restored through the humanists' own efforts to rediscover the heritage of antiquity. Belief that a better world could be manufactured out of the literary remains of Greece and Rome shaped the mentality of the educated classes on both sides of the Alps. These developments led to demands for reform of schools and universities in order to give less attention to some subjects that had dominated medieval education (most notoriously, dialectic) and much more attention to classical languages and literatures. While much of the medieval educational programme persisted long after 1600, humanistic influence on education grew throughout the sixteenth century.

Northern Europe: Christian humanism

This interest in humanistic studies was unmistakably Italian in its origins, but each country took from Italy only what it found attractive. Although many Italian humanists had been deeply religious, Italian humanism in general had been secular. Its goal was to transform education, literature, and even political life; but it did not define a clear set of religious goals. Transalpine Europe had a very different culture. Before humanism could spread beyond a handful of individuals dazzled by contemporary Italy, it had to become something more than a literary enthusiasm. It had to become Christian. Late medieval Northern Europe had developed a number of popular movements seeking personal holiness and Church reform. In order to flourish, northern humanism had to link its Italianate classical interests with reforms that embraced this longing for both personal spiritual renewal and reform of the Church. The earliest northern humanists had not been very spiritual. In Germany, the leaders of the first two generations of humanists, the 'wandering poet' Peter Luder (1415–72) and Conrad Celtis (1459–1505), a man known mainly for propagating the new learning by organizing humanistic societies in German cities, were notoriously dissolute and unstable individuals. Their poems dealt more with drinking and wenching than with holiness. The leading figure among early French humanists, Robert Gaguin (1423–1501), though he was a respected monk, wrote on secular themes such as the early history of the Franks. He had no programme for regeneration of religion through scholarship.

About 1500, however, several humanists began associating a desire to restore classical civilization with determination to bring about a revival of spiritual life and an institutional reform of the Church. Early examples of this new direction were the Alsatian humanist Jakob Wimpfeling (1450–1528) and the dean of St Paul's Cathedral, John Colet (1467–1519). Both of them saw in improved education of lay and clerical elites an effective means to initiate a gradual improvement in the condition of Christendom. Both were attracted by Italian humanism. Yet both were fearful that the study of classical literature would expose schoolboys to pagan influences that might subvert their faith and morals. Their solution was to favour study of the Christian Latin authors of late antiquity. They admitted to their educational programmes only a few pagan authors of outstanding moral reputation, such as Cicero and Vergil, on the grounds that these were acknowledged masters of Latin style and their writings expressed the highest moral values attainable in a pre-Christian world. Dissolute poets like Horace, Ovid, and Martial had no place in their Christian schools.

What none of the early northern humanists had achieved before 1500 was a way of integrating admiration for ancient civilization with efforts to recapture the inner spirit of the ancient Church. The true inventors of Christian humanism were the French humanist Jacques Lefèvre d'Etaples (c.1453–1536) and the Dutch humanist Desiderius Erasmus (c.1467–1536). Like Wimpfeling and Colet, they believed that the best means to regenerate a corrupt Christendom was through better education of future leaders. Both of them wanted to bring about a renewal that would be nourished by scripture and the works of the Church Fathers but also by the noblest elements of classical thought. Erasmus was the more eloquent and the more outspoken about the defects of the contemporary Church that impeded spiritual renewal. He employed his gift for satire in books like *The Praise of Folly* and the *Colloquies*. These works denounced and ridiculed clergymen who exploited simple people by promoting materialistic observances that did little for the soul, but much to enhance the wealth and power of the clergy. Erasmus also was a critic of social injustice and an outspoken pacifist in an age of frequent wars.

Lefèvre spent much of his career teaching at the University of Paris, the centre of medieval scholasticism. Attracted by contemporary Italian culture, he made three trips to Italy (1491–1507) to enrich his understanding of the new learning. He met the leaders of Florentine Neoplatonism, Marsilio Ficino (1433–99) and Giovanni Pico della Mirandola (1463–94). Back in Paris, however, his first move was an attempt to improve the teaching of Aristotle, the traditional philosophical authority, by introducing new translations made directly from Greek to replace the thirteenth-century Latin versions. Lefèvre also edited works of ancient and medieval mystics and Greek patristic authors. After his retirement from teaching in 1508, he turned to the Bible. His *Quincuplex Psalterium* (*Fivefold Psalter*, 1509) and his commentary on the Epistles of St Paul (1512), though less innovative than Erasmus' biblical scholarship, were published first.

The religious programme of Erasmus .

Erasmus, however, was the one whose publications dazzled the idealistic young humanists who aspired to transform the world. He combined study of the classics, the Church Fathers, and the Bible with a conception of personal piety and reform of the Church that swept through the educated classes of Western Europe. As a boy and then a young monk, his interests were mainly literary and linguistic. While studying theology at Paris, he found scholastic learning intellectually stultifying and soon drifted away from theology, becoming one of the many humanistic poets who collected in the French capital.

Sometime between 1498 and 1505, Erasmus was converted from being just a minor Latin poet into the leader of a specifically humanistic and Christian reform movement, determined to recapture not only the literary heritage of ancient Greece and Rome but also the spiritual power of the early Christian Church, as reflected in the New Testament and the writings of the Church Fathers. He articulated an ideology that he named 'the philosophy of Christ' and adopted as the foundation for his career as a Christian scholar. This 'philosophy' held that the crucial part of being a Christian is a highly personal devotion to God rather than external things like dogmas or rituals. This personal devotion must be expressed in a life devoted to the welfare of religion and society. He expounded this ideal in his *Enchiridion militis Christiani* (*Handbook of the Militant Christian*, 1503), which became a popular devotional work. He also concluded that serious scholarship on the Bible and the Church Fathers required mastery of Greek, the language of the New Testament. He sketched out a programme of explicitly Christian scholarship, focused on the Greek text of the New Testament and the Greek patristic authors. His goal was to bring the spirit of the early Christian Church back to life. He also identified the most scholarly of the Latin Fathers, St Jerome, the reputed translator of the Vulgate Latin Bible, as his first object of study. In 1504–5, his discovery and publication of the unpublished *Annotations on the New Testament*, in which the Italian humanist Lorenzo Valla applied his knowledge of Greek to explain obscure passages in the Latin Bible, sharpened Erasmus' determination to probe the Greek text of the New Testament and to bring insights from those studies into his programme of spiritual renewal. His ambitious programme of biblical, patristic, and classical scholarship required more than ten years of hard work, three of them spent in Italy, to reach fulfilment; but in 1516, the most productive year of his life, he brought out the first published edition of the Greek New Testament, a four-volume edition of the letters of St Jerome, and (representing his continuing interest in classical literature) an edition of the Roman moralist Seneca. These publications made him the most famous scholar in Europe, idolized by idealistic young humanists who embraced his goal of bringing about a fundamental (but gradual and peaceful) reform of both the spiritual life and the ecclesiastical structures of Christendom. By then, Erasmus had also published several popular works that sharply criticized contemporary Church and society, especially his great satire *The Praise of Folly* (first published in 1511 but considerably augmented in later editions). He had developed an explicitly Christian type of humanistic scholarship and a characteristically 'Erasmian' vision of religious renewal.

The publications of Lefèvre and Erasmus also caught the unfavourable attention of conservative theologians who regarded their questioning of traditional Latin texts of the Bible and their frank criticism of abuses as an attack on the authority of the Church. Both Lefèvre and Erasmus became objects of suspicion. The ferocity of these attacks increased as theologians began worrying about the spread of the Lutheran heresy. Lefèvre's translation of the New Testament into French (1523) was interpreted as proof of Lutheran sympathies. In the face of these attacks, the ageing humanist retired to the court of his patron Margaret of Navarre and by 1526 had virtually given up active efforts to reform the Church. Like Erasmus, however, Lefèvre was never willing to break with the traditional Church.

Erasmus became more influential than Lefèvre. Humanists young and old hailed his biblical, patristic, and classical publications. By 1520, his works had convinced many young humanists that the triumph of the 'philosophy of Christ' and the reform of the Church had become inevitable. These hopes faded as Erasmus's reform movement became involved with the Reformation. Once it had become clear that the Reformation was dividing the Church, most older humanists joined Erasmus himself in pulling back from any early sympathy for Martin Luther. Erasmus's attack on Luther in *De libero arbitrio* (*On Freedom of the Will*, 1524) was a decisive event, for its reception demonstrated that many young humanists, though they still admired Erasmus's scholarly achievements and his witty satires on abuses in Church and secular society, had ceased to be just humanists and had become Lutherans. Erasmus also retained admirers among humanists who remained Catholic. In the long run, however, as efforts to reunite the Church through negotiation and compromise failed, the Erasmian position became untenable. Many ex-Erasmians began to share the conservatives' opinion that Erasmus' frank denunciation of corruption in the Church and his subjective conception of the Christian's relation to God had undermined the authority of the Church and contributed to the successes of the heretics.

By mid-century, the reputation of 'Christian humanists' in Catholic Europe had sunk even lower. Although the harsh Index of Forbidden Books issued in 1559 by Pope Paul IV was atypical in placing Erasmus among authors whose works Catholics were totally forbidden to print, possess, or read, and although enforcement lapsed after the pope's death in August of the same year, the somewhat more moderate Tridentine Index issued by Pius IV in 1564 was still hostile. In this revised list, only six works by Erasmus (including popular works like the *Colloquies* and *The Praise of Folly*) were totally prohibited; his other publications, including his patristic and even his biblical scholarship, might be lawfully reprinted, but only after objectionable passages had been expurgated and censors had approved a revised text. It remains true, however, that authors whose works were theoretically permissible if expurgated were cited less readily (especially by name) than before the promulgation of the papal indexes and their counterparts in Spain and Portugal. Moderate Catholics lobbied at Rome to preserve access to non-theological works by humanists and even by some Protestant authors, but with only limited success. The Index only confirmed a trend that was becoming evident before 1559: the Christian humanism that galvanized young humanists and alarmed conservative theologians in the period 1500–30 perished as a distinct movement in the middle decades of the century.

That does not mean, however, that humanism in all its aspects disappeared or even declined. Rather, it narrowed its ambitions. Humanism retained and even increased its role in the education of the elite classes of Europe, both lay and clerical. In Catholic lands, the new Jesuit order, which founded its first school in 1548, rapidly became one of the most powerful forces in European education. Erasmus's attacks on clerical corruption and his individualistic piety made Erasmian humanism unacceptable in Jesuit schools. But the non-Erasmian, classical side of humanism became a Jesuit specialty. Except for the brand of theology taught, the Jesuit schools were very much like the best of the Lutheran and Reformed schools organized by Protestant reformers like Philipp Melanchthon (1497–1560) and Johann Sturm (1507–89). Humanism lived on for centuries as the foundation for the education of Europe's elite classes.

Classical scholarship in literature and law

Another major activity of fifteenth-century Italian humanists, the criticism and editing of classical literature, continued to flourish. Italy still produced classical scholars of note, but the centre of humanism defined as a programme of textual scholarship passed north of the Alps, first to France and later (mainly after 1600) to the Netherlands. The decisive figure in establishing French leadership was Guillaume Budé (1468–1540), whose books on Roman law, Roman weights and measures, and Greek lexicography marked new directions in scholarship. Budé's work marks a significant shift of humanism away from Petrarchan or Erasmian dreams of refashioning Christendom. He concentrated his efforts more on methods and factual discoveries than on transcendent and long-term ends that might (or might not) solve the problems of contemporary society. In a sense, Budé represents humanism with the Renaissance faith in the transformative effects of rediscovered ancient wisdom left out. As an official at the French court, Budé advocated the creation of a national institute of humanistic studies like those already established at Alcalá in Spain and Louvain in the Netherlands. In 1530 King Francis I appointed four prominent humanists as royal lecturers—two on Greek language and two on Hebrew—a small beginning for what eventually became the Collège Royal. Several of the royal lecturers became leaders in the rise of French classical scholarship to supremacy. French classical studies reached their peak in the careers of Henri Estienne (1528–98) and Josephus Justus Scaliger (1540–1609). Estienne was the greatest

Greek scholar of the late sixteenth century. His 1578 edition of the Greek text of Plato's works still is the foundation for scholarly citation of Plato, and his *Thesaurus Graecae linguae* (1572), a dictionary of classical Greek, has never been entirely superseded. Scaliger made his reputation with his study of Roman astronomy and the related field of ancient chronology, establishing the time-relationships among the calendars used by various ancient societies to date events.

French humanists also directed their attention to Roman law, as preserved in the *Corpus Juris Civilis* issued by the Byzantine emperor Justinian in 529–34. This line of research, known as legal humanism, stemmed from questions raised by Lorenzo Valla and Angelo Poliziano in the fifteenth century and pursued further by Budé's *Annotationes in Pandectas* (1508). Application of humanistic critical methods to legal texts revolutionized legal history. The legal humanist François Baudoin demonstrated that the Byzantine editors had misunderstood or distorted many of the rulings they collected for Justinian. His contemporary François Hotman in *Francogallia* (1573) challenged the medieval assumption that French law was derived from Roman law; its true origins were native and should be sought in the laws and charters issued by medieval French kings. Other legal scholars such as Pierre Pithou (1539–96) and Etienne Pasquier (1529–1615) continued this work, collecting and publishing the laws and charters of medieval France. Their manuscript discoveries mark the real origin of medieval history.

The search for the esoteric

As time passed and humanists saw that enthusiastic study of the major authors of Latin and Greek literature had not fulfilled their hopes of spiritual renewal through rediscovery of lost wisdom, many of them turned to a far more questionable body of writing, the 'ancient theology' associated with Jewish Cabbala, the Hermetic tracts, and other scraps of ancient theosophy such as the Orphic texts, the Zoroastrian oracles, the Pythagorean hymns, and the Sibylline books. These texts claimed to provide a body of knowledge that renewed the human spirit and led the individual soul toward reconciliation or even quasi-mystical union with the divine. Often, they also claimed to confer magical power over the material world on the soul that understood their secret meaning.

The sixteenth century, when the texts embodying this theosophical literature were becoming available and a genuinely critical assessment of their worth had not yet been made, was the golden age of European occultism. Only with the destructive textual criticism by J. J. Scaliger and Isaac Casaubon (1559–1614) at the end of the century did educated readers begin to abandon the naïve belief that the occultist texts contained a ready-made wisdom that would make all the terrible problems of the contemporary world go away. The modern mentality tends to dismiss the occultist learning of the Renaissance as superstition. Yet learned and sensible scholars, such as Ficino and Pico, studied these texts closely and remained unable to see that they were spurious.

Another name for this occult knowledge is magic, and the German humanist Agrippa von Nettesheim (1486–1535) provided the most comprehensive summary of Renaissance magic in his *De occulta philosophia* (*On Occult Philosophy*, 1533). His magic, strongly influenced by Florentine Neoplatonism, presumed a universe that was hierarchical in structure, one in which mysterious connections linked the parts together in ways that could not be discovered by reason but were communicated in ancient books. Renaissance magic was intended to be more than speculative theory. To the *magus*, the practitioner of magic, knowledge is power; and understanding of the mysterious connections between things located at various levels of the hierarchy could be used to confer power on the *magus*.

Astrology was the most widely practised occult science. The celestial bodies were presumed to affect terrestrial beings, including humans, in ways that could be learned through careful study. When astrologers tried to use celestial influences to predict the future, astrology became a criminal offence, for Church law forbade such attempts as contrary to free will and moral responsiblity, even though many popes, bishops, and kings also sought predictions. Other uses of astrological learning were fully respectable. Students of medicine needed to study the effects of celestial movements on weather, crops, and especially the health of humans and animals, since any competent physician should take them into account when diagnosing illness and prescribing remedies. Another occult science linked to magic was the body of Jewish mystical treatises known as the Cabbala. They claimed to preserve a secret revelation that God gave to Moses. Cabbalistic learning attracted the attention of humanists, ever on the look-out for ancient sources of enlightenment. The most famous Italian student of Cabbala was Giovanni Pico della Mirandola. Like all Christian cabbalists, Pico was convinced that the truths concealed in the Cabbala would prove Christian doctrines such as the divinity of Jesus. Similar ideas appear in the writings of the German humanist Johann Reuchlin (1455–1522), who visited Italy, met both Ficino and Pico, and wrote two books on Cabbala.

Aristotle revived and challenged

Although humanistic influence on education and high culture grew during the sixteenth century, the authority of Aristotle still dominated university studies, a domination that persisted into the seventeenth century. Sixteenth-century Catholic intellectual life experienced a revival of interest in the leading medieval Aristotelian, Thomas Aquinas. The Spanish theologian Francisco de Vitoria (c.1483–1546), who became professor of theology at Salamanca, made Salamanca the first centre for a neo-Thomist tradition that dominated Catholic philosophy until the middle of the twentieth century. Yet humanism itself posed a challenge to Aristotelian philosophy. Aristotle sought to determine absolute truth through logical reasoning. From the time of Petrarch, humanist rhetoricians had criticized scholastic rationalism and had insisted that the proper function of human thought was not the determination of truth but the making of morally sound choices among the alternative courses of action faced by humans in their daily lives. Such decisions, the sort of decisions involved in real life rather than in academic debates, involved not absolute truth but matters on which no decision could be more than probable. Thus humanist rhetoric had an anti-rationalistic and anti-philosophical tendency, and sixteenth-century humanistic reforms of university teaching made dialectic devote greater attention to questions open only to probable—rather than scientifically certain—conclusions. This new direction emerged in *De inventione dialectica* (*On Dialectical Invention*), written in 1479 by the German humanist Rudolf Agricola (1444–85) but not published until 1515. Agricola was dissatisfied with dialectic because it was narrowly focused on formal logic and on theoretical issues relevant only to the interests of academic specialists. His book introduced a large amount of rhetorical material into dialectic. He defined dialectic not as a means of attaining truth but as 'the art of speaking with probability on any topic whatsoever'. From its first publication, *De inventione* became the model textbook that humanists struggled (with considerable success) to introduce for university study of dialectic. *De inventione* marked a limited but influential rebellion against Aristotelian dialectic. An even more hostile criticism of Aristotelianism, involving direct attack on the authority of Aristotle, was found in the publications of Petrus Ramus (Pierre de la Ramée, 1515–72), which aroused fierce conflict in Northern Europe's leading university, Paris. Ramus attracted many supporters, though he was not very successful at defining the system that he wanted to substitute for Aristotelianism.

Despite such challenges, Aristotle still dominated the teaching of natural science, almost to the exclusion of any rival. The continuing hegemony of Aristotle's thought is sometimes cited as evidence that the universities were moribund, irrelevant to intellectual life. Yet there was no other system that could serve as a foundation for teaching natural philosophy. Aristotle's books were effectively organized, broadly comprehensive in coverage of the various sciences, and for the most part, more teachable than any proposed substitutes. The continuing dominance of Aristotle by no means meant that sixteenth-century thinkers followed him blindly. His many surviving works covered a long period of his own life and a broad range of topics. The works most useful for discussion of theology, such as his *Metaphysics*, were very different from those that might attract a natural scientist, such as his *Physics*. There was plenty in Aristotle for nearly everybody.

Italian scientists discovered in Aristotle a philosophy that was materialistic and not particlarly relevant to religion. The naturalistic interpretation of Aristotle by the Arab commentator Averroës not only survived but became more influential from the late fifteenth century. The Paduan professors Nicoletto Vernia (1420–99) and Agostino Nifo (*c.*1470–1538) wrote treatises on Averroës and generally accepted his interpretations, without much concern whether such an Aristotle undermined the biblical account of creation or belief in the immortality of the soul. The greatest representative of this secular Aristotelian tradition was Pietro Pomponazzi (1462–1525). Although Pomponazzi began his career as a Thomist, he concluded that Aquinas's arguments against Averroës were inadequate. His reconsideration of Aristotle's opinion on immortality convinced him that Aristotle did not teach that the individual soul survives separation from the body at death. He stated this view in his book *De immortalitate animae* (*On the Immortality of the Soul*, 1516). Pomponazzi's book on immortality aroused much opposition, but the attacks did not undermine his standing as the leading philosopher of his time.

Where Aristotle could not lead: mathematics and astronomy

Aristotle's neglect of mathematical reasoning and quantitative issues had created problems for Aristotelian scientists as early as the fourteenth century, when natural philosophers at Oxford and Paris found his *Physics* inadequate to explain the motion of projectiles. Their problem was inherent in the scientific thought of Aristotle himself. Even though he taught that sensory experience is the source of the intellect's stock of ideas, he gave little attention to inductive reasoning and the way in which sensory experience is organized into generalizations that can be tested and proved true or false. The proper intellectual method for determination of questions in a mixed science like astronomy, in which observed data had to serve as the foundation of propositions, was a hotly debated issue throughout the sixteenth century.

There was another difficulty for natural scientists inherent in Aristotelian philosophy. For Aristotle, the concept of experience did not imply a modern experiment designed to ascertain whether the consequences that are assumed to follow from a generalization actually do so. Rather, 'experience' meant something that was accepted as true on the basis of common, everyday observation, not a specific observation made to test the validity of a generalization. Indeed, a scientist who appealed to a specific experience, especially one designed by himself, to challenge a generally received opinion could easily be discredited, since 'experience', in the sense of the common experiences that everybody shared, could be cited to demonstrate that the made-to-order experience cited by an innovator represented error or dishonesty on his part.

The developments that eventually led to the new scientific discoveries traditionally labelled 'the Scientific Revolution' involved rethinking these concepts of induction, experience, and experiment. But they also involved a new awareness of the crucial role that mathematics was beginning to play in the work of leading scientists. Experimentation in the modern sense was not the major force behind the great changes in scientific opinion that culminated in early modern science. Mathematics was the real key. This is clearly true of the Polish astronomer Nicolaus Copernicus (1473–1543), author of *De revolutionibus orbium coelestium* (*On the Revolutions of the Celestial Orbs*, 1543), the first major treatise that pointed toward the physical science of the next century. His study of mathematics at Bologna had made him aware of weaknesses in the prevailing Ptolemaic astronomy, which assumed that the earth was the centre of the universe. This theory had been transmitted from the ancient Greeks primarily through the scientific works of Claudius Ptolemaeus (Ptolemy) of Alexandria (d. *c.* AD 151). A Latin translation of Ptolemy's *Almagest* had circulated since the twelfth century and was first printed at Venice in 1515. Most astronomers, however, knew the *Almagest* from a useful summary, the *Epitome Almagesti*, published by the German astronomer Regiomontanus (Johannes Müller, 1436–76) in 1496. In principle, Ptolemaic astronomy was simple, orderly, and harmonious. In reality, however, the celestial movements observed by astronomers did not conform to the pattern predicted by theory. Most troublesome were the planetary orbits, which exhibited a 'retrograde motion' that could be observed but could not be explained. In order to reconcile theory with observation, astronomers introduced a complex set of imaginary mathematical devices that did not follow the theory but could account for the observed positions of celestial bodies. The most common such devices were eccentric circles and epicycles. In terms of theory, these were a defect, justified as something used 'to save the phenomena', that is, to reconcile theory with observation.

Concerned by the complexities and inconsistencies of traditional astronomy, Copernicus undertook a reform of his science. *De revolutionibus* advanced a disarmingly simple suggestion. If the positions of earth and sun in the Ptolemaic diagram of the universe were reversed, with the sun in the centre and the earth reduced to just one of the planets, many of the troublesome complications of the Ptolemaic system would be eliminated. His reformed astronomy got rid of many (though not all) of the contrivances like epicycles and eccentrics but seemed to fly in the face of common sense and could not resolve a number of quite reasonable objections raised against it. Because *De revolutionibus* followed the structure of the *Almagest*, it offered readers not just a few unconventional ideas but a complete, mathematically demonstrated system. That was why it attracted attention even from astronomers who remained unconvinced. Some of their objections were easily resolved, but astronomers also saw real weaknesses in his argument. His system created discord between physics and astronomy, for it invalidated the Aristotelian explanation of gravity as a natural tendency of all bodies to fall toward the centre of the universe. The most valid scientific objection, however, was the absence of parallax in observations of the fixed stars. To most astronomers, Copernicus's theory seemed interesting but unproved. Although some of the scientific objections now seem quaint, few of them were frivolous.

Of all those who pondered Copernicus's ideas, the two most important were the Dane Tycho Brahe (1541–1601) and the German Johannes Kepler (1571–1630). Brahe accepted some of Copernicus's ideas but refused to believe that the sun is the centre of the universe. Convinced by his own observations that there were astronomical phenomena (especially the sudden appearance of a new star in 1572 and a comet that appeared in 1577) that could not be reconciled with established theory, Brahe could accept neither Copernicus's new astronomy nor Ptolemy's ancient one. His alternative proposal came to be known as the 'Tychonic system'. According to him, the earth stands immobile at the centre of the universe. The sun revolves annually about the earth (as Ptolemy taught), but the planets revolve about the sun (as Copernicus taught). This theory provided an explanation for retrograde motion, but it left many questions unresolved. To people looking back from a time after the work of Galileo and Newton, the Tychonic system seems a weak compromise; but many contemporaries found it attractive.

Kepler published most of his work in the next century, but the foundations of his work were laid in the closing years of the sixteenth. He early became a convinced supporter of Copernicus, and his first important book, *Mysterium cosmographicum* (*Cosmographical Mystery*, 1596) made his opinion public. In 1600 he became Brahe's assistant and later his successor, gaining access to Brahe's remarkable collection of astronomical observations. Kepler's later work, which eventually led to his revolutionary proof that planetary orbits are ellipses, was a product of the next century.

The life sciences

Physical science—especially astronomy and physics—underwent the most striking innovations. The life sciences were less innovative. At the outset of the sixteenth century, both physical and biological sciences were ruled by a pair of ancient authorities: Aristotle and Ptolemy in physics and astronomy, and Aristotle and Galen in medicine and biology. But these two areas followed different paths after 1500, a difference illustrated by the directions taken by Copernicus in astronomy and Andreas Vesalius (1514–64) in anatomy. Copernicus was no radical. *De revolutionibus* followed the organizational plan of Ptolemy. The evidence he used to support his heliocentric theory was mostly traditional. He proceeded, however, by challenging the central assumption of all Ptolemaic astronomy, that the earth is the centre of the universe. His 'revolution' in astronomy was therefore primarily conceptual. In the life sciences, however, there was no new theoretical approach. The important changes in these fields involved accumulation of new observations, not making of new theories; and the work of pioneers like Vesalius was descriptive, adding new information that required changes in detail rather than in basic assumptions. Though Vesalius was critical of Galen's reliance on animal rather than human dissections, he offered nothing more radical than an improved account of the topics covered by Galen. Thus in the life sciences, the new direction was cumulative and empirical, not revolutionary and conceptual.

Nevertheless, medicine and biology made important gains between 1500 and 1600. One especially fruitful development involved the study of plants used for medicinal purposes. The editing and publication of three ancient authorities on natural history, Pliny the Elder,

Theophrastus, and Dioscorides, created an urgent need to integrate ancient descriptions of plants with contemporary knowledge. Natural historians like Otto Brunfels (1488–1534), Leonhart Fuchs (1501–66), and Conrad Gesner (1516–56), who were students of nature as well as of ancient texts, wrote encyclopedic herbals that incorporated their own observations. At a purely descriptive level, these publications and their woodcut illustrations drawn from nature helped to integrate ancient with contemporary pharmacology.

Surprisingly, anatomy had received little attention in medieval medicine, even though medical practice was dominated by the humoral theory of disease developed by the greatest anatomist of the ancient world, Galen of Perga (c.129–99 CE). Interest in anatomy increased from c.1500, and at this point, humanists identified Galen's anatomical treatises as another treasure from antiquity that must be rescued from neglect. Several Latin translations were published in the early sixteenth century, and in 1525 the first Greek edition of Galen's works was published. The crucial text in making his anatomical treatises influential was *On Anatomical Procedures*. In 1531 a Paris professor of medicine, Johann Guinter of Andernach (1487–1574), published a Latin translation. One of Guinter's assistants, the young Fleming Andreas Vesalius, became lecturer in surgery at Padua. Unlike most anatomists, he performed dissections with his own hands. In 1538 he and a Dutch artist produced a set of anatomical illustrations based on Galen for use in teaching. But as Vesalius continued performing dissections, he became critical of his source. His masterpiece *De humani corporis fabrica* (*On the Structure of the Human Body*, 1543) was intended to replace Galen. Vesalius criticized Galen for rashly concluding that structures found in animals could be freely attributed to the human body. His book was influential primarily because its foundation was not earlier texts but the new information acquired in his own dissections. Vesalius's most important contribution to medical science was his insistence that anatomy must be based on careful observation of dissections and not on the pages of any book.

Moral philosophy

Moral philosophy was the only philosophical discipline included among the humanistic subjects. Attendance at one or more courses on Aristotle's *Nicomachean Ethics* was a common requirement for degrees in faculties of liberal arts. Rediscovery of classical texts generated interest in other moral philosophers. Plato, of course, was the greatest discovery. Yet his works on ethics never made it into the university classroom. Platonism attracted mainly the philosophical amateurs—poets and others who admired Plato's literary elegance. The Platonic moral doctrine that proved most influential was Platonic love, presented in Plato's *Symposium*. The *Commentary on the Symposium of Plato* (1469) by the Florentine translator of Plato, Marsilio Ficino, shaped discussions of Platonic love in later Renaissance thought. The theme of love as a force pervading the universe and leading the soul toward spiritual goods and even into the presence of God became a major topos of Renaissance poetry. It appears in the dialogue *Gli Asolani* (1505) by the Venetian humanist and poet Pietro Bembo. A fictional Bembo extols Platonic love in the most influential Renaissance book on good manners, the *Book of the Courtier* (1528) by Baldassarre Castiglione.

A second ethical tradition that attracted much attention was Stoicism. The doctrines of Stoic ethics, expounded by major Latin authors like Cicero and Seneca, were well known throughout the Middle Ages. Cicero and Seneca were primarily interested in the moral doctrines of Stoicism, not in awareness of the materialist metaphysics of earlier Greek Stoicism. What readers found most attractive was the definition of virtue as the supreme goal of life. For the Roman Stoics, virtue was the only truly desirable good. All other supposed goods—health, wealth, happiness, or even freedom from pain and oppression—were morally indifferent. Stoicism also taught that an unalterable natural law, arising from divine reason, governs the universe; and the virtuous act is defined as one that conforms to natural law. The Stoic ethic of self-sufficiency could lead to flight from the world. But the combination of moral self-sufficiency with the command to live in accord with nature could also favour the pursuit of virtue in public life. In the fifteenth century, the usual verdict on Stoic ethics was that its demands were too harsh. Denial of the emotions, the claim that the death of a spouse or a child should leave the wise man totally unaffected, seemed inhumane.

The social, political, and religious upheavals that overwhelmed Europe in the second half of the sixteenth century created an ethical crisis. Stoicism, with its teaching that no external circumstances can inflict harm on the well-ordered soul, offered consolation. Likewise, emphasis on the individual's obligation to fulfil the duties imposed by his status in society was attractive to leaders who struggled to perform their duty in a society torn apart by riots, massacres, and toxic religious and political hatred. The most influential author who promoted Stoic moral philosophy as a remedy for such a world was the Netherlandish philosopher Justus Lipsius (1547–1606). Though he published important works of classical scholarship, his most famous book was *De constantia* (*On Constancy*, 1574), an adaptation of Roman Stoicism to contemporary problems. This book became the manifesto of neo-Stoicism. Lipsius's main message was the need to remain steadfast in the face of adversity. He emphasized self-control and internal calm, and the desirability of seeking peace and order by minimizing religious disagreements and conforming outwardly to any prevailing religion or government that would maintain public peace. The violent upheavals that afflicted France at the same period prompted a similar growth of interest in Stoicism there. Guillaume du Vair (1556–1621) was the outstanding figure of French neo-Stoicism. Like Lipsius, he found in Stoicism a doctrine of self-control that helped him endure violence. Unlike Lipsius, who avoided involvement in public affairs, du Vair was a magistrate who remained in his judicial position at a time of great peril. His essay *La Philosophie morale des Stoiques* (*The Moral Philosophy of the Stoics*, 1584) ranks love of country as second only to the love of God. He criticizes those who abandon public office in the face of danger, a judgement repeated in his *De la constance et consolation ès calamitez publiques* (*Of Constance and Consolation in Public Calamities*, 1590). The French essayist Michel de Montaigne (1533–92) found Stoicism attractive at an early stage of his own development but abandoned it, alienated by its demand for impassivity and elimination of all emotion.

Political thought

Political theory was a branch of moral philosophy. Innovative political theories are usually a response to contemporary political crises, and the sixteenth century was full of those. There were two main centres of political breakdown, and each of them inspired important works of political philosophy. The first crisis was in Italy. The decision of Charles VIII of France to invade Italy in 1494 to enforce his hereditary claim to the Kingdom of Naples upset the political equilibrium that had prevailed since the creation of the Italian League in 1455. The French invasion drew in the armies of King Ferdinand of Aragon, who had a rival dynastic interest in Naples; and the Italians could not get rid of one or the other of the rival foreign powers. The French invasion also led to the overthrow of Medici rule over the republic of Florence and initiated a period of instability that did not end until the transformation of the republic into a hereditary duchy in 1532.

The principal reaction to this double crisis was the work of Niccolò Machiavelli (1469–1527). Excluded from office after the restoration of Medici control in 1512 on account of his anti-Medicean political record, he turned to writing in vain hopes of gaining the favour of the new rulers. *The Prince* (1513) was his principal literary work. Traditionally, such books discussed the education of princes and counselled rulers on the morally correct conduct of government. Machiavelli explicitly rejects this function. He aims not to discuss what rulers ought to do but rather what they must do if they are to achieve the one essential goal of any government, 'to preserve the state'—that is, to retain power and maintain social stability. Machiavelli endorses many actions that the Aristotelian, Stoic, or Christian moral codes of the time would condemn. A ruler may do virtually anything that is truly necessary for the survival of his state: lie, cheat, murder, wage aggressive wars, or terrorize. Thus Machiavelli teaches that rulers live by ethical rules far different from those that govern private individuals. This ethical dualism explains why, from the initial publication of *The Prince* in 1532, Machiavelli acquired a reputation as a defender of political immorality.

His willingness to exempt rulers from ordinary moral law is the source of the common but unjustified notion that there is no ethical system in Machiavelli's thought. A careful reading of *The Prince*, and consideration of his second and less known book dealing with republics, *Discourses on the First Ten Books of Titus Livius*, reveals that he does apply an ethical measure, the general interest and social stability of the total community, to the actions of rulers. The *Discourses* also show that he still preferred the moderate republican regime that he served during his political career before 1512. His willingness to accept an authoritarian prince when he wrote *The Prince* resulted from his conviction that republican government is possible only among a people possessed of 'virtue', a term that implied willingness to put the general interest ahead of personal advantage. He judged that, in his generation, the Florentines were too divided by political factions and too morally corrupt to rule themselves. He found in Polybius, an ancient historian of Rome, both a theory of the cyclical rise and fall of good and bad governments and an idealized picture of the Roman republic as a 'mixed constitution' which by balancing the interests of a strong ruler, a powerful aristocracy, and a politically active people had preserved its republican constitution and conquered the Mediterranean world. In discussing the degree to which fate determines the outcome of human decisions and the degree to which human reason can affect outcomes, he estimates that about half of political results are due to wise policy, while the other half are determined by conditions beyond the control of anyone. While this may sound pessimistic, it is far less hopeless than the conclusions reached on the same question by his fellow citizen Francesco Guicciardini (1483–1540) in his *History of Italy* (completed in 1540; published in 1561–64). Guicciardini suggested that our belief that by acting rationally we can influence the success of our actions may be entirely illusory. Both Machiavelli and Guicciardini faced the capital fact of their time, that the Italian states were losing control of their own destiny in the face of foreign invasions.

During the first half of the sixteenth century, most countries of Western Europe experienced a striking growth of royal power. In France, between 1484 and 1560 the crown never summoned the traditional representative assembly, the Estates-General, into session. Royal officials treated the supreme judicial body, the Parlement of Paris, with something verging on contempt. After 1560, the struggle of the Protestant minority to survive efforts to exterminate heresy forced them to develop theories that justified armed resistance. Since they remained a minority, Huguenots had to use arguments that did not offend moderate Catholics. The Huguenots initially appealed to a traditional constitution that they (and many disgruntled Catholics) judged to be under attack by ambitious politicians who exalted the king's power by undermining ancient institutions that protected the people from tyranny. Huguenot rebels insisted on their loyalty to the king himself but charged that he was virtually a prisoner of the ultra-Catholic Guise faction.

This situation changed radically, however, after the massacre of thousands of Protestants on St Bartholomew's Day, 24 August 1572. The queen mother, Catherine de Médicis, and her son, King Charles IX, openly endorsed the massacres. Thus the Huguenots could no longer pretend to be trying to rescue their king from extremists. A number of Huguenot propagandists published tracts justifying armed resistance. In the short run, the most influential of these was *Francogallia* (1573) by François Hotman (1524–90), a humanist and legal scholar. He knew that his propaganda must not alienate moderate Catholic citizens who also had been dismayed by the massacres. So *Francogallia* concentrated on opposition to political innovations that offended many influential Catholics, especially the contempt that royal officials showed for the Estates General and the Parlement of Paris. *Francogallia* claims that the monarchy was originally created by representatives of the people and that the Estates retained an ultimate right to revoke the royal title if the king violated his fundamental obligation to protect the lives and properties of the people.

But the Huguenot cause needed a theory that was less vulnerable to counter-attacks based on a different reading of French constitutional history. Some apologists for resistance looked to a very different tradition of political thought. This was the medieval concept of natural law, which had flourished in the constitutional theories of conciliarists (many of them French) during the Great Schism. Successors to that tradition, such as Jacques Almain (1480–1515) and the expatriate Scot John Mair (*c.*1467–1550), taught that ultimate power in any polity always remains with the people. The ruler's powers are only delegated to him under the terms of a contract stipulating that he use them for the welfare of the community. Natural law gives the community a right to resist a tyrant. Both Almain and Mair were vague, however, about precisely who might lawfully initiate an attempt to depose a tyrant.

This scholastic idea that the prince is never more than a supreme magistrate commissioned by the people provided the kind of secular political doctrine that was needed to justify armed resistance to something as monstrous as a king's complicity in the massacre of his own subjects. Since the Huguenots could no longer pretend that Charles IX was the prisoner of a cabal of radical Catholic politicians, they now justified resistance as a defence of their inalienable rights under natural law to defend themselves and the whole nation against unlawful authority. A number of political tracts pursued this line. The most influential was the treatise *Vindiciae contra tyrannos* (*Defense of Liberty Against Tyrants*), published in 1579. It is now generally attributed to a leading Protestant nobleman, Philippe du Plessis de Mornay (1549–1623). His use of medieval sources is striking. He cites Thomas Aquinas, the medieval Italian jurist Bartolus, the Byzantine compilers of ancient Roman law, and the decrees of the fifteenth-century councils of Basel and Konstanz which opposed papal claims to absolute power. A delicate question in any such justification of rebellion is the question of who has the legal and moral right to initiate action. Mornay derives all government from a complicated twofold contract involving God, king, and people. The king's violation of the contract between king and people is his primary argument. Yet a tyrannical king may not be resisted by any private individual or even by the general body of the people acting collectively. As individuals, all Christians are bound to render passive obedience. Active resistance is justified only through collective action exercised through established leaders who represent the nation, such as members of the nobility, assemblies of estates, judicial bodies, and municipal councils. Mornay's theory is designed to minimize the chances that lawful resistance will end in anarchy. The *Vindiciae* represents the respectable main line of Protestant resistance theory, but natural law and popular sovereignty could also be used to justify a more aggressive defence of revolution. The most striking example was the dialogue *De jure regni apud Scotos* (*On the Law of the Monarchy in Scotland*, 1579) by the Scottish humanist George Buchanan (1506–82). Buchanan derived all governmental authority from a simple contract between king and people and assumed that the people retain a right to revoke the monarch's power if he becomes a tyrant. He eliminated Mornay's concept of mediated authority. The people do not relinquish to any body of representatives their power to defend their rights. Buchanan's theories were far too radical for his time, but they had a great future in seventeenth-century England.

Throughout the period 1562–84, French Huguenots were the ones who struggled to develop theories justifying resistance to royal authority. But the death of King Henri III's last surviving brother in 1584 meant that the succession would pass to the king's cousin Henry of Bourbon, king of Navarre and leader of the Huguenot armies. Thus French Catholics faced the prospect of having a Protestant king. Radical Catholics adopted ideas about political obedience, resistance to kings, and the origin of royal authority that were remarkably similar to those used by radical Protestants and were in fact derived from the same late medieval philosophers.

Although ideas of natural rights, political contract, and resistance to tyranny flourished during the second half of the sixteenth century, the future of continental politics favoured the kind of monarchy that is conventionally labelled 'absolutism'. The dreadful experience of the civil wars in France and the Netherlands created a fear of civil disorder that made authoritarian monarchy acceptable and aroused hostility to all theories of constitutional liberties that might be used to justify revolution. The arguments favouring absolutism ran in two directions. One was the theory of the divine right of kings. Since the biblical injunction (Romans 13: 1–7) enjoining obedience to established political authority constituted the main obstacle faced by Christians who wanted to justify resistance to tyrannical rulers, divine-right theorists insisted that the biblical commands were absolute and that they provided no exceptions. The authority of the secular state, even a pagan or heretical one, came directly from God and so was holy. The king's right to rule was not bestowed by the people but by the Almighty. Hence it could be neither restricted nor resisted by those whom God had placed under its authority. The most prominent defender of divine right was himself a king, James VI of Scotland, in his political tracts *The Trew Law of Free Monarchies* (1598) and *Basilikon Doron* (*The Royal Gift*, 1599).

The second theoretical justification of absolute monarchy was more rationalistic. Its ablest representative was the French jurist Jean Bodin (*c.*1530–96). He produced two major works on politics and history: *Methodus ad facilem historiarum cognitionem* (*Method for the*

Easy Comprehension of History, 1566) and *Six Livres de la République* (*Six Books of the Commonwealth*, 1576). In the *Methodus*, Bodin favoured a powerful monarchy but still, like most legal thinkers, thought of the royal authority as limited by certain traditional laws and customs. Even in the *Methodus*, however, Bodin was critical of the concept of a 'mixed constitution' in which monarchical, aristocratic, and popular elements each has a guaranteed constitutional voice so that power is divided and no one branch can become all-powerful. By 1576, when the *République* was published, Bodin had strengthened his objections to mixed constitutions and had reversed opinion on several points. The breakdown of civil society after 1572 convinced him that preservation of the people's liberties was far less important than maintenance of social order. Hence he now rejected nearly all limits on royal power.

The foundation of the *République* is Bodin's concept of sovereignty. He was the first thinker to develop this idea fully; he claimed to have invented it. Simply put, sovereignty is the power to make law, without the need to secure consent from anyone or to observe any preliminaries or formalities. Law is nothing but a declaration of the sovereign's will. When Bodin calls the sovereign absolute, he means that, even if the sovereign is oppressive, no subject has a right to break his laws or to raise any opposition in the name of justice. Although Bodin is concerned mainly about contemporary France, his theory is applicable to any form of government. Sovereignty is the specific characteristic that constitutes any state, and if there is no sovereignty, there is no state. Sovereignty does not have to be in the hands of a king. It is found wherever the ultimate power to make is law is located. It lies in the hands of the nobles in an aristocracy and in the hands of elected representatives in a republic. But sovereignty has to exist somewhere in every government. If the locus of sovereignty is unclear or disputed, political conflict and social disorder are inevitable. Bodin prefers monarchy, because sovereignty is in the hands of a single person. Only one will is involved, and hence there is no difficulty in determining law. In aristocracies and republics, creating a single will—that is, making law—is more difficult. Those who insist that the parlements or estates must give consent to royal legislation are really trying to shift sovereignty from the king to the judges or the estates. A sovereign king is not bound by the laws; he makes them. Despite his clarity on this general principle, Bodin confuses the issue by acknowledging certain limits on the sovereign. The most dangerous limitation is Bodin's insistence that the sovereign is bound to respect the private property of his subjects. This defence of private property is understandable from Bodin's point of view, for the purpose of the state is to preserve the social order. Since society is made up of families and families cannot exist without property, the social order depends on respect for private property, even by the king. Although this restriction is justified by Bodin's conception of the family as the foundation of the social order, his doctrine of property rights consituted a potential threat to sovereign power.

Challenges to knowledge: forms of scepticism

Educated Europeans at the end of the sixteenth century faced many challenges to assumptions about the world that their ancestors took for granted. The most shocking of these was the Protestant Reformation and the consequent end of religious unity. In Northern Europe, the Christian humanism that flourished at the beginning of the century had foundered amidst the ideological struggles of the 1520s and 1530s. The humanism that survived was more cautious, shorn of its grandiose aspirations to cultural rebirth and spiritual renewal, concerned mainly with education and scholarship. The frustrating search for new ways to regenerate religious, political, and social life through the study of antiquity left many educated people uneasy. Nothing seemed certain anymore. Syncretists like the Florentine Neoplatonists had expected that increased knowledge of ancient philosophy would reveal that, at bottom, all ancient philosophies were one. On the contrary, it had proved that ancient philosophers were just as divided as contemporary ones.

Some thinkers remembered that the Greek sceptics had questioned whether the human mind has any ability to discover absolute truth. Medieval philosophy had shown little interest in such ideas, but one sceptical work of a major Latin author, the *Academica* of Cicero, was widely available though not given much attention in the Middle Ages. Cicero defended the moderate (or Academic) scepticism of the Platonic New Academy, which maintained that human reason can distinguish the more probable from the less probable but cannot know the truth of any proposition with absolute certainty. A more radical form of ancient scepticism, Pyrrhonism, objected even to the Academics' conclusion that nothing could be known with certainty. Pyrrhonists advised that, when faced with uncertainty, the philosopher can only suspend judgement. This form of scepticism was even less known in the Middle Ages than Academic scepticism. Only one ancient Pyrrhonist author, Sextus Empiricus, survived. Except for one little noticed book by Gianfrancesco Pico della Mirandola (1470–1533), there is no firm evidence of direct use of Sextus' works until 1562, when a Latin translation of his *Outlines of Pyrrhonism* was published. Nevertheless, sceptical ideas were in the air even in the first half of the century. There are references to Pyrrhonists and sceptics in the *Tiers livre* (*Third Book*, 1546) of the most popular French prose author, François Rabelais (*c.*1494–1553). Rabelais's references are particularly significant, since although he was a learned man, he was writing a vernacular book addressed to a popular audience. The French philosopher Omer Talon (1510–62) in his *Academica* (1548) used Cicero's defence of Academic scepticism to justify attacks by Petrus Ramus on Aristotelian philosophy. Like virtually everyone who defended scepticism in this century, Talon argued that scepticism merely shows that Christian faith, not Aristotelian philosophy, is the true way to knowledge of God.

The growing interest in scepticism found its clearest expression in the works of two French authors, one famous and the other nearly forgotten. The obscure one was Francisco Sanches (1552–1623), who taught philosophy and medicine at Toulouse. His book *Quod nihil scitur* (*That Nothing is Known*, 1581) is a systematic attack on the Aristotelian concept of knowledge. It offers a detailed criticism of the foundations of Aristotle's trust in reason and presents a genuinely philosophical argument, quite unlike earlier dabblers in scepticism. But Sanches seems to have had little influence.

Michel de Montaigne, though far less consistently sceptical, was very influential. The reason is partly that he was a great writer. There is much besides scepticism to be found in his *Essays* (1580–8), which offer rambling discussion of a multitude of topics. The *Essays* are especially important because both they and their author were rooted in the culture of Renaissance humanism. As a child, Montaigne was brought up to speak only Latin. He received the best humanistic education available at the best classical school in France. His mastery of ancient literature is evident in everything he wrote. Yet his essay 'Of Education' insists that book-learning, though desirable, is far less important than good morals and clear thinking. Familiarity with the classics, one principal aim of humanistic education, is all very well but has no real value unless the knowledge is assimilated, not just memorized.

Although he knew Sextus' *Outlines of Pyrrhonism*, Montaigne's position on human knowledge comes more from the anti-philosophical tendencies of humanist rhetoric than from Sextus or any other philosopher. Rhetoric was the art of persuasive oratory. It challenged the intellectual processes that claimed to determine absolute truth, the goal of Aristotelian philosophy. Instead, rhetoric addressed decisions that were moral rather than scientific, such as the determination of public policy or issues of everyday life when an individual had to choose between alternative courses of action. Humanist rhetoricians thought that questions involving absolute truth rarely if ever arise in the life of either an individual or a political community. 'Absolute truth' of the sort sought by Aristotelian logic was mostly a matter for idle speculation among academics. Such rhetorical reservations about the ability to achieve certitude had already been applied by Erasmus against Martin Luther and by the humanist Sebastian Castellio against John Calvin.

Montaigne was the heir to this humanistic tendency. His experience of the violence caused by the Reformation reinforced his sceptical tendencies. The Pyrrhonist scepticism of Sextus Empiricus probably was what led him to write the most overtly sceptical of his essays, 'An Apology for Raymond Sebond'. Sebond, a fifteenth-century Spanish theologian, contended that speculative questions of all sorts, including the existence of God and the divine attributes, could be determined by reason. A Church court forced him to recant because he left no room for faith. Montaigne 'defended' Sebond by arguing that his rationalistic arguments were just as valid as the conclusions of rationalistic philosophers in general: that is, not valid at all. Montaigne borrowed from Sextus Empiricus a devastating critique of the human senses, showing that the senses, which according to Aristotle are the source of all human ideas, are unreliable and thus that reasoning based on human ideas can never determine any speculative question. Montaigne's essays also express a cultural relativism derived from reports of European explorers. In his essay 'Of Cannibals', he suggests that Brazilian cannibals who cook and eat their vanquished enemies are no more irrational and unnatural than European Christians who plunder, torture, and massacre their fellow citizens in the name of religion.

Montaigne's writing is full of references to classical authors. He declares his admiration for the wisdom of the ancients. Yet truth is not neatly contained in the texts where his humanist precursors had sought it. The optimistic Renaissance faith in the regenerative power of ancient culture has disappeared. Ultimately, he concluded, absolute truth is beyond the grasp of the human mind. Like all sceptics of this period, Montaigne claimed that the consequence of recognizing the limitations of human reason is reliance on the truth revealed by God. For a generation after him, Pyrrhonist scepticism actually became the favoured philosophical defence of Catholicism in France.

Towards the seventeenth century

The works of the sceptics prepared the way for seventeenth-century philosophers who were not content to accept scepticism as a final outcome of intellectual discourse. Both of the first two major authors who confronted the problem of knowledge were influenced by Montaigne. René Descartes (1596–1650), who began his new philosophy by embracing Pyrrhonist scepticism, is a figure of the new century. Much more a product of the closing sixteenth century is Francis Bacon (1561–1626), who agreed with the attack on Aristotelian rationalism but attempted to define a new direction in philosophy in *The Advancement of Learning* (1605). Like Aristotle and in opposition to the sceptics, Bacon reaffirmed the value of sensory experience. He attempted, though without great success, to define a new logic that could guide the mind from sensory experience to valid scientific generalizations. Far more bluntly than Montaigne, Bacon dismissed classical learning as worthless for philosophical and scientific investigations, though still useful for other purposes. In a work that he never completed, *The Great Instauration*, he declared: 'It must be plainly avowed that the wisdom which we have derived principally from the Greeks is but like the boyhood of knowledge, and has the characteristic property of boys: it can talk, but it cannot generate, for it is fruitful of controversies but barren of works.' In one sense, this passage is just another Renaissance attack on Aristotle. In a deeper sense, however, it marks the end of the Renaissance faith that wisdom can be rediscovered by searching through the literary remains of ancient Greece and Rome. For Bacon, the Renaissance confidence in the classical tradition had come to an end: the ancient Greeks represent not the mature wisdom of the human race but its callow, prattling, and immature youth.

5

The turmoil of faith

Euan Cameron

If any age in the history of European Christianity witnessed tumultuous change, it was the sixteenth century. In 1500 the people of Western Europe belonged to an international Church theoretically serving them all. Though flexible and diverse in many ways, that Church was so nearly universal that few of Europe's people need consciously have thought of themselves as Western, Latin, and Catholic Christians. Although there were cells of a few dozen or a few hundred Waldensian or Lollard 'heretics' in isolated pockets across Western Europe, structured heresy had shrunk to a fraction of its earlier levels. Even the Church in Bohemia, in semi-schism since the time of Jan Hus, had reached a means of coexistence with Rome. In complete contrast to this near-uniformity, by 1600 many, perhaps most of Europe's people were acutely conscious of being Roman Catholics, Lutherans, or reformed. Those only moderately educated were expected to know why they were as they were. Adherence to one or another of the major or minor confessions in the West defined not only one's conscience but one's political allegiance. States were ranked against each other in a variety of barely stable leagues and alliances, poised to turn Central Europe into the bloodbath which ensued from 1618 onwards.

The beliefs of the majority

And yet one must beware of overstating the case. We are only beginning to realize how important and how durable a body of beliefs lay just beneath the surface of European culture. These beliefs were not separated off into some sort of compartment known as 'popular culture' or 'popular religion'. They overlapped, mingled, and interacted with the officially sponsored religious beliefs and activities. They reflected the everyday concerns, needs, and insecurities to which most if not all early modern Europeans were exposed.

The vast majority of Europe's people lived in a relatively close relationship with the land. Their security, their lifestyle, at times their very existence depended on the fertility of the soil, the survival and fecundity of their livestock, and a favourable climate at critical times of the year—all things that became increasingly problematic as the sixteenth century wore on. People also relied upon sustaining sufficient health and vigour in themselves and their families and household to perform the necessary routine tasks. They needed access and use of the soil free from robbery, the presence of armies, or the ever more intrusive demands of taxation. These factors lay outside the real control of most if not all of the people most of the time. There were no naturally effective means to ensure their own welfare or to guard against misfortune. So people would seek supernatural assistance, in ways which included, but also overflowed beyond, the resources offered by the established Church.

Catholic theologians around c.1500 contributed to this sense of dependence on supernatural aid against evils potentially of supernatural origin. In 1505 the university theologian Martin Plantsch preached a series of sermons in the parish Church of St George at Tübingen. Plantsch argued, quite conventionally, that demons could harm people by raising storms to destroy their crops, by stealing grain and wine from their stores and milk from their cattle, and by causing sickness, sterility, or impotence in people or animals. Sorcerers frequently caused the same misfortunes by using spells, charms, images, and medicinal or poisonous substances (though these instruments were merely tokens prompting the demons to cause the problems). Typically, many people reacted to the experience of misfortune by seeking help from a variety of supernatural sources, including some far outside the Church's sanctions. Plantsch argued that to seek help from popular healers, 'cunning folk', and magicians was a disastrous error. All the evils that people suffered derived, ultimately, from the providence of a caring God. God permitted evil to occur to tempt the feeble in faith, and to test the fortitude of the saints. People were warned to avoid any form of remedy or protection that itself savoured of demonic magic or sorcery. Instead they should use the spiritual remedies approved by the Catholic Church, along with traditional medicine. So, Plantsch encouraged the people of Tübingen to apply holy water to their sores, wounds, and even their homes and buildings. They could place consecrated palm-fronds on the fire to drive away thunderstorms, 'as long as this was for the honour of God'. They could deploy an arsenal of waters, candles, and consecrated bread dedicated to particular saints, to cure the ailments specifically linked with those saints: St Antony's water against 'morbid fire', St Peter Martyr's water against fevers, or St Blasius's candles against sore throats.

In the course of the sixteenth century the Lutheran and reformed Protestant churches would, with striking unanimity, reject the framework of thought from which these consecrated remedies came. Protestant theologians argued that neither Church rituals nor magical ceremonies could change the properties of material objects. However often consecrated, water and salt remained just water and salt. Yet most people still saw the causes of their misfortunes in supernatural, even in demonic terms. Contemporary sources concur that ordinary people continued to believe that hostile looks and thoughts could cause disease and even death. They still resorted to a range of popular and empirical cures for their misfortunes outside the limits of conventional medicine or conventional religion. They believed that various divinatory techniques could discover lost goods and detect the thieves responsible. Lists of these prescriptions and remedies were copied between the sceptical Renaissance physician Johannes Weyer, the Lutheran writer Johann Georg Godelmann, and the Jesuit theologian Martín Del Rio. However much they disagreed on ideology, these authorities concurred in the 'data' they presented about the beliefs of the uneducated.

By the beginning of the sixteenth century a new resource against demonic magic had arisen in Western European society. Those believed to have caused harm by magic were accused of belonging to a demonic subculture, the 'heresy' of witches. The European witch-hunt began before 1500, but it only revealed its worst and most spectacular aspects after 1600. For much of the sixteenth century it was overshadowed by the events of the Reformation, which threw ecclesiastical justice into much confusion. Long before the early modern period people feared that their neighbours could, if they wished, cause serious and even mortal harm by focusing their ill-will upon them. What changed in the 'witch-hunts' was that various law officers, religious and secular, centralized or (more often) local and provincial, offered to deal with suspected 'witches' through criminal justice, as an alternative to counter-magic or negotiation. In the fifteenth century, the justice offered came chiefly, though not exclusively, from priestly inquisitors. Inquisitorial writers fused their mental images of heretics and magicians, creating a 'stereotype' of the witch who belonged to a real and visible society, met regularly to worship the Devil, and performed hostile sorcery with demonic help. This image was disseminated in numerous genre paintings as well as learned treatises around 1500. It informed learned theory and (to some extent) jurisprudence, but had more limited impact on popular ideas. However, it was chiefly in the later sixteenth century, and in specific types of territories (certain prince-bishoprics in Germany, the Saarland, parts of the European borderlands, Switzerland and Swabia) that witches were systematically hunted out by inquisitorial procedure. By that stage secular tribunals rather than ecclesiastical judges often presided over the trials. Local provincial authorities were most likely to conduct the 'craze' type of investigation, characterized by the indiscriminate use of torture, and thus by a domino-effect of consecutive accusations. Highly centralized legal systems, like the Italian or Spanish Inquisitions or the Parisian Parlement, generally adhered to stricter rules of evidence, allowed delays and appeals, and consequently made fewer victims.

In one important respect the beliefs of the various theological elites and the majority of the people joined hands. Whenever the order of nature seemed violently disrupted, the hand of God was seen to be at work. People from all kinds of backgrounds took note of marvels, misbirths, eclipses, comets, and other portents or signs of divine anger or warning. Two of the most notorious misborn animals, the 'papal ass' found dead in the Tiber in 1496 and the 'monk calf' born in Freiberg in Saxony in 1522, provoked considerable learned discussion and interpretation. A woman gave birth to three grotesquely misshapen offspring at Augsburg in 1531, duly described in the literature. Fish were occasionally caught in the Baltic with curious messages in their scales, or misshapen bodies. In the 1530s and 1540s, when Protestant Germany was repeatedly threatened by armed conflict over religion, various visions were reported in the skies: knights in armour, towers, lions, bears, and dragons. Comets, which appeared unpredictably in the otherwise perfect and stable heavens, could only be signs that God was giving dire warnings to the people.

Shared Catholicism on the eve of the Reformation

On the eve of the Reformation the piety of Western, Catholic Europe had assumed certain distinctive features. At its heart lay principles that had been growing in importance throughout the Middle Ages. The saving work of Jesus Christ was mediated through sacrificial and sacramental ministry by the priests of the Catholic Church. In the Church, as the Fourth Lateran Council had put it in 1215, Jesus Christ was both priest and sacrifice; outside the Church no one whatsoever was saved. So Jesus Christ, crucified for the sins of humanity, stood at the centre of late medieval Christianity. Late Gothic representations of his sacrifice, in panel paintings, limewood sculptures, and statuary, dwelt with gruesome, sometimes almost pornographic detail on the physical horror of his suffering. The Stations of the Cross gave structure and narrative form to a meditation on the passion story which had long since been elaborated beyond the Gospel accounts. At one level, this dwelling on the passion was intended to arouse the believer to an empathetic and therefore meritorious contemplation of the results of his or her own sin. However, one cannot read late medieval representations of the passion without including their Eucharistic connotations. At the foot of the cross in Matthias Grünewald's famous Isenheim altarpiece, the lamb of God bleeds directly into a chalice. Conversely, the miraculous Eucharistic wafers preserved in the German field-shrine at Wilsnack shed drops of blood from the body of the crucified God-man into which they had been transubstantiated. In other words, the sacrifice of Christ was not an event more than fourteen centuries old: it was a miracle daily repeated and re-enacted on every altar in Christendom.

Historians habitually analyse the twin doctrines, of Eucharistic presence and Eucharistic sacrifice, as separate components in medieval thought. In reality, of course, each one supported and reinforced the other, and each grew to ever greater significance as 1500 approached. Because Christ became so accessible, tangible, and visible in the Eucharist, the Eucharist became the most natural way to confer divine grace on individuals and communities. Christian worship focused more and more on the elevation of the host, the display of the consecrated host in a monstrance, or the procession of the host through the community on the feast of Corpus Christi (first invented in Liège in 1246 but only widely popular when patronized by popes from the early fourteenth century onwards). On the other hand, priests and laity became ever more certain that the benefits of a sacrificial mass could be quantified and multiplied. The more masses said, other things being equal, the greater the grace that was bestowed. This was not a new idea on the eve of the Reformation: priests had been warned not to celebrate one mass for multiple beneficiaries in the later thirteenth century. However, it was chiefly in the fifteenth century that this principle sanctioned multiple obit masses, perpetual chantries, and whole colleges of priests dedicated to no other purpose than hastening departed souls through purgatory by manifold repetition of sacrificial Eucharists. Such a height did this 'accounting for the hereafter' attain that those who bought only a *moderate* number of post-mortem masses in some parts of Europe have fallen under suspicion, in historians' eyes, of being Waldensian heretics.

Yet when looked at from another perspective, pre-Reformation religion does not seem so Christ-centred after all. Christ might be visible to all as bread on the altar. Yet when Jesus was not depicted on the cross as an awful warning of the consequences of sin, he was shown presiding at the Last Judgement, an even more awful warning of the fate awaiting those who disdained the Church's means to atone for their sins. The role of the gentle, sympathetic protector fell increasingly to Jesus's mother. The Virgin Mary became in the last decades of the Middle Ages far more than an example of meek submission to the divine will. In the sermons of the Tübingen theologian Gabriel Biel (d. 1495) she appeared as the co-redeemer of mankind. In devotional prayers, engravings, and sculpture she sheltered sinful humanity from the rigours of divine judgement. Desiderius Erasmus (c.1467–1536) observed that so universal was the cult of the Virgin, that vows made to her were thought worthless unless they specified which particular manifestation of the Blessed Virgin at which shrine received the votary's intentions. He also imagined the Virgin weary of the endless petitions of mortal people: they supposed that her power over the infant Jesus was such that 'if he did deny the petitioner something, I for my part would refuse him the breast when he was thirsty'.

While the Virgin Mary was supreme over all the saints, the duty of intercession and patronage in some measure belonged to them all— and would continue to do so in Catholic Europe throughout the century. Saints and their cults punctuated the second half of the liturgical year, breaking the religious monotony of 'ordinary time' in the summer and autumn with patronal festivals. They covered with their identity and their protection those communities which housed their relics, or simply thanked them for past deliverances from drought, flood, pestilence, or other misfortune. Great prestige was at stake in the gathering and display of relics. In bastions of late Gothic culture such as Germany, it causes no surprise that a conventionally devout prince like Friedrich III of Saxony should assemble a large and exotic collection of saintly fragments. But even the sardonic and cynical Renaissance Pope Pius II (d. 1464), author of one of the most unblinkingly secular analyses of the papal court ever written, took naïve pleasure in the translation of the head of St Andrew from Patras to Rome in April 1462.

A serious theological point underlay the sometimes frantic efforts of later medieval people to associate themselves and their loved ones with any and every manifestation of the sacred. Human beings could not save their own souls. Even at its most works-righteous, the medieval Church never actually claimed that Christians 'earned' salvation. The saints needed divine help like everyone else. That help came, ordinarily, through the system of penitential purifications. Since 1215 Western Christians had been legally obliged to make at least once a year (normally in Lent) a private confession of their sins to their parish priest or his substitute or assistant, and to perform a work of satisfaction or 'penance' assigned at the discretion of the confessor. The system had elaborated and grown beyond the capacity of many parish priests to cope. Specialist confessors (often friars), even private confessors, guided their penitents through the maze of individual moral rights and wrongs prescribed in the intricate and massive volumes of confessors' manuals like the *Angelica* and the *Sylvestrina*. Fearsomely judicial at first sight, the system actually combined ethical legalism with a medicinal, therapeutic aspect. For those who found the rigours of penance too great, it was often possible to commute one's 'work of satisfaction' into something a little easier or more congenial. By going on pilgrimage to certain shrines, or even by devoutly contemplating an image, one could earn 'indulgence' to delete some of the penance owed here or in the hereafter. When popes proclaimed jubilee or other special indulgences, even more easy relief was offered for a means-tested sum of money. When Martin Luther (1483–1546) challenged indulgences in 1517, he began from a thoroughly conventional medieval question: was it a good idea for sinners to be relieved of their penitential burdens in this spurious way? Was not completing one's penance (literally) better for the soul?

The 'Luther-Movement'

One thing is clear about the Reformation of the sixteenth century. No single figure, no single ambition or objective, no single social, political, or religious movement brought it into being. Its outcome depended on enormously complex and unpredictable interactions between personalities, events, beliefs, and attitudes. Yet it is impossible to separate the early history of the Reformation from the personality of Martin Luther. As an Augustinian eremite of the Observant wing of the order, he sprang from the revival in traditional ascetic piety at the end of the Middle Ages. As a philosophical nominalist, he combined a rigorously critical attitude to theological language with a sense that a transcendent God might have done it all differently. As a product of the Northern Renaissance, he knew that classical literature and above all classical languages had important things to say to his own time. He slipped easily into the language of German ecclesiastical nationalism, all the more when he met representatives of the papal curia's feeble theology. Yet he was more than the sum of his many parts. It was unusual for a university theologian to turn out a brilliant publicist and pamphleteer. It was abnormal for a student of the Renaissance to believe that religious doctrines must (a) be discerned with absolute, critical clarity and (b) be disseminated even to the ordinary mass of the people. It was almost unique for someone of such ability and stature to set his conscience and his insights against the common opinion of Western Christendom, and be ready to give up his life for his certainties.

The initial controversy over indulgences related only tangentially to the theological issues of the developed Reformation. The archbishop-elector of Mainz, Albrecht von Hohenzollern, was to be allowed to recoup some of the huge costs of his confirmation in his see from the proceeds of a reissue of the indulgence originally offered to help the rebuilding of St Peter's at Rome. Such indulgences already aroused religious scepticism in some quarters and financially motivated resentment in others. But pastoral concerns dictated Luther's response. Was it really beneficial to sincere Christians to forego penitential prayers and offerings, even if an indulgence made them unnecessary? Initially, Luther intended to make a discreet and respectful protest to the archbishop, and at the same time to invite the theological academy to discuss the issue. Only when no constructive response came from Mainz did he begin to circulate his *Ninety-Five Theses*. Yet embedded in the technical school-Latin of the theses were hypothetical versions of what sceptical laypeople might have been thinking. 'Why does the pope not empty purgatory for love of souls rather than money?' 'Why are masses still said for the souls of those supposedly already freed from purgatory?' 'Why do indulgences commute penalties according to a "tariff" of penances long since in disuse?' Luther did not himself ask these questions, but he imagined others doing so. The theses contained the seeds of a publicity campaign, and the printer-publishers who issued them as printed broadsides without Luther's approval saw that.

The 'indulgence-dispute' turned into a crisis through repeated blunders and mishandlings. Elements in the Dominican order saw the Augustinian theologian's critique as an outrage. Papal theologians saw the implied slight to the pope's spiritual power as intolerable. Luther became progressively more disillusioned as one after another emissary from Rome, including Cardinal Cajetan, one of the greatest Dominican theologians of the age, proved pathetically unable to answer his arguments. The Roman hierarchy painted itself into a corner by aligning itself with the most discredited and exclusive elements in the religious culture. By the time of Luther's excommunication in 1520, only the most single-minded defenders of the papal court—of whom there were few enough in Germany—remained hostile to Luther's cause. Confronting the Emperor at Worms in 1521,

Luther was a German hero. It may be doubted whether the young Emperor Charles V could have dared hand him over to the Roman authorities even if he had not promised him safe-conduct.

Meanwhile Luther had been evolving in ways quite separate from the issue of indulgences. Since beginning his lectures on scripture at Wittenberg in 1513 he had wrestled continually with the theological understanding of how souls were saved from sin. Fairly rapidly he became convinced, like others in his order, that 'justification', the process that makes people righteous and acceptable before God, came as a gift from God, not as a fruit of human response. If Luther's thought had stopped there, there need have been no Reformation, since such a belief was entirely within the spectrum of acceptable Catholic views. The real crux was somewhat technical, but can be expressed thus. Did God enter the soul of a person and make it more holy, in order then to accept it? Or did God arbitrarily decide to regard people as 'covered' by the merits of Jesus Christ, as 'extrinsically' free from sin irrespective of their *real* spiritual condition? In 1515–17 Luther was presenting both of these options, intermingled and interchangeably, to his students. By 1518–19 his thought had moved on further, not by a sudden epiphany, rather by the gradual adoption of one interpretation to the exclusion of all others. God's decree to save, to 'justify', rescued *inherently unworthy* souls through no intrinsic quality of their own. 'God's righteousness' given to the believer really meant God's arbitrary *acquittal* of the sinner before judgement.

By 1520 this insight was clearly not just radical theology. It also by its inner logic required a completely different concept of worship and the Christian Church. If God decreed that human beings be saved through preaching a gospel of radical forgiveness rather than dispensing sacraments of purification, what need of a ritually and legally separate sacrificing priesthood? What was the point of an elite of celibate priests, monks, and nuns, mortifying the flesh in the futile belief that they became holier by so doing? By the time he wrote his scathing assault on the traditional view of the sacraments in the *Babylonian Captivity of the Church* (1520) Luther himself had seen the implications. So entrenched were wrong ideas about the purpose of Christian worship that to correct them

it would be necessary to abolish most of the books now in vogue, and to alter almost the entire external form of the churches and introduce, or rather reintroduce, a totally different kind of ceremonies. But my Christ lives, and we must be careful to give more heed to the Word of God than to all the thoughts of men and of angels.

In that last phrase, Luther committed all the political outcome of his movement to God. He would preach and teach the truth, and let events take their course. This was typical of the man, but not always to the same extent. In his own territory of Wittenberg he could see things differently. In the winter of 1521–2 Luther spent time in the protective custody of his prince at the Wartburg. In that remote castle he wrote feverishly and began his epoch-defining German New Testament. During his absence friends and colleagues started to put his ideas into effect: they changed the order of the mass, gave the chalice of wine to laypeople as well as clergy, emptied monasteries, and destroyed 'idolatrous' images and altars. Luther saw that one fetishistic religion risked being replaced with another no less fetishistic. He returned to Wittenberg in March 1522 and told his followers to pause, think, and teach. Unless there was teaching and understanding, changes to outward religious behaviour would achieve nothing. He would cling to this need for mass religious instruction, despite the practical difficulties it posed, for the rest of his life. Wittenberg moved towards reformed worship in the baggage-train rather than the vanguard of the Reformation.

Community and city reformations in the Germanic world

Luther rapidly became a public icon, a figure celebrated in woodcut engravings and *Flugschriften* across Germany and beyond. Various groups of people saw his cause as their own. Critics of the higher clergy and bishops, for example, lesser nobility like Franz von Sickingen or Hartmuth von Cronberg, warmed to his critique of clerical arrogance and privilege. Renaissance literati appreciated his campaign to displace Aristotle and Peter Lombard with the Greek and Hebrew Bible and the Fathers. But it was perhaps in the atmosphere of independent corporate cities and towns that the most natural

—if transient—coalition was formed between Luther's theological message and current trends in social and political thought.

The cities of the Empire in the later Middle Ages were communities apart. Like cities elsewhere they were legal entities, governed by their corporations and defined by the circuit of their walls. More than that, however, those of the German Empire and the Swiss Confederation were *de facto* sovereign states. Many of them ruled small hinterlands. They made alliances, hired soldiers, took part in police actions and minor wars. Above all they had issues to resolve with the Church. Some had become 'free cities' by expelling, centuries earlier, the diocesan prince-bishop who nominally presided over them. With their strong sense of corporate responsibility and mutual aid, they chafed at the clergy's fiscal and legal privileges. For decades before the Reformation, cities like Nuremberg and Strasbourg had sought patronage over the principal town churches, or cajoled the clergy into voluntary surrender of their immunities in return for *Schirm*, a form of civic insurance protection afforded to full citizens. Many towns hired a stipendiary city preacher outside the normal system of benefices: Zürich recruited Huldrych Zwingli (*c*.1484–1531) as its *Leutpriester* or stipendiary priest before he turned to the Reformation. Medieval towns thought of themselves as one community under God, not two divided communities of laity and clergy. There was a fortuitous but historically crucial overlap between their aspirations and Martin Luther's new concept of Church and ministry.

Between 1521 and 1525 the towns and cities of the Empire witnessed a nearly unique experiment in public religious debate. One key to this was the rise of a relatively free and enormously prolific printing press. Printing technology was already some sixty years old by 1520. For those initial decades printed books had, generally, been manuscripts produced by other means: there had been relatively few innovations in format. With the advent of Luther, publisher-printers speedily discovered that one or two sheets of paper folded down into quarto size would yield material for a pamphlet of some sixteen pages or more. The pamphlet or short tract filled the space between the learned tome and the single-sheet woodblock broadside, which had previously been the favoured format for popular cheap print. Luther's early works, especially his sermons, fitted this format perfectly. Soon his controversial pieces also appeared as handy quartos. Other ecclesiastical writers such as Erasmus printed their works in similar form; they were then joined by an army of contoversialists, including laymen like Hans Sachs and laywomen like Argula von Grumbach and Katharina Zell. Luther vastly outwrote, outpublished, and outsold anyone else in these years of intellectual ferment. Just as important, however, was his creating a space in which to ask new questions. Could one be saved without indulgences? Did a Christian community have the right to call, install, and dismiss its ministers?

Most people, even in the most sophisticated of towns, were illiterate. But pamphlets did not work on their own, but in conjunction with noisy and well-attended sermons. These were accessible to all in the towns and the surrounding countryside who might come to hear them. Reforming spirits did not have a prerogative on preaching: traditionalists responded in kind. In the early 1520s many towns found their preachers, from both sides of the Reformation debates, so fiery and disruptive that they attempted to calm them down on civic authority. In at least seventeen towns in Germany and the Swiss Confederation preachers were told to confine themselves to expounding scripture and avoid mutual acrimony. The injunctions failed, as they always do. More importantly, these edicts gave the city fathers the responsibility to police their own understanding of 'scripture'. City fathers' sense of civic duty and the reforming preachers' encouragement of lay self-esteem coincided. At Zürich in January 1523, Huldrych Zwingli confronted the bishop of Konstanz's vicar-general when the latter argued that no theological disputation could be allowed to take place in the presence of laymen. Zwingli answered:

in this very hall we have a Christian assembly gathered together . . . Since, therefore, in this our assembly there are great numbers of true faithful people both from our own district and from beyond, and these are just like so many pious and learned bishops . . . I see no reason whatever to prevent us here and now from lawfully disputing the Vicar's opinion on these matters.

It took several years at least for the process to work through to its conclusion. Fortified by the regularly reinforced conviction that their acts were godly rather than sacrilegious, city communities seized control of their ecclesiastical establishments and the miscellaneous hospitals, almshouses, and other welfare structures that went with them. Priests turned into civic ministers, married, and integrated into the citizenry. The mass was replaced by a reformed order of service. Sooner or later all the houses of vowed religious orders were closed down and their property confiscated. A confused pattern of private and corporate charity was replaced, in theory, by systematic and rational poor relief and public schooling. The political processes in the towns and cities varied. The Reformation might be born in political strife (the Baltic cities), compulsive hesitation on the part of the magistrates (Augsburg), or even after opinion polls taken of the citizen body (Ulm, Konstanz, Memmingen, and elsewhere). No one analysis fits all cases: they shared only passionate concern for civic religion.

A historically fateful fault-line began to open up in the early Reformation between the towns and cities of the north and the south of the Empire. The divide was neither clearly political nor clearly theological. Rather it concerned the methods used in installing the Reformation. In northern Germany, Luther and even more his close friend Johannes Bugenhagen (1485–1558) fostered a reform movement that was liturgically quite conservative. It favoured traditional forms where they could be preserved, fostered gradual change, and forbad wholesale destruction of images. After centuries of Lutheranism some north German churches retain their late medieval altarpieces to this day. In the south Huldrych Zwingli at Zürich, and Martin Bucer (1491–1551) at Strasbourg urged a more thorough 'cleansing' of the medieval order. Images were stripped out and the liturgy progressively purified of non-scriptural elements. Luther came to see this Swiss and south German style of Reformation as a menace: it was too preoccupied with sudden and drastic change, too confident of the power of human reason, too arrogant in questioning the divine paradoxes of the Eucharistic presence. Luther was not an architect of institutions, and would never have seen a unified 'reformed communion' as necessary in the first place. However, the rifts and misunderstandings of the later 1520s began the process that would leave Europe with two potentially antagonistic Protestant blocs.

The urban Reformations were a fascinating cultural phenomenon, but outside the Swiss Confederation they were not militarily defensible. South German cities, which used to lean on the Emperor against the princes, turned to the leagues formed from 1531 onwards by their former enemies, the territorial princes. When the Emperor attacked the princes in the 1540s those same princes would leave the free cities to their fate. They would lose their distinctive forms of worship and theology: some would lose their freedoms as well.

Peasants, princes, and monarchs

Self-governing towns and cities did not have a prerogative on strong sense of community and mutual responsibility. In the fervid atmosphere of the early 1520s rural communes across central and southern Germany began to see their social and cultural aspirations through a lens ground by the Reformation context. If God had entrusted the means of salvation to a community, choosing and appointing its own pastor, must that community not also own the rights to the use of lands, woods, rivers, and other natural resources? Should not the lords and knights have to prove their territorial claims based on the community's prior consent? Mingled with this pragmatic village-commune thinking were more radical elements, drawn from visions of the millennium and prophecies of a new Christian order. This brew boiled over in the spring of 1525, following several months of turmoil in Swabia. In the south of Germany bands of 'peasants' (actually farmers, villagers, and some townspeople) assembled in arms to protest against their predicament, clustering in and around the town of Memmingen. Further north, in Thuringia, leagues of ordinary people, some led or inspired by the apocalyptic visionary Thomas Müntzer, gathered at Frankenhausen. The articles of the Swabian peasants circulated round Germany in, inevitably, a quarto-format printed pamphlet, inspiring numerous imitators.

The 'Peasant War' of 1525 was doubly a misnomer. It was not restricted to 'peasants', and it was barely a war at all. The Swabian peasants dispersed after talks, and those of Thuringia were massacred by trained troops outside Frankenhausen. However, it had a dramatic effect on the attitudes of the German nobility and princely elites. During the early 1520s the aristocracies of Germany had generally stood aloof from the religious debate. Those who, like Duke George of Saxony, tried to confiscate German Bibles suffered Luther's withering scorn. The events of 1525 showed that benign neglect was no longer an adequate policy. Although spontaneous expressions of reformed commitment still appeared, especially in urban settings,

Germany after 1525 presented a more hierarchical, more controlled environment. The time for greater assertion of aristocratic control had arrived. There were already precedents for princely control over the territorial Church, just as there had been precedents for city magistrates' control over the churches in the towns. Some prince-bishops had become vassals of princes for their secular estates; some great princes had acquired ecclesiastical patronage like the crowned heads elsewhere in Europe. Especially in the north and east of Germany, there were undeniable attractions to the princes in rounding off the borders of their large principalities by absorbing enclaves of ecclesiastical lands.

Nevertheless, the 'princely Reformation' proceeded slowly, and was less fertile in new religious concepts than its urban counterpart. In Luther's homeland of Electoral Saxony, ruled by the 'Ernestine' branch of the Wettin dynasty, the territorial Church was organized through a process of state-sponsored visitations (1528) leading to new ordinances in the 1530s. A precocious attempt by Philip of Hesse to organize his Church at the Synod of Homburg in 1526 failed to stick. Over time, territorial churches coalesced under 'Church ordinances' sponsored by the princely regime: a particularly detailed example was the Nuremberg–Brandenburg–Ansbach Church ordinance of 1533. By the early 1540s the network of Lutheran principalities in Germany was largely complete. It had taken as long as it did because of political calculations and dynastic rivalries. Many of the princely families of the *Reich* were divided into rival branches, each ruling their own patch of territory: when one branch reformed, the other tended to delay Reformation at least until a new ruler acceded.

The most important contribution of the princely Reformation to the stock of reformed ideas lay in the area of political thought. Throughout the later Middle Ages the problem *par excellence* in the German Empire had been law and order. In the absence of an effective central authority, the choice lay between ever stronger princely power, and a network of leagues and confederations between lesser powers with political responsibility. When princes realized that their patronage of Reformation posed risks to their survival, they responded in the traditional way by banding together with the like-minded. In the late 1520s cities and princes expressed their solidarity with the Reformation in the 'Protestation' made at the Reichstag of Speyer in 1529; they subscribed the definitive Lutheran 'Confession of Ausgburg' in 1530, where last-ditch talks to reintegrate the Empire's churches ran into the sand. By the early 1530s a Protestant defensive League, including Lutheran and south German reformed states, had been formed as the League of Schmalkalden. During its existence it acquired some embryonic attributes of statehood, holding assemblies, gathering money and troops, and sending embassies abroad to foreign powers. Yet it posed a theoretical problem for the reformed theologians. Martin Luther's initial opinion had favoured regarding the *Reich* as a single kingdom under the rule of the Emperor. Anyone, knight, peasant, or prince, who resisted the Emperor with force broke a divine commandment. By 1530 Luther and his colleagues had been cajoled into accepting that, at least on grounds of secular law, the constitution of the German Empire was more complex. Germany was a polity where princes might legitimately defend themselves and their subjects against an unjust act by the Emperor, or indeed any external aggressor. Towards the end of his life Luther would add his own apocalyptic cast to this body of thought: the pope was a fairytale monster of depravity to be resisted by the whole community, and any ruler who took his side had no legitimacy.

Resistance theory was one thing: resistance practice was another. By 1546 Charles V had emasculated the Protestant League by blackmailing Philipp of Hesse and seducing the disgruntled Duke Moritz of Albertine Saxony away from the alliance. He was thus free to attack the forces of Electoral Saxony and Hesse. After defeating them in battle in 1547, Charles then proved utterly unable to win the peace through his vision of a moderate, partly reformed but still Catholic order of worship. Lutherans and Catholics in the Empire were too far apart to be forced into a shotgun marriage that adulterated both their principles. In the early 1550s Charles V suffered a mental breakdown, and entrusted his brother Ferdinand with negotiating a system for the coexistence of Catholics and Lutherans in the Empire. This solution was substantially agreed by 1552 and formally adopted by the Peace of Augsburg in 1555. The subtle diversity of the pre-1546 German religious context was replaced by a stark choice between doctrinaire Lutheranism and hierarchical Catholicism.

Meanwhile various sovereigns in Europe had engaged with Lutheranism, with a diverse range of outcomes. The consequences were clearest cut in Scandinavia. In the kingdom of Denmark (which also included Norway, the southern tip of modern Sweden, Iceland,

and Schleswig-Holstein) a sequence of civil conflicts and *coups d'état* culminated, by 1536, in the establishment of a Lutheran Church order under Christian III (1534–59). In Sweden, independent of the Danish crown from the early 1520s, the authoritarian and sometimes capricious Gustav I Vasa (1523–60) gradually instituted a state Church with Lutheran characteristics from 1527 onwards, though he deliberately avoided entrusting his clergy with too much independent authority. In France the spendthrift and often unpredictable Renaissance monarch Francis I toyed with aspects of reforming ideas when the ultra-Catholic theology faculty of Paris threatened his own ideological ascendancy. Both he and his son Henri II made repeated overtures to and alliances of convenience with Lutheran princes, to further their lifetime obsessions of resisting the military power of the Austro-Spanish Habsburg dynasty. However, they also punctuated their reigns with episodes of fierce persecution of Protestants. In England Henry VIII (1509–47) found himself at odds with the papacy over his matrimonial problems. He and his ministers spent much of the 1530s in intermittent dialogue with the political and religious leadership of Lutheranism. He even allowed a putatively semi-Lutheran set of articles of doctrine to be presented to the Convocation of the clergy in 1536. However, the king hankered after alliances with the first rather than the second division of European powers, and could not resist dabbling in theology himself to the exasperation of his own Archbishop Cranmer and Philipp Melanchthon alike. On his personal choices the prospects for a Lutheran England soon foundered.

The refugee paradigm

In the latter half of the sixteenth century the religious geography and alignments of Europe were transformed by the advent of a new route to Reformation. John Calvin (1509–64) did not set out to found a distinctive new type of religious Reformation—indeed, the idea would probably have horrified him. This serious, gifted, intelligent, and almost unbelievably diligent Frenchman had embraced the reforming message in 1533, in a conversion process which (unlike Luther) he rarely introspected. After a brief apprenticeship in Basel he published the first edition of his manual of reformed theology, the *Institutio*, a little like the *Common Places* of Melanchthon, whom he resembled somewhat in temperament. Calvin was then drawn, almost by physical force, into the unwelcome task of helping to steer the Reformation of the French-speaking ex-episcopal free city of Geneva from 1536, under the protection of the Swiss canton of Berne. His resoluteness and exceptional gifts as a writer, teacher, and preacher earned him a unique ascendancy among small-town reformers. His stature grew first to rival, then to surpass, that of his colleague Heinrich Bullinger at Zürich. With the homogenization of the German Protestant Churches under Lutheranism, the Swiss cities were left by c.1550 as the sole representatives of the non-Lutheran 'reformed' tradition. Of those only Geneva and Zürich retained international significance—and Zürich was hemmed in from further expansion by its frontiers with its Catholic neighbours, frozen since 1531.

Calvin was a brilliant organizer, expositor, and systematizer of reformed theology, a religious diplomat of genius, and a mentor to the reformed world. But he did not design Geneva's role in the Reformation: that was a product of circumstances. In the middle 1550s Geneva, like Strasbourg, Frankfurt-am-Main, and other Central European towns, became a destination for religious refugees from France, the Low Countries, Italy, England. In that same period Calvin had gained a degree of moral ascendancy over the town that he had struggled for before in vain. He achieved his objective of enforcing moral discipline through excommunication quite independent of the magistrates, something never attempted in Zürich. A sequence of political mischances forced Geneva to set up its own Academy, comprising both a school and a seminary, in 1559.

So, the refugees who streamed into Geneva found a city organized as a model centre of Reformation like no other. Once there, they could be trained for ministry to export what they saw to other corners of Europe. In the 1540s Calvin had seen his French compatriots hesitate on the sidelines of Reformation, living inertly as token Catholics and waiting for better times according to the principle known as 'Nicodemism'. He viewed this as a dangerous act of dishonesty, supping with the Devil in the hope of safety. Surely exile was a better alternative. Better still, potentially, was to set up reformed worship even within a hostile state, in secret initially at least, and see how many joined the banner. Here Calvin differed diametrically from Luther. Luther had positively discouraged initiatives by private individuals to found secret churches; Calvin supported them. Calvin's approach made sense in areas of Western Europe that were much more politically homogeneous than Germany: France, the Low Countries (a Spanish-Habsburg territory since 1548), and the British Isles. His ideas also appealed in parts of Eastern Europe where Slavic reformers sought something different from their German neighbours' Lutheranism.

The reformed paradigm known later as 'Calvinism' reversed the chronological order of the early Reformation. In the 1520s–1530s, a given community's decision to embrace the Reformation message came first; the details of liturgy, confessions, and church structure were worked out *after* the decision in principle had been made. Under 'Calvinism', in contrast, an ideal-type or model of reformed Christianity was available to be, as it were, taken off the peg *before* the community or state decision was made. That did not mean that 'Calvinism' was *invariably* associated with 'Reformation from below' or indeed with religious revolution. In Scotland a group of nobles and leading ecclesiastics organized an aristocratic *putsch* in 1560 against the French-born queen mother-regent, with the assistance, given reluctantly and very late, of Elizabeth I of England. The resulting national Church if anything strengthened rather than weakened the integrity of the realm—though not always in terms congenial to the monarch. In England, the Protestant spirits among clergy and nobility had already embraced reformed rather than Lutheran Protestantism in the reign of Edward VI. Edward's half-sister Elizabeth found, on succeeding the Catholic Mary I in 1558, that she had to work with a pre-set reformed orthodoxy; however, she proved extremely adept at drawing its ideological teeth and forcing it to work within a national Church that retained its medieval structures. Most striking of all was the alliance forged from the 1560s onwards between 'Calvinist' principles and princely authoritarianism in parts of Germany. Led by the Electors Palatine at Heidelberg, numerous German princes sought with varying degrees of success to enforce the austere, rational, cerebral forms of Genevan worship on their previously Lutheran subjects.

Nevertheless, the 'reformed' pattern of Protestant Church-building found itself in revolt against the Valois monarchy in France, and the

Habsburg regime in the Low Countries. Right at the beginning of the process, a tiny minority Church in the Alps set a poignant example of religious resistance. From 1555 onwards Geneva had flooded the Alpine valleys of western Piedmont, held by 'Waldensian' heretics, with reformed ministers. Suddenly furtive dissent turned into public worship. The duke of Savoy first threatened these people, then attacked them with force. Exploiting the terrain, the Waldensian Protestants defended themselves so effectively that the duke made peace in 1561 and allowed them their reformed enclave. This statistically insignificant victory for 'Reformation from below' had immense psychological impact. It was reported across Europe in pamphlets and martyrologies just as the French and the Flemish were beginning their own struggles for recognition. In France the struggle for an established Protestant Church was fairly clearly, from 1562 onwards, about just how much privilege and how wide a distribution the minority reformed Church would achieve. So unstable were monarchy and society that only after more than thirty years of intermittent bloodshed was this issue brought to an acceptable compromise under the ex-Protestant Henri IV in 1598. In the Netherlands the struggle for Protestantism meshed with the complaints of the Flemish nobility about Habsburg placemen in government, the aspirations of Flemish and Brabanter artisans to live and work free of Habsburg domination, and the political ambitions of the noble house of Orange-Nassau. Though the reformed were a minority as they were in France, in the Netherlands that minority became the voice of a nascent Netherlandish 'national' sentiment and the natural governing class, at least in the northern provinces where the revolt became entrenched after the mid-1580s.

The 'Calvinist' mode of Reformation also proved remarkably attractive in parts of Eastern Europe. The German communities of the east from the Baltic coast to the *Siebenbürgen* of Transylvania had, initially and in some cases decisively, dabbled in Lutheranism. Sections of the Slavic and Magyar nobilities found it congenial to adopt a form of Protestantism different from their Teutonic neighbours: so Polish nobles like the Leszczyński and Tarnowski defended their political right to uphold Calvinism in their spheres of influence, and Magyar Calvinist leaders including Martin Santa Kálmáncsehi and Péter Méliusz Juhasz organized a Calvinist synodical structure to rival the Lutheran one. As in Germany, it was essentially nobles and towns that had anything resembling free choice of confession. Moreover, the roots of reformed Protestantism proved in some areas to be relatively shallow. Those who, like the Radziwiłł in Poland, had dabbled in Calvinism proved just as ready to dabble in more exotic heresies, including the earliest forms of antitrinitarianism or Socinianism (see below, 'On the margins of the confessions').

Despite the huge geopolitical discrepancies between different parts of the 'Calvinist' world, certain attitudes to the Christian Church marked them off. The reformed believed that their Reformation was complete where the Lutheran Reformation was incomplete. They prided themselves on rejecting all that savoured of 'idolatry' in traditional worship. They aspired with varying degrees of success to a vigorous ecclesiastical discipline. They tended to be internationalists: where Lutherans thought in terms of the national or provincial interest, the reformed thought in terms of a grander, more abstract 'cause'. The following century would witness the fatal results of these incompatible views of Protestant politics.

Catholicism chooses its path

It was not foreordained that a 'Roman Catholic Church' should arise as an antagonistic rival and ideological counterweight to the reformed Churches. At various points before c.1550 it seemed possible to envisage a reintegration of the fractured visions of European Christianity into one institution. Catholic Christianity after 1520 was shaped through a series of political and ideological choices. It is now clear that the traditional image of the Renaissance Church as uniformly decadent, luxurious, undisciplined, staggering unconcerned towards the Reformation precipice, will not stand up. Among regular and secular clergy as well as some laypeople, campaigns were run to encourage devotional life and ascetic piety. As part of those campaigns, religious reformers wrote to denounce the laxity of unreformed religious orders, the low standard of many of the secular clergy, or the wasteful way in which the Church was administered. Fair or unfair, these complaints testify to the vigour of reforming sentiment rather than the lack of it. It is less clear whether these waves of moral uplift and denunciation of vices should be dignified as a 'pre-reform' movement, as a distinct phase in Catholic history. It may be better to say that such criticism ran like a continuous thread throughout the Middle Ages.

One characteristic of Catholicism c.1500—only in later periods would it be seen as a flaw or a vice—was a certain openness about doctrine. On many theological questions, not least the doctrine of justification, the Church had yet to pronounce a definitive theological position. In the first three decades of the sixteenth century some of the most spiritually and intellectually gifted minds in Italy, many of them friends of the Venetian nobleman and future cardinal Gasparo Contarini, formed beliefs about justification that were at least verbally very close to the reformers'. They did not draw the same lessons about worship and the Church as the Protestants did, at least not initially; indeed their theological piety tended to be somewhat self-absorbed and introverted, fitted to religious salons and discussion groups rather than preaching or pamphleteering. Until the 1540s those who held a more liberal attitude towards doctrine were probably in the ascendancy, morally and numerically, in the highest councils of the Church. Set against them were a handful of rigorists, best exemplified by Giovanni Pietro Caraffa, the future Pope Paul IV, who ranked 'heresy', meaning any dogma dangerous to the hardest of hard-line orthodoxy, as just another serious disciplinary failing alongside simony or moral depravity. The spiritual and rigorist wings could agree on the need for moral regeneration, but could not agree on what kind of response to the Reformation challenge should form part of such regeneration.

The debates were moot for much of the 1520s and 1530s. The Roman curia could not mount any sort of united response to the Reformation for some twenty years after the Italian wars flared up again in 1522. Without peace between Austria and France, the promised general council could not meet and the vital assistance of Catholic sovereigns could not be relied upon. In the early 1540s several factors changed the landscape. In Germany, the most distinguished representatives of liberal Catholic thought tried their hardest to reach agreement with moderate Lutherans in conferences at Hagenau, Worms, and Regensburg in 1540–1, and failed. In Italy, the spiritual wing handed a political victory to the rigorists when two of its chief representatives defected to Protestantism in 1542; the same year saw the founding of a permanent Office of the Inquisition in Italy for the first time. Also in 1542, Pope Paul III finally managed to organize the summoning of the long-promised and often-postponed general council, though it would not meet at Trent until 1545. Meanwhile, the Emperor was gearing up his military machinery to attack the Lutheran League in Germany.

The decisions taken in the Council of Trent, which met over 1545–7, 1551–2, and 1562–3, should therefore be read against this background of a tide ebbing away from conciliation. In its fourth session on 8 April 1546 Trent effectively prejudged all the other discussions on doctrine by declaring that it received 'with an equal affection of piety and reverence' both the scriptures and the historic traditions of the Church: doctrine and practice must be continuous, not discontinuous across history. The fourth-century Latin Vulgate translation of the Bible, attributed to Jerome and the source of many of the turns of phrase on which medieval theology depended, was declared authentic (with an implied superiority over the Hebrew and Greek originals). The little remaining room for manœuvre was then further confined by a skilfully drafted decree on justification. This interesting decree effectively canonized the interpretation of St Thomas Aquinas and the neo-Thomists, to the dissatisfaction alike of those who favoured the late medieval nominalist approach and those who (like the English presiding delegate Reginald Pole) inwardly favoured something much closer to the Reformation insights. The remaining decrees undergirded the continuance of traditional sacramental and disciplinary practice: theological inquiry was bound to support, not challenge, established custom.

And yet Trent changed Catholicism. In parallel with the consolidation of traditional doctrine ran a programme to make pastoral control over the dioceses more effective. Bishops were required to reside in their dioceses, to preach and to supervise the faithful. None of this was remotely new. Medieval councils had made the same stipulations, and some bishops had tried to fulfil them. What was new was the degree of authority conferred on bishops to ride rough-shod, if need be, over the exemptions and privileges held by all sorts of bodies within the Church. Diocesan bishops were given power to act without all the restraints and impediments that had often made even residence intolerable to their later medieval counterparts. Reforming synods and visitations, attempted sporadically in the past, became standard and regular practice. Not all of this was gain. The archetypal reforming prelate, Carlo Borromeo of Milan, aroused significant hostility in his relentless push for reform. Other bishops found it more pastorally effective to reconcile rather than provoke the unreformed. It has also been argued that the rise of the better educated and culturally more remote model of the parish priest, hearing confessions anonymously in the box popularized by Borromeo, may have opened up a greater gulf between priests and people.

The history of Catholicism in the sixteenth century must not be written solely in terms of the response to challenges, whether doctrinal or disciplinary. In important parts of Europe, most of all in the Iberian peninsula, religious life continued according to the principles laid down in the Middle Ages. Here the 'good of souls' meant the continuation and development of spiritual and ascetic principles long since established. This environment fostered movements of monastic renewal and observance, and the significant mystical and visionary traditions represented by figures like Teresa of Ávila and John of the Cross. It also sheltered a continuing growth in neo-Thomist theology that drew on medieval models without interruption. This was also the environment in which the Society of Jesus was born. Ignatius Loyola sprang from a late medieval Spain that still thought of itself as a frontier land for Christianity, where knightly and Catholic values mingled in the military orders. The society of priests regular for which he and his companions secured papal endorsement in 1540 was dedicated to works of pastoral consolation through education and *Jesuits* hearing confessions, as well as missions among non-Christians. A cogent argument can be made that none of this, in its origins, had much to do with combating Protestantism.

However, within a few years of its inception the Society of Jesus found itself heavily committed to religious and broader education. Ignatius recognized that a key part of education lay in instilling the 'correct' doctrines of the Church in a clear summary form for the benefit of even the youngest students. The Council of Trent, meanwhile, had embraced the need to have all those destined for priesthood educated through vocational seminaries. The outcome of these parallel ambitions was that the Jesuits became sucked into the work of training the Counter-Reformation priesthood. Their seminaries filled what would otherwise have been a gaping void if the Church had relied only on bishops' initiatives. Their missionaries went on heroic, sometimes suicidal missions to parts of the Americas and Asia to win over non-Christians; they also embarked on (sometimes just as suicidal) missions within Europe to win over non-Catholics and confirm Catholic minorities in their resistance. In the next century, Jesuit priests would play vital roles in the confessional politics of Europe. They established lines of communication with zealous Catholic rulers, including their former students Maximilian, duke of Bavaria, and Emperor Ferdinand II. They helped foster an alliance between Catholic doctrine and the power of the state that would shape the image of Catholicism in the seventeenth century.

On the margins of the confessions

The overwhelming majority of Europe's people were included within one or another of the mainstream confessional Churches. However, there also arose religious movements where self-selecting communities of devotees separated themselves from the wider society and formed Churches entirely apart. In this respect they went further than most medieval heretics, who usually retained some vestigial practice of traditional community worship. These voluntary 'gathered Churches' have since inspired great scholarly interest, because they seem to foreshadow modern society: their religion was voluntary and self-selecting as ours is. However, those parallels are somewhat misleading. To exclude oneself from the wider community and join a gathering of the elect, in the sixteenth century, required either enormous spiritual certainty, expectation of the imminent end of history, or positive willingness to abandon one's life for one's beliefs. The heady atmosphere of sixteenth-century Anabaptism bears little resemblance to the cool relativism of post-Enlightenment liberal Churches.

What became known as 'Anabaptism' was a product, in part, of the ferment of religious ideas and experiments in the early 1520s. Religious thinkers in northern Switzerland and southern Germany aspired completely to redefine and rethink Christian community. They rejected two important nuances shared by all the mainstream reformers. First, they did not agree that the saved, the elect, were also sinners in need of social discipline who might be indistinguishable to human eyes from the rest. Secondly, they did not accept that reformation should be an experience for whole communities rather than just the saved. Therefore, they wished to form an immediate, thoroughly reformed community composed only of the wholly regenerate. Gradually, though not immediately, such groups came to define themselves through the ritual of believers' baptism. The first leaders of the primordial 'Anabaptist' community were driven out of Zürich in the early 1520s and gathered supporters in the hinterland. They formed contacts with other like-minded people who emerged in southern and western Germany. 'Anabaptism' is now generally reckoned to be a bundle of multiple parallel movements, aware of each other but not necessarily all sprung from the same source.

For most sixteenth-century people, Anabaptism came to be associated with one spectacular and highly untypical example. Rebaptism had become suddenly popular in the province of Holland in the early 1530s. Under persecution from the Habsburg authorities, many followers fled and gathered in the episcopal city of Münster in Westphalia, which was in the grip of a relatively conventional city Reformation. The Anabaptists at Münster fell under the influence of an apocalyptic visionary named Melchior Hoffman, then in prison at Strasbourg. Under siege from the prince-bishop, their leadership passed to a brutal and eccentric dictator named Jan Beukelszoon of Leiden, whose arbitrary and bloody rule made Münster a byword before his defeat and execution in 1535.

Even before the Münster episode, forces within Anabaptism were working towards an approach to community survival that did not have the second coming and the end of history as its precondition. By the middle of the sixteenth century, two forms of Anabaptist community would prove themselves as viable even in the face of general hostility. The first was the movement of the followers of Menno Simons, known as 'Mennonites', who formed quietist, pacifist, reclusive communities in the more remote provinces of the Netherlands. The second was the 'Hutterite' movement, named (as so often happened) not after its first founder but after Jakob Hutter, who took the Anabaptist communities in the villages of Moravia under his guidance. The Hutterites pioneered an experiment in community living based on the absolute sharing of all property. Neither of these forms of religious dissent were entirely stable, socially or ideologically. In a community which aspired to real regeneration, disputes, disagreements, and scandals, which occurred quite often, could cause real crises. Both movements were fragmented and out of communion amongst themselves at one time or another. Members of both ran a high risk of martyrdom if captured; some actively prepared for and expected it.

Often included with the so-called 'radical wing of the Reformation' is another quite different kind of animal. The mainstream reformers had remained committed to much of the traditional Western Catholic inheritance from late antiquity, in the shape of the Latin forms of the three traditional creeds, Nicene Trinitarian doctrine and Chalcedonian Christology. This was not unthinking traditionalism: both Luther and Calvin could write eloquently about why the received Western view of the Godhead and Christ was true. Others were not so orthodox. Amongst those who embraced reforming views in Italy, a significant proportion—though not all, as used once to be assumed—drifted beyond Protestantism to something more exotic. Many of these Italians, of whom Lelio and Fausto Sozzini were possibly the most famous, left Italy to seek security in the almost unregulated religious world of Eastern Europe. There they mingled with and influenced indigenous reforming thinkers who had opened theology up to the most radical of revisions. In the 1560s there formed in Poland what became known as the 'minor' or antitrinitarian Church, soon gathered into a community at Raków on the estate of a supportive nobleman. In Transylvania, an Ottoman protectorate on the debatable borderlands between Habsburg and Turkish Europe, the drift towards 'Unitarianism', a belief-system that rejected Jesus Christ as a person of the Godhead, became both explicit and formally tolerated by the local authorities. In the eighteenth century, the survivors and descendants of these movements would exert considerable influence in the Europe and America of the Enlightenment. For the time being, such influence was far off; mere survival and the avoidance of lethal schisms was enough to ask.

Conclusion

In religious terms, the late sixteenth and early seventeenth century often seem like an age of iron. Where the Reformation had opened questions up, the era of confessional orthodoxy, in Protestant and Catholic countries alike, closed them down again. Yet attempts to draw a sharp distinction between the 'Reformation era' and the 'confessional era' have often failed to yield results. The point is this. Modern commentators are often attracted to the early Reformation because of its diffuseness, its openness, its possibilities. Yet that diffuseness was never intended to be permanent: it was a by-product of the search for a higher truth, not an end in itself. Sixteenth-century religious people believed that absolute truth could be extracted from the texts of scripture, and that once extracted, it should be proclaimed and defended absolutely. The rigidity and militancy of the 'confessional era' was a natural consequence of the Reformation, not the betrayal of its ideals. The tragedy of the seventeenth century was that it took so long for everyone to perceive that no one set of dogmas ever could—or even should—attain complete ascendancy.

6

Europe and a world expanded

D. A. Brading

Expanding territories in the sixteenth century

In *The Wealth of Nations* (1776), Adam Smith declared that: 'The discovery of America and that of a passage to the East Indies by the Cape of Good Hope are the greatest and most important events recorded in the history of mankind.' He added that, although the full range of benefits and misfortunes effected by these discoveries had yet to be manifested, it was already clear that certain European countries had encountered extensive and rapidly growing overseas markets for their manufactured goods. At the same time, Smith frankly confessed that: 'To the natives of both the East and West Indies, all the commercial benefits which can have resulted from those events have been sunk and lost in the dreadful misfortunes which they seem to have occasioned.'

But Smith's assumption that European colonization in Asia and America could be coupled together as markets for manufactures cannot be easily applied to the sixteenth century, since the Iberian explorers and conquerors of that epoch were largely animated by a quest for spices and precious metals, not to mention human souls. At that time European industries produced few goods that could be sold in Asia, or that could find many purchasers in America. Moreover, the character and outcome of Iberian colonization differed radically in the Old and the New World. In the Americas both Spaniards and

Portuguese conquered and settled broad swathes of territory and quickly established European forms of production, eventually creating thriving export industries in sugar and silver. By contrast, the Portuguese entered Asia as predatory interlopers and established a maritime commercial empire based on superior sea power that was sustained by the exchange of precious metals for pepper and other spices.

Indeed, if the Americas be removed from consideration, then it was the three 'gunpowder empires' of Islam, the Ottoman Turks, the Safavids of Iran, and the Mughals in India, that were the most obviously engaged in territorial expansion during the sixteenth century. It was then that the Ottomans subjugated the Arab world, which was to say, Syria, Egypt, and Mesopotamia, and then, in 1529, besieged Vienna and soon after annexed the kingdom of Hungary. In India the Mughal dynasty, which employed Persian as their court language, employed both Iranian and Turkish mercenaries in their conquest of northern India. In 1565, the three Muslim sultans of the Decaan defeated and destroyed Vijayanagra, the last great Hindu kingdom, whose capital had housed, so it was estimated, half a million inhabitants. So, too, it was during the sixteenth and early seventeenth centuries that Islam consolidated its religious conquest of Sumatra and Java, not to mention the lesser islands of the Indonesian archipelago. In effect, a common Islamic culture, Arab and Iranian, came to govern South and South-East Asia.

It was only on the frontiers of this expansive Islamic world that Christian powers succeeded in wresting control of a few provinces from Muslim control. In 1492, the Catholic kings of Spain, Isabel of Castile and Ferdinand of Aragon, completed the reconquest of the populous emirate of Granada, employing cannon to destroy its hitherto impregnable chain of mountain fortresses. But, although both they and their heir, the Emperor Charles V (1517–54), dispatched several expeditions to North Africa, they failed to secure any foothold on that continent. Moreover, although King John I of Portugal, the founder of the Avis dynasty, captured and held the Moroccan port of Ceuta in 1415, most subsequent Portuguese expeditions which entered North Africa failed to obtain any substantial or lasting success. Indeed, in 1578, the last scion of the dynasty, the young King Sebastian, suffered a tragic defeat in which he and thousands of his subjects suffered untimely death. Curiously enough, it was at the other end of Christendom that Ivan the Terrible (1533–84) proclaimed himself tsar of the third Rome, obtained the appointment of the first orthodox patriarch of Moscow, conquered the southern Tartar khanates of Kazan and Astrakhan in the 1550s, and threatened the Crimea, then held by a Muslim ruler subject to the Ottomans. It was thus two great regions, Russia and Iberia, which once had been devastated by Muslim invasion that, in the sixteenth century, exhibited the greatest animosity to Islamic power. So too, the theocratic temper of Ivan the Terrible and Philip II of Spain (1554–98) found monumental expression in the incomparable edifices of the Kremlin and the Escorial.

The Iberian powers and the first oceanic explorations

If the Iberian powers dominated oceanic exploration and conquest, it was largely thanks to Prince Henry, the younger son of John I of Portugal, who employed his inheritance and the resources of the military Order of Christ, of which he was the head, to settle the Atlantic islands and to dispatch a series of naval expeditions to reconnoitre and chart the western shores of Africa. In 1425, he introduced colonists to the uninhabited islands of Madeira and Porto Santo, leasing them to sub-donatories charged with their development. In 1439 he arranged for the occupation of the Azores, followed by the Cape Verde Islands, as his ships pushed southwards to Gambia and Senegal. It was in 1444 that Prince Henry inaugurated the Atlantic slave trade, sending ships to seize unsuspecting natives. By the next decade, however, his agents in Senegal purchased slaves, exchanging them for horses at the rate of seven Africans to one beast. By the time Henry died in 1460 over 2,500 miles of coastline had been visited. Where he failed was in his attempt to conquer the Canary Islands, a task which was vigorously assumed by the licensed agents of the Catholic kings in the 1480s. It was under John II of Portugal (1481–95) that the Portuguese established a fortified 'factory' on the island of São Jorge de Minha off the coast of Guinea, and then pushed southwards along the coast to modern Angola. This whole cycle of patient, coast-hugging exploration, which stretched over fifty years, culminated in the voyage of Bartholomew Dias who, in 1487–8, patiently followed the African coasts down to Walvis Bay in modern Namibia, only then to be blown into the open ocean, spending thirteen days out of sight of land, until he reached the eastern shores of South Africa, thereby opening the route to India.

When the Iberians reached India and the Americas they sailed in ships, caravels in particular, which embodied the fusion in ship design of the Mediterranean galley, with its narrow build and lateen sail, and the square-rigged 'round' ships of the Atlantic coasts. There finally emerged the familiar ship of the sixteenth century with its three or four masts, the fore and main masts square-rigged, and the mizzen with lateen sails and with raised 'castles' at one or both ends. But oceanic navigation depended on the systematic use of the compass, by observation of the South Pole Star with quadrant and astrolabe, by daily dead reckoning of progress and, obviously, by a diffusion of naval charts and arithmetic calculation. In effect, as the Portuguese moved southwards there emerged a cumulative, collective body of empirical knowledge, preserved in charts, divided by the lines of latitude and longitude, and supplemented by the practical experience of currents and winds. The third element in all this was the application of artillery to ships, which were provided with medium-sized guns placed below decks in the waist of the vessel, with portholes which could be closed in high waters. When Francis Bacon in *The New Organon* (1620) declared that the art of printing, the use of gunpowder, and the nautical compass had changed 'the face and condition of things across the globe', he implicitly recognized the role of European 'floating fortresses' in both Asia and America. Moreover, thanks to the 'print revolution' of the fifteenth century, news of the overseas discoveries and conquest of the Iberian powers was rapidly transmitted across Europe.

The feats of sailing across the Atlantic or the Indian Ocean, no matter how audacious, would not have changed the history of the world had not the Iberian monarchs acted swiftly to convert 'discovery' into empire by the dispatch of an entire series of armed expeditions to defend and enlarge their new possessions. Both in Portugal and Castile the crown attracted the service of the nobility, ranging from aristocrats in command to a swarm of impoverished gentlemen, and petty *hidalgos*, who sailed for the Indies in search of fortune. At all times these men were as liable to build a personal fortune as to serve the king's interest, but on both scores they helped to develop the colonial economy. At the same time overseas trade and production were often funded by the commercial and banking system of Europe, with Genoese merchants in Lisbon and Seville acting as the intermediaries. The early arrival of gold from Hispaniola and pepper from India was the subject of immediate comment in financial circles in Flanders, south Germany, and the Italian republics: lines of credit were then extended across the oceans. Indeed, the very ability of the Iberian kings to sustain their overseas empires depended in part on the loans and credit of the international banking system, especially in the case of Spain which, under Charles V, became the centre of the leading monarchy in Europe.

When Christopher Columbus, a Genoese mariner with long experience of Portuguese trade in Africa, ventured across the Atlantic in 1492, sailing with three small ships and ninety men through uncharted seas for thirty days without landfall, he expected to arrive at the western shores of Asia. Once, there, so he wrote, he expected to convert the great khan of Cathay to Christianity and thereafter form a grand alliance against Islam in order to liberate Jerusalem from Muslim rule. On reaching the Caribbean, he took possession of Hispaniola and other islands in the name of his patrons, the Catholic kings of Spain. Upon his return, these monarchs obtained from Alexander VI a papal bull in 1493, which granted the kings of Castile dominion over the islands and mainland of the ocean sea, albeit upon condition that they promote the conversion of the inhabitants of these newly discovered lands. The following year, with papal approbation, they signed the Treaty of Tordesillas with John II of Portugal, by which the two Iberian powers divided the possession of the overseas world, fixing the limits according to crudely drawn longitudinal lines. It was thanks to this treaty that when, in 1500, Pedro Alvares Cabral, blown off course while on route to India, discovered Brazil, he immediately claimed possession for Portugal. But it was not until 1519–23, when Ferdinand Magellan, a Portuguese mariner who had served in Indian waters, attempted to circumnavigate the world on behalf of Charles V, that the limits between the two Iberian powers in Asia were identified. Magellan entered the Pacific via the straits that bear his name, only to fall prey to native attack in the Philippines, leaving Sebastian del Cano to complete the voyage home after almost three years at sea.

Although news of Columbus's discoveries spread rapidly through Europe, it was left to a Florentine adventurer, Amerigo Vespucci, who had accompanied a Portuguese expedition to Brazil, to define their true significance in his *Novus mundus* (*c.*1503), a brief account written in elegant Renaissance Latin. For here was the celebration of the existence of a new continent, filled with immense trees and dense forests, populated with countless species of birds and beasts unknown to ancient naturalists, where even the heavens displayed a different constellation. Moreover, the natives of these lands went stark naked, dwelt freely together, holding everything in common without the constraints of law, religion, individual property, and unmolested by obedience to any lord or king. Sexual relations were governed by a similar freedom, with promiscuity the rule and marriage unknown. Although in his subsequent *Letters* Vespucci admitted that the natives engaged in constant warfare and ate the flesh of their captives with gusto, his first image of a tropical paradise where man lived a natural life, was destined to haunt the mind of Europe. It was in tribute to Vespucci's exuberant description that, when in 1507 Martin Waldseemüller was commissioned to frame a map of the world, the German cartographer boldly named the newly discovered continent 'America', albeit applying the term only to the southern land-mass.

Despite being named admiral and viceroy by the Catholic kings, Columbus proved unfit to govern the unruly Castilian adventurers who entered the New World, so that Nicolas de Ovando, a nobleman and knight of the military Order of Alcantara, was named governor of Hispaniola (1502–9), arriving with thirty ships and 2,500 men. Soon the island was endowed with a royal treasury, a high court, and a bishopric. But to exploit its resources, Ovando introduced the institution of *encomienda*, an arrangement whereby a specific number of lndians were entrusted to a Spanish settler and obliged to work for him free of charge and to offer him tribute in kind, all in return for protection and instruction in the Christian faith. In practice, this distribution of the native population was a charter for their virtual enslavement and so onerous were the demands placed on them that many were driven to an early death, since they were unaccustomed to daily labour and needed to supplement their diet of cassava bread made from manioc, by hunting for wild life. As the supply of ready labour dwindled, the Spaniards raided the lesser islands of the Antilles, enslaving their inhabitants on the pretext that they were guilty of cannibalism. For all that, the profits from gold-placer mining on Hispaniola were sufficient for the Spaniards to launch expeditions to conquer and settle Puerto Rico, Jamaica, and Cuba in the years 1508–11. It was only in 1513 that the Spanish crown dispatched a further expedition headed by Pedrarias Dávila, who led some 2,000 men, many of them veterans of the Italian wars, to take possession of Darien in modern Panama. To mine the gold deposits they found, these conquerors enslaved the hapless natives of this region and used hunting mastiffs to murder all who resisted their demands. Such was the devastation wrought by the Spaniards in the Caribbean, not to mention the impact of epidemic diseases that, by the 1520s when sugar plantations were established in Hispaniola, it was necessary to import slaves from Africa. In this last phase, the techniques of production developed by the Portuguese in the islands of Madeira and São Thomé were introduced into the New World.

The conquests of Mexico and Peru

The character and scale of Spanish colonization was dramatically transformed in 1519–21, when Hernán Cortés, an *encomendero* of Cuba, succeeded in overthrowing the Aztec empire. The first conquerors of México-Tenochtitlan were never to forget the grandeur of this island-city of 150,000 inhabitants, which was dominated by the great stepped pyramid temple where scenes of human sacrifice were regularly celebrated. The central basin of Mexico encompassed, so it is estimated, up to a million inhabitants, supported by an intensive agricultural system of irrigated terraces and floating rafts of vegetation which yielded two harvests a year. In effect, the Spaniards encountered an advanced civilization, completely autochthonous, with society divided between a sedentary peasantry, urban centres which housed artisans, a warrior nobility, and a distinctive priesthood, not to mention pyramid temples, palaces, and imperial dynasties. But it was also a civilization which, despite its great skill in agriculture, depended on human muscle for freight and traction, and which had yet to use metal implements or weapons, let alone the wheel. The Mexica were a warrior tribe, relative newcomers to the Central Valley, whose empire was the last political flourish of a civilization which had developed irregularly across two thousand years. Although Cortés wrote exultantly to Charles V that: 'Your Highness . . . may call himself once more emperor, with a title and with no less merit than that of Germany', Mexico did not offer the conquerors any immediate treasures, since the imperial tribute collected by the Aztecs consisted of a great many bins of maize and bundles of cotton cloth, topped up by the jaguar skins and eagle feathers worn by warriors.

Barely had Spain time to digest the thrilling news from Mexico than in 1532–5 Francisco Pizarro, a veteran *encomendero* of Darien, led a small expedition into the Andean highlands and seized control of the Inca empire. And here the conquerors lit upon a copious quantity of gold and silver, offered as ransom for the Emperor Atahualpa, whom they had captured and later executed. Moreover, whereas the Mexica had created a predatory dominion sustained by terror, the Incas demanded from their conquered peoples great contingents of labourers, who were employed not merely to build fortresses and temples, but also to carve out terraces and irrigation channels that greatly increased agricultural production. So, too, they distributed flocks of llamas across their empire, which stretched from Ecuador to northern Chile. To sustain their armies they built a great series of storehouses filled with arms, cloth, and foodstuffs, and constructed two roads, one on the coast, the other through the mountains, that connected the far-flung frontiers to the capital city of Cuzco. To this day, the skill and massive presence of their stonework impresses all visitors to Machu Picchu and Cuzco. But, like their Mexica counterparts, the Incas lacked metal implements and weapons and the use of the wheel. With the violent advent of the Spaniards their dominion crumbled, its conquered peoples abandoning their former allegiance.

The conquest of these great empires was achieved by a relatively small number of conquerors—Cortés entered Mexico with 500 men and Pizarro had 169 men—armed with steel swords, crossbows, arquebuses, with relatively few horsemen and still fewer small cannon. The conquerors usually referred to themselves as 'companions' rather than soldiers, and were described by a contemporary as 'men of quality, born poor, obliged to observe the military rule, a rule more strict than that of the Carthusian Order and more dangerous'. When engaged for an expedition, an *entrada*, they constituted a *compaña*, a free company reminiscent of those that had fought in France during the Hundred Years War, which were united by the expectation of plunder, but subject to the authority of their captain or *caudillo*, who maintained a loose but summary discipline. In effect, conquest and settlement gathered a momentum which was sustained by an ever-growing number of adventurers who swarmed into the New World, most of whom were to die an early death, but leaving survivors who formed a hardy breed of frontiersmen, as capable of enduring the rigours of climate and privation as of sustaining the demands of warfare. In all this, the only role played by the Spanish crown was to grant the captains who led these ventures a *capitulación*, a license to subdue and administer a given territory, albeit with the obligation of dispatching a fifth, *the quinta real*, of all precious metals to the king.

It was not the windfall profits of conquest, however, that the conquerors of Mexico and Peru took as their object, but rather the pacification and distribution of the native population into *encomiendas*. Moreover, unlike the Caribbean grants, the *encomiendas* in Mesoamerica and the Andean zone were based on ethnic communities and district lordships, so that the mobilization of labour and the collection of tribute could be delegated to the native nobility. It followed that the *encomiendas* distributed by Cortés and Pizarro were large, since in Mexico they generally comprised at least 5,000 tributaries, male Indians aged between 18 and 55, and in Peru they could include as many as 10,000 tributaries. It was the obligation of *encomenderos* of the first generation to establish their residence in a Spanish city close to their grants, where they generally served as councillors and magistrates, so that although an *encomienda* did not provide its possessor with any jurisdiction, civil or criminal, the role of *encomenderos* as councillors and urban magistrates allowed them to allocate vacant lands, once held by temples or the imperial dynasty, and to regulate the flow of native labour when required. In effect, the *encomenderos* constituted a colonial nobility who maintained open table and, in Peru at least, supported about ten other Spaniards, using them for various tasks.

The central importance of *encomiendas* for the first conquerors can be demonstrated by examining their range of enterprises. In New Spain, as Anáhuac was renamed, Hernán Cortés pitched his capital and built his palace amidst the ruins of México-Tenochtitlan, anxious to inherit the cosmological prestige of the Aztec city. In the distribution of *encomiendas* he awarded himself 23,000 native tributaries and, with their free labour, mined for silver at Tasco; engaged in gold placer-mining in Oaxaca; planted sugar along the Gulf of Mexico; built ships at Tehuantepec for trade with central America and Peru; opened fields for the cultivation of wheat; and imported cattle, horses, and sheep for breeding and use. In Peru, Francisco Pizarro ignored the claims of imperial Cuzco and built a new capital in Lima, situated on the Pacific coast close to Callao. He allocated himself over 25,000 tributaries in *encomienda* and used their services to plant coca along the western flanks of the Andes, wheat and maize in the mountain valleys, and sugar along the coast. So, also, he operated ships on the Pacific coast to Panama and opened stores for trade in Lima and elsewhere. His brother, Hernando, who received 6,250 Indian tributaries, planted coca and dispatched large contingents to work in the silver mines of Potosí. It is estimated that the *empresa*, or combined enterprises of the Pizarro brothers, came to employ no less than 400 Spaniards to manage their multifarious concerns, with lines of credit stretching from Seville to Cuzco. In effect, the *encomenderos* moved rapidly to install the foundations of a European economy in the New World, with the advantage of employing wageless, drafted labour.

The Church in New Spain: ethical responses to conquest

In 1524, Hernán Cortés knelt in the dust before the assembled nobility of Mexico City, Spanish and Indian, and kissed the hand of Martin de Valencia, the ascetic leader of a Franciscan mission composed of twelve friars, who had walked barefoot from Veracruz. These mendicants, soon to be joined by Dominicans and Augustinians, were entrusted with the conversion of the native peoples. To this end, the friars levelled temples to the ground, smashed idols, burnt codices as signs of necromancy, and banned any further celebration of pagan rites. Any lord or priest who sought to preserve the old religion was liable to be whipped, imprisoned, exiled, or, on rare occasion, burnt. By way of replacement, the friars exploited the full resources of the Catholic liturgy and the splendour of their new churches to attract the Indians, celebrating the chief feasts of the Church calendar with great pomp. During the late 1540s, these mendicant friars were further entrusted with the grand resettlement of Indian communities, concentrating scattered hamlets into towns, each built on a grid system, which radiated from a main square dominated by the parish church and the council chambers of the native nobility.

The Franciscans in Mexico were animated by a desire to return to the primitive simplicity of the early Church and interpreted the conversion of the Indians of New Spain as divine recompense for the Protestant heresy of Northern Europe. From the start, they summoned the sons of the native nobility to live in their convents and later used these young disciples as interpreters. They dedicated great efforts to learning native tongues and, with the help of their native disciples, devised catechisms, hymns, and sermons in the leading languages. Later they published grammars and vocabularies and pursued exhaustive enquiries into native religion, culture, and history. In their churches they used the native painters, whom they had trained, and formed choirs and small orchestras for their liturgy. The first book to be printed in the New World was published in Mexico City in 1539 by Juan de Zumárraga, its first bishop, and was a summary of Christian doctrine 'in Mexican language and Castilian'.

Although the conquests of Mexico and Peru obviously caused considerable loss of life and disrupted the social order, by and large the worst excesses of the Caribbean were avoided, especially since both the *encomenderos* and friars relied on the native nobility to mobilize Indian labour. But the situation was transformed by the advent of epidemic diseases, their impact rendered all the more violent by the isolation of the American hemisphere, which left the native peoples without immunity or resistance to smallpox, measles, typhus, pneumonic plague, and yellow fever. During the very siege of México-Tenochtitlan, its inhabitants lay dying of smallpox, which was to spread to Peru even before the Spaniards entered that country. The result was a demographic catastrophe. In New Spain the native population fell from an estimated 10 million in 1519 to less than a million souls in 1600. The trend was much the same in the Andean zone, more pronounced on the coast, less rapid in the high mountain valleys, but eventually of much the same magnitude. In places, the poor diet of the native peasantry prior to the conquest, the subsequent disruption of the command economy in agricultural production, and the introduction of European livestock, all contributed to magnify the disaster.

It was the horrors of Spanish exploitation in the Caribbean and the rapid disappearance of the native population that drove Bartolomé de las Casas (1483–1566), a one-time *encomendero* and Dominican friar, to launch a lifelong campaign to defend the rights of the Indians and condemn the abuses of the conquerors. It was thanks to his virulent tract, later published as *Brief Account of the Destruction of the Indies* (1552), that in 1542, Charles V promulgated the New Laws, which emancipated all Indian slaves and abolished the right of *encomenderos* to demand free labour service from their Indians, who henceforth only paid tribute either in cash or kind. Equally important, all labour undertaken by Indians for Spaniards had to be paid for by a daily wage. Despite a flurry of settler protests, these provisions were eventually enforced. But, such was the uproar provoked by the charges of Las Casas that, in 1551–2, the emperor convoked a 'debate' between the Dominican and Juan Ginés de Sepúlveda, a humanist priest, over the justice of the Spanish conquest. What rendered the occasion so fascinating was that the arguments centred on the nature of the Indians, which was to say, whether they were 'servile' and incapable of true self-government, and whether the government of the Incas and Mexica was 'tyrannical' or benevolent. To support his defence, Las Casas was driven to assemble a mass of information concerning the pre-conquest regimes, which he characterized as equal in justice and civility to their counterparts in the classical world of Rome and Greece.

Whereas the first viceroy of New Spain, Antonio de Mendoza (1535–51), applied the New Laws with great caution, by contrast, in Peru, the incoming viceroy sought to despoil leading *encomenderos* of their grants and provoked a rebellion led by Gonzalo Pizarro, which threatened royal dominion. It was left to Philip ll (1554–98) to convert these overseas kingdoms into profitable possessions. After careful visitation by trusted lawyers, he appointed two noble stewards of the royal household, Francisco de Toledo (1569–81) and Martín Enríquez (1568–80), as viceroys of Peru and Mexico. Both these men proved successful in increasing the flow of revenue to Spain and strengthened royal authority by the appointment of *corregidores* and *alcaldes mayores*, district magistrates, who henceforward became responsible for the collection of Indian tribute, thereby reducing the *encomenderos* to the level of crown pensioners. At the same time the number of royal treasuries and high courts was increased. It was in this same period that the Inquisition was established in both these countries.

Establishing a hispanic society in the New World

The most striking achievement of this epoch occurred in Peru, where Viceroy Toledo conducted a thorough-going enquiry into the practice and principles of Inca government, concluding that their rulers knew that 'the inclination and nature of the Indians was to be idle and indolent' so that coercion was necessary if the peasantry was to be mobilized for labour service. The first result of his enquiry was a massive resettlement programme whereby Indians were concentrated into towns dominated by the parish church. At the same time, the authority of the *kurakas*, the Indian lords, was reinforced and their loyalty assured by payment of a salary deducted from royal tributes. Any nostalgia for the Incas was countered by the judicial murder of Tupac Amaru, the last ruler of a small mountain principality. More important, Toledo moved decisively to reinvigorate the mining industry at Potosí, where the *encomenderos* and *kurakas* had exhausted the richest deposits. He conducted experiments to demonstrate that low-quality ores could be refined by mixing them with mercury and other ingredients and thereby transformed the industry, since Spanish entrepreneurs replaced the simple clay furnaces of the Indians with large refining mills with elaborate patios, vats, and water wheels. He also located abundant mercury deposits at Huancavelica in central Peru and leased its production to independent miners.

Finally, Toledo invoked Inca precedent and revived a *mita*, a compulsory labour levy comprising one-seventh of all adult males, recruited from fourteen provinces, an area stretching from Potosí almost to Cuzco, which yielded 13,500 men for work at Potosí. By this time the mines employed a good number of skilled workers who were attracted by high wages, so that the function of the *mita* was to provide a mass of cheap labour paid less than half the rate offered to long-term workers. But the result of technological innovation, capital investment, and labour mobilization was a dramatic increase in production so that, whereas the royal fifth had fallen to less than 200,000 pesos a year by 1569, ten years later it had risen to more than a million pesos. It was the influx of silver principally from Potosí during the 1580s that rescued Philip II from bankruptcy and enabled him to pursue his military adventures in Europe. In effect, the toil of the Andean peasantry financed the Spanish monarchy's hegemony and, as we shall see, enabled Europe to maintain its commercial balance in Asia.

In New Spain the demographic catastrophe, so evident with the renewed plague of 1576, drove the *encomenderos* and other Spanish settlers to obtain land grants from the viceroys in central and southern regions, and thereby slowly create great estates, some used as mere sheep farms, others devoted to the cultivation of wheat and maize, and a few, in semi-tropical Morelos, to sugar-planting. They obtained labour by a system of *repartimientos*, whereby local magistrates distributed 10 per cent of the available Indian male population, albeit only for limited distances. The silver mines in central Mexico, such as Tasco, Pachuca, and Real del Monte, all benefited from these labour levies. However, the discovery of plentiful silver deposits at Zacatecas in 1546, followed by the location of smaller camps, all situated in the northern territories far beyond the confines of the sedentary peasantry of Mesoamerica, led to the emergence of a different form of labour recruitment. With no Mexica precedent of long-distance labour levies, the miners of Zacatecas were obliged to attract free, migrant Indian workers from central Mexico by offer of high wages, men who came in groups and settled with their compatriots in a number of hamlets surrounding the city. For their part the Basque miners who dominated the industry became royal governors in these northern territories, obtained vast land grants, and developed great sheep farms. Indeed, the conquest of New Mexico in the 1590s was entirely funded by the sons of these Basque miners.

If the dispatch of the royal fifth enabled Philip II to enlarge his credit with German bankers such as the Fuggers, the produce of the American silver mines sustained transatlantic commerce. Over 80 per cent of exports from Mexico and Peru consisted of precious metals, mainly silver, supplemented by dyestuffs and fine wood. In return, the colonies imported mainly luxury textiles, at least 65 per cent of the value, accompanied by wine, paper, and iron-goods.

Owing to the attacks of French privateers, from 1564 onwards the Atlantic trade was conducted in two annual convoys, the one sailing to Veracruz, the other to Nombre de Dios in Panama, where the cargo was transported across the Isthmus and then shipped to Lima. Such was the importance and profits accruing from this trade that many Spanish merchants established permanent residence in Mexico City and Lima, and often maintained additional stores in provincial cities and the leading mining centres. It was then but a small step for wealthier merchants to advance credit to silver-miners and thus become involved in production. The social standing of these great import merchants was recognized by the foundation in 1592 of a merchant guild, a *consulado*, in Mexico City, with a counterpart in Lima set up in 1613. These bodies were to be dominated by immigrants from Spain until the advent of independence. Their leading members often purchased haciendas and, in wealth, came to equal or surpass the great landlords and silver-miners.

By 1600 the Spanish empire in America comprised the two viceroyalties of New Spain and Peru and eleven high courts, *audiencias*, situated in Guadalajara, Mexico City, Guatemala, Panama, Santo Domingo, Santa Fé de Bogotá, Quito, Lima, Charcas (modern Sucre), Santiago de Chile, and Manila. All save Guadalajara were destined to become capitals of sovereign republics. In the spiritual sphere, the same territories maintained six archbishops, thirty bishops, and 906 cathedral canons. In New Spain there were 149 district magistrates and in Peru about 70. There were royal treasuries in the capital cities, the ports, and the mining camps. This majestic imperial edifice had been created by the toil of the Indian peasantry, assisted in places by the labour of 75,000 African slaves imported in the sixteenth century, but also by the enterprise and energy of 56,000 registered Spanish colonizers, a quarter of whom, in the last four decades of that century, were women. Obviously, many more Spaniards may have arrived and some scholars pitch their estimates as high as 250,000, even if half that number appears more probable, since in the 1560s New Spain only counted 10,000 Spanish *vecinos* or householders, half of whom resided in the capital. In the same decade about 6,000 Spaniards lived in Peru, only one in eight of whom was a woman. By the close of the century there was abundant reference to the growing number of *castas*, individuals of mixed ethnic origin, mestizos and mulattos, as they were known, who came to form an intermediary group between the two communities, the two *repúblicas*, of Indians and Spaniards.

By 1600 there was also evidence of the first stirrings of a creole consciousness, which is to say, the first memorials written by Spaniards born in America, descendants of the conquerors and *encomenderos*, who protested bitterly against the loss of their inheritance and the growing wealth of immigrant merchants. The arrival of the Jesuits in 1569–71 in both Mexico and Peru had led to the immediate establishment of a series of colleges, which provided education for young creoles and enabled them thereafter to qualify in the universities founded in 1551 in both Mexico City and Lima. It was the graduates of these institutions, often members of an impoverished elite, who swarmed into the ranks of the clergy or who clamoured for appointments in the civil bureaucracy. Here indeed was an entire hispanic society, recreated in the New World.

The Portuguese empire

In July 1497, Vasco da Gama (1469–1524), a Portuguese nobleman and knight of the military Order of Santiago, departed from Lisbon with three small ships, a supply vessel and 190 men. After reaching the Cape Verde islands, he pushed well out into the Atlantic and then sailed south before following the trade winds eastwards, spending ninety days out of sight of land before reaching South Africa. After passing the Cape of Good Hope, he ventured northwards and passed four months visiting the petty Muslim sultanates that dotted the African coast from Mozambique to Malindi. There he hired a Muslim Gujarati pilot, who steered the expedition across the Indian Ocean, reaching the port of Calicut on the Malabar coast in May 1498. If nine years had lapsed between the return of Bartholomew Dias and the departure of Vasco da Gama, it was in part caused by a royal succession crisis and in part owing to the upset of the discovery of America. It was left to Manuel I (1495–1521), a cultivated, visionary monarch who dreamt of liberating Jerusalem by forming an alliance with Prester John the legendary Christian king of 'India', to renew the quest of a direct passage to that still mysterious land. When Vasco da Gama returned from India, reaching Lisbon in July 1499, King Manuel immediately assumed the grandiose title of 'Lord of the Conquest, Navigation and Commerce of Ethiopia, Arabia, Persia and India' and communicated news of the 'discovery', a term Amerigo Vespucci was to dispute, to the pope and the Catholic kings of Spain.

If discovery seemed an inappropriate term, it was because Vasco da Gama and his men found that the ports of the Indian Ocean were filled with Muslim traders and their ships. Indeed, when one of their party was sent ashore in Calicut, he met 'two Moors from Tunis who knew how to speak Castilian and Genoese', who exclaimed: 'The Devil take you! What brought you here?' To which he replied: 'We come to seek Christians and spices'. In effect, much of India was an extension of the Middle East and bound to that region by centuries of commerce as well as by religion. To be sure, the Portuguese hoped to find news of Prester John and, when they first entered the Hindu temples of Calicut, identified their cult as an aberrant form of Christianity. Any hopes of an alliance against Islam were soon dashed by the contemptuous manner in which the Hindu ruler of Calicut, the Zamorin, dismissed Vasco da Gama's paltry gifts as unworthy of a merchant, let alone the envoy of a monarch.

When Vasco da Gama returned to India in 1502, he was accompanied by thirteen ships and a thousand men, and carried silver from Europe and gold dust he had obtained in East Africa. In order to avenge an attack on a previous Portuguese expedition, he bombarded Calicut, by then persuaded that Hinduism was but a form of paganism. So, too, he attacked and sunk a Muslim pilgrim ship returning from Mecca, despite promises of ransom money. In a word, he extended the Portuguese war against Islam to the shores of the Indian Ocean. For all that, he used his silver and gold to purchase a rich cargo of pepper and spices and, when he departed, left five ships and their crews to defend the 'factory' he had established in Cochin. In these early years of 'discovery' 1501–5, King Manuel dispatched no less than eighty-one ships and 7,000 men to Asia.

It was left to Alfonso de Albuquerque, effective viceroy in 1509–15, to lay the foundations of Portugal's maritime empire in Asia. By then, expeditions had ranged across the Indian Ocean, attacking Muslim shipping and ports, thereby provoking the Mameluke rulers of Egypt to dispatch a large fleet to counter their raids. But this fleet, composed of galleys, was destroyed by the Portuguese in 1509. More important, Albuquerque captured the island city of Goa in 1510, and the next year stormed Malacca (Merlaka), the populous port which dominated the straits between modern Malaya and Sumatra. And in 1515, after failing to take Aden, the fortified port which guarded access to the Red Sea, he took Hormuz, an island port at the opening of the Persian Gulf. Thereafter, the Portuguese demanded that all ships that frequented these ports should obtain a *cartaz*, or pass, and pay customs duties in return for which, at times, escorts were provided. In addition to these strongly fortified ports the Portuguese installed a chain of smaller trading 'factories' around the Indian Ocean and, in 1521, took virtual control of Ternate in the Molucca Islands, the source of rich spices. If this 'empire' was established at such little cost, it was largely owing to the superiority of Portuguese ships and the artillery that converted the swift caravels and heavy carracks into 'floating fortresses'. Even when the Ottomans conquered the Arab world and dispatched successive fleets to dislodge the Portuguese, they were roundly defeated in 1533 and again in 1554. Moreover, the Portuguese monarchy did not merely establish a regular dispatch of ships to Asia, they maintained a small fleet in the Indian Ocean and used the resources of Goa to build ships locally.

In its first phase, the economic basis of this far-flung empire was the exchange of silver, first German then American, for pepper and other spices, which is to say, a trade between Lisbon and Goa, which was monopolized by the Portuguese king and carried by ships owned by that king. In the early years, pepper from India accounted for over 90 per cent of Asian exports, supplemented by cinnamon from Ceylon and nutmeg, cloves and mace from the Molucca Islands. Profits were remarkably high and the distribution across Europe of these spices was handled by merchant syndicates based in Antwerp. As was to be expected, the crown fell progressively into debt as these syndicates advanced monies well before the arrival of the Asian products. The royal monopoly was soon diluted by renting cargo space to individuals and, in 1570, finally abolished. It should be emphasized that at no time did the Portuguese monopolize the entire spice trade, since Asian and Middle Eastern demand remained strong and, by the 1550s, even the European market was supplied in part through the Red Sea. Moreover, in the period 1580–1640, for which exact figures exist, the convoys sailing between Lisbon and Goa chiefly carried cotton and silk cloth from Gujarat, which accounted for 62 per cent of their cargo value, compared to pepper and spices at 15 per cent, and diamonds and other precious stones at 14 per cent.

The Portuguese empire in Asia was expected to be self-sustaining and hence the royal monopoly was but one part of its commercial activity. There was a great deal of trade within Asia itself carried on, as before, by both Muslim and Hindu merchants as well as by Portuguese merchants. Thus, horses were imported from the Middle East via the Persian Gulf and Gujarati textiles found markets in Sumatra and Java, not to mention East Africa. Moreover, the exploitation of the Far Eastern trade was left to private enterprise. Following the opening of relations with Japan, Macao was settled in 1555–7 and a profitable trade was established when Japanese silver production boomed, since it could be procured by sale of Chinese silks and porcelain, and then exchanged for gold at a premium in China. Furthermore, in 1567, a Spanish expedition from Mexico occupied the Philippines and established the capital at Manila. In the years which followed, a valuable Pacific trade emerged with Indian textiles and Chinese silks and porcelain exchanged for Mexican silver, with a great galleon sailing every year across the ocean. A significant role in this trade was played by a large community of Chinese merchants who settled in Manila. By the close of the sixteenth century, the Portuguese commercial system in Asia still flourished and, by then, had attracted the intervention of New Christian merchants and capital, which was to say, of converted Jewish trading families, many of whom had relatives settled in Amsterdam, the new financial capital of Europe.

Although the Portuguese crown successfully claimed possession of Brazil in 1500, it was not until 1533 that John III divided its vast coastline into fifteen donatory captaincies, thereby allowing noblemen to undertake its colonization on an individual basis. What transformed the venture, most obviously in the north-east, was the introduction of sugar-planting. Indeed, when the king, in 1548, appointed the first royal governor in Salvador de Bahia, he instructed him to establish a crown-owned sugar mill and plantation. By then, of course, the Portuguese had developed such plantations in Madeira, worked by slaves imported from the Canary Islands, and on the island of São Thomé, where the slaves were brought in from West Africa. In Brazil, plantations were chiefly concentrated in Pernambuco and the zone around the great bay of Bahia. Up to the 1570s the labour force was composed of local Indians, some enslaved and others supplied by Jesuit-administered free villages, all of whom, however, were liable to succumb to European diseases. It was only in the two last decades of the sixteenth century that the importation of African slaves and the production of sugar rose rapidly, so that the country soon became the leading source of sugar consumed in Europe, far surpassing the output of the Spanish Caribbean. The emergence of Brazil was thus essentially a seventeenth-century phenomenon, and was consummated in 1695 when extensive gold deposits were discovered in Minas Gerais, inland from Rio de Janeiro.

Like their Castilian rivals, the Portuguese kings possessed the rights and obligations of the *Padroado*, the right of ecclesiastical appointments in their overseas empire. In 1534 Goa became a bishopric which, in 1577, was converted into an archbishopric and endowed with a splendid cathedral. The Jesuits arrived in 1542, opened a college, and began mission work. Other religious orders soon followed. The most obvious Christian flock was the Portuguese, who married local women and so raised a generation of mestizos in all leading cities. But there also existed a community of Christians in southern India, some 30,000 in number, who employed ancient Syriac in their liturgy and were Nestorian in belief. Although relations between these St Thomas Christians and the Portuguese were initially amiable, conflict arose when imperious prelates sought to demand that they abjure their Nestorian beliefs, and even replace Syriac by Latin, demands which were to divide this community into two separate communions. The most striking missionary achievement occurred in 1535–7 when the Paravas, a fisher-folk living on the tip of the sub-continent, converted *en masse*, in part to avoid Muslim dominion. By and large, the Portuguese failed to attract many converts to Christianity in Asia owing to the superior charm of Islam and the enduring power of Hinduism. It was only in the Philippines that Christianity advanced and that was because, with the exception of Mindanao, the native population of these islands had yet to be invaded by Islam, and had no advanced form of religion or state formation. Moreover, the Spaniards were to remain entrenched in this colony for four centuries.

Other European powers

If the Iberian powers dominated European expansion in the sixteenth century, their hegemony was challenged by French, English, and Dutch explorers, privateers, and merchants. In the years 1534–42, Jacques Cartier made three voyages up the river St Lawrence, sailing a thousand miles inland to reach the sites of modern Quebec and Montreal, but permanent exploitation of his discoveries did not occur until the next century. So too, French privateers and merchantmen entered the Caribbean and, in 1555, launched an attack on Havana. They also traded along the coast of Brazil and, in 1555–60, a French expedition, led by the Chevalier de Villegaignon, occupied an island in the Bay of Rio de Janeiro before being ejected by the Portuguese. Only with the voyage of Samuel de Champlain in 1603 was an attempt made to settle Canada. The English were more successful in their piracy. After the Spaniards treacherously attacked the English fleet that had harboured in San Juan de Ulúa in 1568, its leaders, Sir John Hawkins and Francis Drake, opened hostilities, with the latter landing in Nombre de Dios and seizing the silver train from Peru as it crossed the Isthmus of Panama. In 1577, Drake led an expedition of three ships and 160 men to circumnavigate the world, during which he passed the straits of Magellan and then raided along the Peruvian coast, capturing a galleon loaded with silver. Thereafter, he pushed northwards, reaching Vancouver, and harboured in the Bay of San Francisco. He then sailed across the Pacific, purchased spices in the Moluccas and finally landed the *Golden Hind* in Plymouth, after a journey of two years, ten months. Thomas Cavendish repeated the circumnavigation of the world in 1586–8 and captured the annual Spanish galleon that sailed between Acapulco and Manila. Other English privateers raided Spanish possessions in the Caribbean, including an attack on Santo Domingo in 1585 led by Sir Francis Drake, when these English Protestants desecrated churches and held citizens for ransom. Both Hawkins and Drake died at sea in 1595 in an unsuccessful expedition designed to take Panama. It was not until 1600 that the East India Company was founded and the first merchant voyage to the Indian Ocean dispatched.

The heirs of the Portuguese in Asia were the Dutch. With the

Protestant revolt of the northern Netherlands from Philip II in 1567, open warfare between Spain and the Dutch was destined to last for many decades, albeit mitigated by the necessities of trade. But when Philip also became king of Portugal in 1580, the Dutch extended their attacks to include Portuguese factories and trade in Asia. The Dutch East India Company was founded in 1595 and, in the same year, dispatched the first fleet to sail via the Cape of Good Hope directly to the Spice Islands. Thereafter, the Dutch systematically attacked Portuguese possessions and, although they failed to take Goa and Macao, they effectively seized control of the trade of the Indonesian archipelago. It was much later, in 1631–52, that the Dutch West India Company occupied Pernambuco and exploited its sugar plantations, only finally to be ousted by militia forces raised in Brazil, a sure sign of the growing vitality of creole society in this great dominion. Indeed, when the Dutch occupied Luanda, a Portuguese colony in modern Angola, founded in 1576, it was an expedition launched from Brazil that recaptured the town in 1648.

Europeans in Africa

But what of Africa in all this? Throughout the sixteenth century the Portuguese maintained a chain of fortified ports and islands on both sides of the continent. But, whereas in America epidemic disease assisted Iberian conquest, in Africa endemic fevers often impeded European colonization. Nor did Africa possess any great commodity such as silver or spices which might have demanded active exploitation. In any case, African states and tribes had iron weapons and a warrior tradition, so that subjugation was no easy matter. In consequence, apart from some ivory and gold-dust, the great African export was slaves. It should be noted that within African society, slaves rather than land were the chief form of personal wealth and that they were largely acquired through warfare. It was thus to be expected that African rulers would sell slaves in order to obtain horses, luxury textiles and iron-ware, both for implements and weapons. But, whereas prior to the 1520s most slaves sold to the Portuguese were sent to Europe or employed in the sugar plantations of Madeira, the Canary Islands, and São Thomé, in the years which followed, increasing numbers were dispatched to America. It was estimated that for the entire period 1451–1600 some 254,000 slaves left Africa, of whom 75,000 went to Spanish America, 50,000 to Brazil, and a surprising 76,000 to São Thomé. The sixteenth century thus witnessed the foundation of what in the next three centuries was to form the greatest enforced migration in human history. In all this the Portuguese acted as initiators, purchasing their human cargoes in African ports.

Thanks to the slave trade and missionary ambitions, individual Portuguese travelled across the continent, albeit without lasting effect. Thus, for example, the king of Kongo, Alfonso I (1506–43), converted and accepted Catholicism as his state religion, even if he still maintained a large number of wives. But, after his death, enthusiasm waned and only the most rudimentary form of Christianity survived in that region. The most decisive Portuguese intervention occurred in Ethiopia where, in 1541–3, a well-armed expedition of 400 men led by Cristóvão da Gama, son of the great navigator, finally succeeded in liberating the country from a recent Muslim invasion. For twelve years Imam Ahmed ibn Ibrahim al-Ghazi (1506–43) nicknamed Ahmed Gran, a Muslim leader, had ravaged and conquered Ethiopia, destroying its ancient churches and monasteries, burning its invaluable manuscripts, enslaving many, and forcing thousands of his new subjects to convert to Islam. In effect, he treated the Ethiopians in much the same way as, or worse than, the Spaniards dealt with the Mexica and Incas. Although the young king and his queen mother led an effective resistance, it was the weaponry and cannons of the Portuguese that played the decisive role in saving this ancient monarchy and its African form of Christianity from destruction, even if their leader and most of his men died in battle.

The Society of Jesus in the wider world

When the Iberian powers boldly crossed the oceans of the world, they often drew upon the assistance of other Europeans and, indeed, acted as the spearhead of European economic expansion. But the participation of other Europeans was prominent in the sphere of the religious orders and particularly among the Jesuits. Since its foundation in

1540, the Society of Jesus undertook the challenge of preaching the Christian gospel to all nations across the world. As early as 1542, the future saint, Francis Xavier, a Basque by origin, landed in Goa and, after working for some years in India and the Molucca Islands, entered Japan in 1549, from whence he dispatched glowing reports about its inhabitants. From the start, he sought to obtain the favour of the feudal lords, who in this period were engaged in perpetual strife. When the Jesuit mission expanded and obtained the conversion of one such *daimyo*, followed by others, the floodgates of conversion opened and the new Church came to comprise 300,000 souls. With the arrival of Alessandro Valignano as visitor of Jesuit missions in Asia, a concerted campaign was launched to learn Japanese thoroughly, to print translations of Christian catechisms and other works, to admit Japanese as candidates for the priesthood and as Jesuits, and finally to respect local customs and dress. In effect, Valignano introduced the perspectives of Italian humanism and rejected the innate Iberian suspicion of the good faith of all 'New Christians', be they former Jews or Buddhists. At the same time, the Jesuits did not hesitate to destroy Buddhist and Shinto temples in the areas they dominated. A cultural backlash occurred, however, the reflection in part of political change, and in 1587 Christians were persecuted and their priests subject to martyrdom, so that only a small remnant survived, and that in secret.

The most remarkable attempt by a European to penetrate and comprehend a non-Christian culture occurred in China, where Matteo Ricci (1552–1610), a learned Italian Jesuit, entered that country in 1583 and succeeded not merely in mastering the language but also the Confucian classics. By the time he arrived in Beijing in 1601, he had written treatises in Chinese dealing with moral themes and was reputed to be a great scholar. Like other Jesuits of this epoch, he judged Buddhism by its temples and images and condemned it as a form of paganism. But he regarded Confucianism as a philosophy which had attained knowledge of the existence of a supreme god of the universe and espoused a morality that obeyed the tenets of natural law. Indeed, he expressed the confident hope that Confucius himself might well have obtained salvation. The Jesuits in Beijing impressed their hosts by their knowledge of astronomy and geography, not to mention mathematics, and their mission was to endure until the eighteenth century.

The wider world in European literature

As was to be expected, both Spanish and Portuguese chroniclers celebrated the discoveries and conquests of their nations with considerable exuberance. In Portugal's national epic, *The Lusiads* (1572), Camões, who had spent years in Asia, lauded the exploits of his compatriots as heroes who had mastered the elements as well as waging war against the infidels. So too, Francisco López de Gómara, the humanist chaplain of Cortés, composed a *General History of the Indies* (1552), in which he boldly declared: 'the greatest event since the creation of the world, apart from the incarnation of He who created it, is the discovery of the Indies, which is thus called the New World'. He further pronounced a brazen eulogy of the Spaniards when he exclaimed that 'Never at any time did a king or people move or subject so much in so short a time as we did . . . as much in warfare and exploration as in preaching the gospel and the conversion of idolaters'. It was perhaps only to be expected that, although he recognized the grandeur of México-Tenochtitlan, he portrayed its society as worshipping the Devil and engaged in massive human sacrifice and cannibalism.

This glorification of the conquerors, however, was challenged by Las Casas who, towards the end of his long life, declared that Cortés and Pizarro should have been hanged as common criminals. His *Brief Account* was translated into most European languages and was much cited by the Protestant enemies of Spain. But his exploration of the religion, culture, and government of the Incas and Mexica influenced subsequent historiography, despite being preserved only in manuscript. In his *Monarchy of the Indies* (1615), Juan de Torquemada, a Franciscan who learnt Nahuatl as a boy, employed a great range of manuscript chronicles, native codices, and Las Casas's research to portray pre-hispanic Mexico as a glittering Babylon, which is to say, as an advanced civilization with a strict morality, but irredeemably stained by idolatry. He also celebrated the foundation of the Mexican Church, emphasizing the dedicated labours of his Franciscan brethren. For all that, the overall effect of his work was to preserve the memory of the Mexica and Toltec past and fix the foundation date of Mexico City not in 1521, but in 1325. New Spain thus was defined as the successor and heir of the Mexica empire, rather than starting *de novo* at the conquest.

In Peru, El Inca Garcilaso de la Vega (1539–1616), the son of an Inca princess and a leading conqueror, applied his knowledge of Renaissance historiography, acquired during his residence in Spain, to portray the former rulers of Peru as a caste of Platonic guardians. In his *Royal Commentaries of the Incas* (1609), he declared that the emperors and their *amautas*, the native sages, had achieved knowledge of the one, true God, but taking account of the material inclinations of their subjects, they encouraged monotheism by promotion of the cult of the sun. They governed their conquests in a benevolent fashion, seeking the welfare of the population at large, and in all cases following the tenets of natural law. In effect, they brought civilization to the natives of Peru. Here was a version of events which found immediate welcome among the Jesuit-educated native elite of Cuzco and, indeed, when in 1780 a remote descendant of the Incas raised the banner of revolt, he implicitly appealed to Garcilaso's patriotic history. By then, many creole intellectuals, both in the Andes and in Mexico, accepted the pre-hispanic civilizations of their countries as the classical foundation of their history. So in Mexico at least, when independence was finally achieved in 1821, it was defined as the recovery of freedom by a nation already in existence in 1519. This claim was a legal fiction to be sure, but it was also a persuasive historical myth.

Conclusion and commentary

Euan Cameron

Historians conventionally locate the sixteenth century within a longer phase in European development known to the academy as the 'early modern'. This is an expression that is easy to mock as a contradiction in terms or a piece of hindsight. Yet despite the quibbles that can be raised about it, this description of the period endures. It endures because it reflects a perceived reality. The sixteenth to the eighteenth centuries, taken in their entirety, display a distinct trajectory. This trajectory would ultimately lead Europe to embrace a highly diversified and largely unregulated global consumer economy, a free traffic in ideas, the emancipation of the physical sciences from metaphysical speculation, religious toleration, and a political system based on pragmatism, collective sovereignty, and shared responsibilities as much as on precedent, privilege, and the immunities of special interests. None of these trends was fully complete by 1800, let alone 1600. For most of the period few if any Europeans envisaged these outcomes as desirable or even possible. No collective or individual choices were made with the specific intention of bringing them about. They belong in what past historians have called 'the logic of events' if they belong anywhere.

The question, then, is whether by 1600 one can discern signs of movement that indicate where that logic of events would ultimately lead. In other words, how does the story described above continue into the seventeenth century? Do the events and movements perceptible in the next century demonstrably continue trends seen in the sixteenth, such that the sixteenth can legitimately be called a part of 'early modernity'? Or are the processes of post-1600 rather separate and distinct developments driven by their own internal logic? In the economic sphere, the lessons are predictably mixed. Tom Scott has demonstrated that several important 'trends' traditionally assigned to the entire early modern period, such as the increasing enclosure of commons in English agriculture, the radical enserfment of so many peasants in Europe east of the Elbe, or the growing market in mass consumer goods especially in England and the Netherlands, were actually characteristic of the seventeenth century and not of the sixteenth. Even more importantly, Scott stresses that the most prominent or distinctive features of one phase in the economy may not necessarily also be the most important indicators of future developments. For instance, it has been traditional to regard 'commercialized' agriculture and the 'putting-out' system of textile production as the drivers of economic progress later in the early modern period, because of their supposedly greater flexibility and responsiveness to market forces. However, Scott argues that proto-capitalist agriculture or proto-industrialized manufacturing (in so far as these terms are appropriate anyway) do not automatically develop into full-blown capitalism or industrialization. On the other hand, in certain areas, most notably the development of credit instruments and the increasing use of the joint-stock company to fund international trade, there was a genuine link between earlier and later developments. In England only the first stirrings of joint-stock company capitalism were evident before 1600; the success of permanent companies with funded capital came after. However, the trend had been set.

One of the most important lessons in this area is that developments in one sphere of human activity often influence those in another. The source of the distinctiveness of England and the United Provinces of the Netherlands, in economic terms, lay in a political decision. In neither country was the government entrusted by its constituents with the level of arbitrary and permanent taxation that would allow the government to issue bonds against future tax revenues; so nobles and bourgeois alike were not discouraged from investing commercially. Elsewhere in Europe, most notably in Spain, France, and the papacy, such bonds were issued in such quantities and at such high rates of interest that a great deal of investment capital was drained out of commerce and manufacturing. In some countries the legal restrictions on what activities a nobleman could undertake without losing tax privileges aggravated this trend, though their impact can also be overstated. In the case of France the prodigious bubble created by the crown's indebtedness would grow and grow until it finally burst in the critical year of 1789. In this instance a political fact—that England, for example, had only hand-to-mouth and irregular direct taxation until after 1688— had a clear socio-economic impact as well as important political consequences.

Politics is perhaps the area where it is least fruitful to search for patterns or clear lines of development—at least in the sense that the relative rise and fall of this or that dynasty or nation follows no obvious logical necessity. Nevertheless, in the theory and ground rules of politics, not to mention the techniques by which one power sought to exert pressure on another, one can discern some trends. It is however exceedingly difficult to know what to make of that cliché of sixteenth-century political writing, 'reason of state'. Contemporaries were ambivalent about it, and one suspects that there was little agreement as to what it meant. In so far as it implies that arbitrary rule or decisions based on crude expediency can be justified by the good of the body politic, it would be hard to prove that the currency of this concept made politicians in the sixteenth or seventeenth centuries any more unscrupulous, cynical, or treacherous than those of previous ages. However, 'reason of state' may fit into the general tendency for the intellectual analysis of human activities to fragment into autonomous disciplines. Politics was no longer a specialized branch of religious ethics. However, the trends in the seventeenth century would, once again, send conflicting messages. In that century some of the most unblinkingly pragmatic analyses of politics would be published and debated. Thomas Hobbes's *Leviathan* combined the absolutism of a Bodin with the logical deductiveness of a Descartes. (On the other hand, Robert Filmer produced as late as 1680 a political theory based on the supposedly 'natural' patriarchal authority of Adam and his descendants.) However one approached the problem, it seems clear that the sixteenth century had posed the question of what 'sovereignty' was, and the seventeenth expended much energy in trying to answer that question. Changing theories, however, may be very poorly reflected in practice. Some of the most overtly authoritarian rulers of the seventeenth century, figures like Emperor Ferdinand II or later Louis XIV, would pay constant heed to the advice of spiritual confessors and other religious guides. Both were perfectly prepared (in 1629 and 1685 respectively) to make political decisions that manifestly contradicted their material and pragmatic interests, apparently under the influence of religious considerations.

On the other hand, the military developments of the seventeenth century show obvious extrapolation from the sixteenth. The size of armies, and the consequent importance attached to provisioning and to lines of supply, increased throughout the seventeenth century. Infantry battles between massed forces of pikemen required an increasingly mathematical, calculating, drilled approach to the conduct of battle. When the possession of a key fortress was at issue (as in the final phases of the Dutch war for independence from Spain) siege warfare became enormously protracted, since fortifications were effectively impregnable to the existing forms of artillery. Some of the less effective conventions of sixteenth-century warfare were reformed under Maurice of Nassau and Gustavus Adolphus of Sweden. Guns were adapted as weapons for use in the field rather than for siege warfare.

Perhaps the clearest trend of all across the early modern period is that those Europeans able to do so spent progressively more and more money on all kinds of goods and all kinds of activities. Governments expended on courts, armies, building, administrative personnel, and conspicuous consumption. Individual people across a broadening band of the social scale spent money on clothes, books, houses, and their furnishings and equipment. The amount of excess resources and labour devoted to decorating all of these consumer goods increased; decorative fashions evolved and mutated with ever greater speed. The quantitative significance of luxuries imported from far corners of the world (sugar, spices, silks) is always prone to be exaggerated, sometimes because of the warnings of moralists. Martin Luther complained in 1520 that

even if the pope had not robbed us Germans with his intolerable exactions, we should still have our hands more than full with these domestic robbers, the silk and velvet merchants. In the matter of clothes, as we see, everybody wants to be equal to everybody else, and pride and envy are aroused and increased among us, as we deserve. All this and much more misery would be avoided if our curiosity would only let us be thankful, and be satisfied with the goods which God has given us.

There is however no doubt that even these items, from the relatively small-scale noble-oriented but still significant trade of the sixteenth century, became increasingly important as the seventeenth century went on.

In the sphere of 'natural philosophy', what would later be called 'science', the relationship and lines of descent from the sixteenth to the seventeenth century are complex and problematical. At one time the relentlessly teleological historians of 'science' could point to the rise of mechanical and mathematical cosmologies in the very late sixteenth to seventeenth centuries, and argue that the 'mechanical philosophy' was the one trend that mattered. At the opposite extreme stood the occultism, the esotericism, the search for the 'ancient theology' through the Hermetic or cabbalistic corpus. All these pseudo-subjects had proved to be a sequence of blind alleys for European knowledge. More recently a reaction has set in against this tracing of outcomes to causes. Historians have deployed great ingenuity to show (i) that many 'occult' modes of thinking contained within them the germ of experimental thinking, especially in what would later be called the life sciences; and (ii) that many of those who espoused and participated in the 'mechanical philosophy', from Johannes Kepler to Isaac Newton, were also intrigued by more esoteric and speculative modes of thought. Some cultural relativists who stress the continuing vitality of the speculative strains in late Renaissance thought object to the historical priority traditionally assigned to mechanistic thinking on ideological grounds: 'scientific' is 'modern' and therefore hegemonic and anti-liberal. At its worst this mode of historical thinking can descend into shallow postmodernism or adversarial point-scoring.

However, there is a serious point at issue as well. Early modern thinkers could not know which lines of inquiry would prove fruitful, so inevitably they explored many possibilities which may now seem curious. There was no obvious way to resolve whether magnetism or gravity would better explain the forces binding the universe together. Secondly, thinking people were groping, from the Renaissance and Reformation onwards, towards a new epistemology. By what criteria could something be known to be 'true'? For the Middle Ages, truth was defined primarily by authority (especially scriptural authority) and 'right reason', which in practice meant the rules of academic logic including the principle of non-contradiction. Luther at his critical hearing at Worms in 1521 insisted that, to be disproved, he must be shown to be in error 'by the testimony of Scripture or evident reason'. As the sixteenth century progressed, some forms of textual authority declined (such as that of many medieval theologians and philosophers) while others, like that of the texts of reclaimed and restored antique writers, may have gained. However, in the midst of all this some appropriate place in the hierarchy of knowledge had to be found for the accurately recorded datum or the verifiable and repeatable experiment. Charles Nauert quotes at the very end of his chapter Francis Bacon's dismissal of Greek philosophy as 'the boyhood of knowledge . . . fruitful of controversies but barren of works'. Bacon wrote in the early 1600s, at the very outset of the project to accumulate descriptive proto-scientific knowledge, and was one of the most effective propagandists for that movement. Yet his propaganda pieces are almost inconceivable without the successes of the descriptive botanists, zoologists, and anatomists of the sixteenth century, without Fuchs, Gesner, or Vesalius. Careful meticulous description of data found in a stable world, populated by clearly distinct species, marked one of the most important initiatives that the sixteenth century bequeathed to the seventeenth.

The transition from the sixteenth to the seventeenth century is in some ways clearer in the area of Christian history than in many others. The period from around 1560 to the latter half of the seventeenth century is known as the 'confessional age'. Depending on one's theological or ecclesial standpoints, this era can appear as either the fulfilment or the betrayal of the Reformation. If the Reformation and/or Counter-Reformation 'restored' correct Christian teaching, the confessional era set those teachings in concrete. On the other hand, if the Reformation era was about diversity in ideas and beliefs, about the freedom of the individual to think and write his or her thoughts according to the dictates of conscience, then the confessional era was a disaster. Spiritual freedom and adulthood was given to at least some of Europe's people only to be brutally snatched back from their grasp. At the same time, German historians especially have defined 'confessionalization' as a programme of systematic moral and dogmatic supervision of the population of the territorial state under the leadership of a religiously engaged prince, something that can be observed in Protestant and Catholic territories alike. It was not only spiritual freedom that became a casualty of the confessional era.

Such antithetical portraits of an era are far too crude. First, as stated earlier, there is no clear rift in purpose and intent between the first reformers and the second and subsequent generations of systematizing confessional theologians. Remaining forever in the fruitful, exciting, heady chaos of the early 1520s was never a plan or an option. The religious leaders of the sixteenth century were already committed to concepts of 'truth' that did not readily allow for pluralism. That they disagreed over what that one truth actually said was their misfortune, not their ideal. Secondly, even in the 'confessional era' it was perfectly possible for the heady chaos of the 1520s to break out all over again, given the right set of circumstances. In England in the 1640s and 1650s the religious authority of the national Church and the episcopate broke down just as it had done in Germany in 1521–5. Exactly the same consequences followed: the printing presses boomed with all sorts of controversial writings; exotic and diverse varieties of sects emerged; lay men and women wrote and preached in all sorts of contexts formerly thought inappropriate. Moreover, after it was all over England witnessed the same sort of 'disciplining' reaction in 1662 as had occurred in Germany after 1525. Finally and most importantly, 'confessional orthodoxy' never won more than a partial victory. No confession succeeded in obliterating its rivals. Even the most fragile and apparently defenceless growths such as Mennonites and Hutterites clung on to life. Ultimately princes abandoned the attempt to compel their subjects to submit to their rulers' faith choices. And for as long as the Almighty seemed disposed to permit more than one incompatible mode of Christianity to continue and even to flourish, so the possibility became more and more thinkable that, after all, maybe it was not just one faith that was true. By 1699 the Lutheran Pietist Gottfried Arnold could even write:

The invisible universal Church, . . . is not linked to a specific visible society, but rather is spread and scattered throughout the whole world amongst all people and congregations . . . It is very difficult, then, to say which of the external Church-congregations should be named as the true Church.

Those who in the early twenty-first century maintain theological websites extolling the unique purity of orthodox Lutheranism or Calvinism or Tridentine Catholicism should take note.

David Brading's review of the history of sixteenth-century Europeans' dealings with the wider world has proved startlingly prescient of future developments. The sixteenth century was not just an age of discovery and encounter with the strange: it was an age of commercial exploitation and imperial expansion. There was of course something economically naïve about the first phase of this development. The concentration on importing 'treasure', gold and silver bullion, from the Americas in vast quantities made no long-term economic sense, even if its inflationary consequences have been exaggerated. Yet the Spanish empire was not unique in this folly: Walter Ralegh, extolling the virtues of his largely imaginary 'large, rich, and beautiful empire of Guiana' in his pamphlet of 1596, envisaged an English 'Contractation House' being set up, like its equivalent at Seville, to record the arrival of cargoes of South American treasure in England.

It would be a mistake to contrast the sixteenth century as the era of treasure-plundering with the seventeenth as the age of plantations and commerce. Spanish treasure-fleets sailed on through the seventeenth century, while the English and the Dutch after 1600 embarked on the same mixture of colonial enterprises that their Hispanic rivals had done in the previous century. They replicated European communities across the ocean; they traded for luxuries with exotic peoples; and they founded exploitative plantations based on forced or enslaved labour to supply the home market with raw materials. In all of this the European powers discovered something peculiar about holding colonies far below the horizon. It was possible to fight minor colonial wars with each other at a sufficiently low level of intensity that these need not always impinge on the relations of the mother countries back in Europe.

Every age in some way or another poses questions that succeeding ages have to try to answer. However, that cliché is more than usually applicable to the relationship between the sixteenth century and the seventeenth. The sixteenth century was, as suggested earlier, an age of rapid and painful adjustment to previously unthinkable uncertainties and dilemmas. Unexplained and traumatic economic expansion tested the traditions of agricultural and commercial life to destruction. Political 'sovereignty' ceased to be confined within the medieval convention of the parallel hierarchies of papacy and empire. The scholastic synthesis of metaphysics and natural philosophy forfeited its exclusive claim on the allegiance of intellectuals in both the intellectual and the religious sphere. It became progressively clearer that in some areas of knowledge one must leave the authority of the ancients behind. Above all, Europeans could no longer be secure about the means to approach the creator in whom the vast majority appear to have believed. Two conflicting and competing systems, of sacramental purification and imputed righteousness through faith, became embedded in the structures of Church and society. Finally, Europeans had to confront the opportunity and the challenge that a whole vast world of continents and peoples presented to them. The only way, it seemed, to vindicate the unique validity of the European perspective was impose that perspective as normative on all those peoples of the world whom Europeans could discover and dominate. So of course the seventeenth century had to discover new responses to these challenges. It was quite predictable that some of the response would consist in grasping after greater control, in seeking to discipline, regulate, codify, and systematize these responses. In turn, and inevitably, those attempts to control the unruly confusion of human affairs would throw up new challenges and further disrupt European peoples' sense of their place in the world. Out of that struggle would emerge the tumultuous and unforeseeable transformations of the 'early modern' epoch.

Further reading

1. The Economy: Tom Scott

The economy of Europe in the sixteenth century cannot be analysed in isolation as a discrete entity. Profound changes in the later Middle Ages, too readily seen as an age of economic crisis, bore upon the sixteenth-century economy, which in turn decisively shaped developments in the centuries beyond. Accordingly, few works devote themselves to the sixteenth century alone.

Head and shoulders above all other recent surveys stands Robert S. DuPlessis, *Transitions to Capitalism in Early Modern Europe* (Cambridge, 1997), which, despite its title, is suitably cautious about seeing the hand of capitalism at every turn. It also contains a comprehensive annotated bibliography. DuPlessis, controversially but correctly, all but dispenses with tables, graphs, and figures, in marked contrast to the previously authoritative account by Peter Kriedte, *Peasants, Landlords and Merchant Capitalists: Europe and the World Economy, 1500–1800*, tr. Volker R. Berghahn (Leamington Spa, 1983), which is saturated with statistical material, often sloppily and confusingly presented. Kriedte's attempt to reconcile Marxist with neo-classical approaches to the early modern economy was path-breaking at the time, and his conceptual insights remain valuable. Kriedte's work is set in context in an important historiographical review by William W. Hagen, 'Capitalism and the Countryside in Early Modern Europe: Interpretations, Models, Debates', *Agricultural History*, 62 (1988), 13–47. A recent attempt to rethink the fundamental assumptions underlying both Marxist and non-Marxist accounts has been offered by Peter Musgrave, *The Early Modern European Economy* (Houndmills and New York, 1999). Conceived as a bracing polemic, the book suffers from a lack of detail, despite its repetitiousness, and is guilty both of exaggeration and a reluctance to identify precisely whom or whose interpretations he is denouncing. The much older account by Hermann Kellenbenz, *The Rise of the European Economy: An Economic History of Continental Europe 1500–1750*, tr. Gerhard Benecke (London, 1976) was always theoretically deficient, but can still be quarried for factual information, especially on the German lands. Readers may still refer to the relevant volumes of *The Cambridge Economic History of Europe*, but vol. iv. *The Economy of Expanding Europe in the Sixteenth and Seventeenth Centuries*, ed. E. E. Rich and C. H. Wilson (Cambridge, 1967), and vol. v. *The Economic Organization of Early Modern Europe*, ed. E. E. Rich and C. H. Wilson (Cambridge, 1977) are now in need of substantial revision. Of more use nowadays is the

Handbook of European History 1400–1600: Late Middle Ages, Renaissance and Reformation, i. *Structures and Assertions*, ed. Thomas A. Brady, Jun., Heiko A. Oberman, and James D. Tracy (Leiden, 1994), especially the contributions by Bartolomé Yun, John H. Munro, James D. Tracy, and Jan de Vries.

For the emergence of a 'world-economy' from the sixteenth century onwards see Immanuel Wallerstein, *The Modern World-System*, i. *Capitalist Agriculture and the Origins of the European World-Economy in the Sixteenth Century* (New York, 1974); *The Modern World-System*, ii. *Mercantilism and the Consolidation of the European World-Economy, 1600–1750* (New York, 1980), a work in thrall to its own model-building. Although containing useful insights, the analysis suffers from inadequate knowledge of Eastern and East-Central Europe. In essence, it represents the projection onto a global canvas of the celebrated study of the Mediterranean world in the sixteenth century by Fernand Braudel, *The Mediterranean and the Mediterranean World in the Age of Philip II*, 2 vols., tr. Siân Reynolds (London, 1972–3). This work, criticism of which is regarded in certain quarters as tantamount to blasphemy, is an astonishingly uneven achievement. Sprawling and discursive, it is sustained by the sensitivity towards economic and historical geography which informed all members of the *Annales* school, but it remains beholden to the view that the New World made a significant economic impact on continental Europe in the course of the sixteenth century. Braudel's *Capitalism and Material Life, 1400–1800*, tr. Miriam Kochan (London, 1973) is both weak on theoretical analysis of capitalist economics and short on empirical detail. It has been reissued in a revised translation and under a new title *The Structures of Everyday Life: The Limits of the Possible* as vol. i of *Civilization and Capitalism*, 3 vols, tr. Siân Reynolds (London and New York, 1982). Taken together, the volumes display the same strengths and weakness as Braudel's study of the Mediterranean world. The classic narrative of the economic supremacy of north-western Europe by Ralph Davis, *The Rise of the Atlantic Economies* (London, 1973) remains stimulating, even if its agenda has been thrown into question, not least by the brilliant demolition of European exceptionalism (although primarily concerned with the period beyond the sixteenth century) in Kenneth Pomeranz, *The Great Divergence: China, Europe, and the Making of the Modern World Economy* (Princeton and Oxford, 2000).

A detailed list of works on the so-called late medieval economic crisis would be out of place here, but it forms the bedrock of the debate over capitalist transformation initiated by Robert Brenner. The contributions are gathered in T. H. Aston and C. H. E. Philpin (eds.), *The Brenner Debate: Agrarian Class Structure and Economic Development in Pre-Industrial Europe* (Cambridge, 1985). For decades the debate has languished, but has recently been revived in an important collection of essays on the economy of the Low Countries by Peter Hoppenbrouwers and Jan Luiten van Zanden (eds.),

Peasants into Farmers? The Transformation of Rural Economy and Society in the Low Countries (Middle Ages–19th Century) in Light of the Brenner Debate (Turnhout, 2001). Several contributors combine dense empirical detail with ambitious theoretical reflection; the vast concluding essay by Robert Brenner represents a palpable shift from his arguments first advanced in 1975. Four other wide-ranging collections of essays on specific aspects of the European economy are: Maarten Prak (ed.), *Early Modern Capitalism. Economic and Social Change in Europe, 1400–1800* (London, 2001); S. R. Epstein (ed.), *Town and Country in Europe, 1300–1800* (Cambridge, 2001); Tom Scott (ed.), *The Peasantries of Europe from the Fourteenth to the Eighteenth Centuries* (London and New York, 1998); and Sheilagh Ogilvie and Markus Cerman (eds.), *European Proto-Industrialization* (Cambridge, 1996). To the latter may be added the useful survey by Myron Gutmann, *Towards the Modern Economy: Early Industry in Europe, 1500–1800* (Philadelphia, 1988). On urbanization, using sophisticated econometric analysis, see Jan De Vries, *European Urbanization 1500–1800* (London, 1984). The recent study by David Nicholas, *Urban Europe, 1100–1700* (Houndmills and New York, 2003), need not, by contrast, detain the discerning. On markets and the institutional framework of economic development see the thought-provoking study by S. R. Epstein, *Freedom and Growth: The Rise of States and Markets in Europe, 1300–1750* (London and New York, 2000).

Prices, wages, and secular economic cycles are discussed in two fundamental works: B. H. Slicher van Bath, *The Agrarian History of Western Europe A.D. 500–1850*, tr. Olive Ordish (London, 1963), and Wilhelm Abel, *Agricultural Fluctuations in Europe from the Thirteenth to the Twentieth Centuries*, tr. Olive Ordish from 3rd German edn. of 1978 (London, 1980). These are, however, both now old, and should be supplemented by two recent articles by Robert C. Allen, 'The Great Divergence in European Wages and Prices from the Middle Ages to the First World War', *Explorations in Economic History*, 38 (2001), 411–47; and 'Economic Structure and Agricultural Productivity in Europe, 1300–1800', *European Review of Economic History*, 4 (2000), 1–25. On climate change see the pioneering study by Christian Pfister, 'The Little Ice Age: Thermal and Wetness Indices for Central Europe', *Journal of Interdisciplinary History*, 10 (1980), 665–96, and the more general survey by J. M. Grove, *The Little Ice Age* (London, 1988).

For Eastern Europe see Daniel Chirot (ed.), *The Origins of Backwardness in Eastern Europe: Economics and Politics from the Middle Ages until the Early Twentieth Century* (Berkeley, Calif., 1989), uneven in quality, but with important essays by Robert Brenner and Jacek Kochanowicz. It complements the earlier collection by Antoni Mączak, Henryk Samsonowicz, and Peter Burke (eds.), *East–Central Europe in Transition from the Fourteenth to the Seventeenth Century* (Cambridge and Paris, 1985), in which the essays by

Leonid Żytkowicz, Marian Małowist, and Jerzy Topolski are of particular note (though the statistical information should be treated with great caution). The thorny issues surrounding the rise of the so-called 'second serfdom' east of the Elbe are not readily accessible to those who do not read German or Polish, but see the discussion in Tom Scott, *Society and Economy in Germany, 1300–1600* (Houndmills and New York, 2002), ch. 6, and William W. Hagen, *Ordinary Prussians: Brandenburg Junkers and Villagers, 1500–1840* (Cambridge, 2002). For Poland, the neo-Marxist analysis by Witold Kula, *An Economic Theory of the Feudal System: Towards a Model of the Polish Economy 1500–1800*, tr. Lawrence Garner (London, 1976) is dense, and suffers from its insistence on the primary significance of export markets.

For western Germany see now Scott, *Society and Economy* (as above) and the essays in Bob Scribner (ed.), *Germany: A New Social and Economic History*, i. *1450–1630* (London, 1996). Among the few regional studies in English see, for Hohenlohe, the outstanding monograph by Thomas Robisheaux, *Rural Society and the Search for Order in Early Modern Germany* (Cambridge, 1989); for Bavaria, the important revisionist study by Govind P. Sreenivasan, *The Peasants of Ottobeuren, 1487–1726: A Rural Society in Early Modern Europe* (Cambridge, 2004); and for the Upper Rhine, Tom Scott, *Freiburg and the Breisgau: Town–Country Relations in the Age of Reformation and Peasants' War* (Oxford, 1986) and his *Regional Identity and Economic Change: The Upper Rhine, 1450–1600* (Oxford, 1997). William J. Wright, *Capitalism, the State and the Lutheran Reformation: Sixteenth-Century Hesse* (Athens, Ohio, 1988) is a somewhat eccentric and unconvincing account. On the Fuggers see Richard Ehrenberg, *Capital and Finance in the Age of the Renaissance: A Study of the Fuggers and their Connections*, tr. H. M. Lucas (New York, 1963)—the latest reprint of a work first published in English in 1896! For Augsburg see Martha White Paas, *Population Change, Labor Supply, and Agriculture in Augsburg, 1480–1618: A Study of Early Demographic–Economic Interactions* (New York, 1981), whose views on the partibility of peasant farms in eastern Swabia remain controversial. For Nuremberg, see Wolfgang von Stromer, 'Commercial Policy and Economic Conjuncture in Nuremberg at the Close of the Middle Ages: A Model of Economic Policy', *Journal of European Economic History*, 10 (1980), 119–29. The best study of the Hanseatic League remains Philippe Dollinger, *The German Hansa*, tr. D. S. Ault and S. H. Steinberg (London, 1970), which has been reissued with an introduction by Mark Casson (London and New York, 1999). There is also a profusely illustrated East German account by Johannes Schildhauer, *The Hansa: History and Culture*, tr. Katherine Vanovitch (Leipzig, 1985).

The Low Countries boast an extensive historiography, though until the appearance of Hoppenbrouwers and van Zanden, *Peasants into Farmers?* (as above) Belgian historians tended, understandably, to concentrate on the efflorescence of medieval Flanders and Brabant, Dutch historians on the early modern rise to mercantile supremacy of the northern Netherlands. For the south see the relevant essays in John H. Munro, *Textiles, Towns and Trade: Essays in the Economic History of Late-Medieval England and the Low Countries* (Aldershot, 1984), and the comparison of Flanders and northern Italy in Herman van der Wee (ed.), *The Rise and Decline of Urban Industries in Italy and the Low Countries: Late Middle Ages–Early Modern Times* (Leuven, 1988). On textiles in general see Marc Boone and Walter Prevenier (eds.), *Drapery Production in the Late Medieval Low Countries: Markets and Strategies for Survival (14th–16th Centuries)* (Leuven and Apeldoorn, 1993). On the 'new draperies' see the outstanding essay by Robert S. DuPlessis, 'One Theory, Two Draperies, Three Provinces, and a Multitude of Fabrics: The New Drapery of French Flanders, Hainaut, and the Tournaisis, *c.*1500–*c.*1800', in N. B. Harte (ed.), *The New Draperies in the Low Countries and England, 1300–1800* (Oxford, 1997), 129–72. On Antwerp the classic study remains Herman van der Wee, *The Growth of the Antwerp Market and the European Economy, Fourteenth–Sixteenth Centuries*, 3 vols. (The Hague [Leuven printing], 1963). The most recent survey of the north is by Jan de Vries and Adriaan van der Woude, *The First Modern Economy: Success, Failure, and Perseverance of the Dutch Economy, 1500–1815* (Cambridge, 1997). See also Karel Davids and Leo Noordegraaf (eds.), *The Dutch Economy in the Golden Age: Nine Studies* (Amsterdam, 1993). On the rural economy of the north see Jan de Vries, *The Dutch Rural Economy in the Golden Age 1500–1700* (New Haven and London, 1974), a brilliant work which has been challenged but not refuted (see de Vries in Hoppenbrouwers and van Zanden, *Peasants into Farmers?* above), still a classic after thirty years—as is Violet Barbour, *Capitalism in Amsterdam in the Seventeenth Century* (Baltimore, Md., 1950) after more than fifty years. More recent studies of Dutch capitalism include Jan Luiten van Zanden, *The Rise and Decline of Holland's Economy: Merchant Capitalism and the Labour Market* (Manchester, 1993), the essays in Maurice Aymard (ed.), *Dutch Capitalism and World Capitalism* (Cambridge and Paris, 1982) and, among his many fine monographs, Jonathan Israel, *Dutch Primacy in World Trade, 1585–1740* (Oxford, 1989). On credit see the ground-breaking study by James D. Tracy, *A Financial Revolution in the Habsburg Netherlands: 'Renten' and 'Renteniers' in the County of Holland, 1515–1565* (Berkeley and Los Angeles, 1985), and the more specialized study by Marjolein 't Hart, *The Making of a Bourgeois State: War, Politics and Finance during the Dutch Revolt* (Manchester, 1993).

There is no lack of English-language works on the French economy after 1600, but the sixteenth century remains largely *terra incognita* unless one has French. On the peasantry and the rural economy see Emmanuel Le Roy Ladurie, *The French Peasantry 1450–1660*, tr. Alan Sheridan (Aldershot, 1987) and the recent useful survey by Philip T. Hoffman, *Growth in a Traditional Society: The French Countryside 1450–1815* (Princeton, 1996). To them should be added the long-range local study by Jonathan Dewald, *Pont-St-Pierre 1398–1789: Lordship, Community and Capitalism in Early Modern France* (Berkeley, Calif., 1987). Guy Bois's study of late medieval Normandy, *The Crisis of Feudalism: Economy and Society in Eastern Normandy c.1300–1550*, tr. anon. (Cambridge and Paris, 1984), written from an unorthodox Marxist perspective, infuses exhaustive local research with wide-ranging theoretical reflection. Unfortunately, his remarks on the sixteenth century are entirely off-beam, and have in fact quietly been abandoned in his recent return to the subject (in French), *La Grande Dépression médiévale: XIVe et XVe siècles. Le Précédent d'une crise systémique* (Paris, 2000). For urban and rural industry there is virtually nothing, apart from Gaston Zeller, 'Industry in France before Colbert', in Rondo Cameron (ed.), *Essays in French Economic History* (Homewood, Ill., 1970), and the now very old comparative study by John U. Nef, *Industry and Government in France and England, 1540–1640* (Philadelphia, 1940), which is no more than an extended essay.

Spanish economic history in the period is somewhat better served, but mainly through monographs rather than by general overviews. An excellent starting-point is Teófilo F. Ruiz, *Crisis and Continuity: Land and Town in Late Medieval Castile* (Philadelphia, 1994), which sets the scene for the debates about the greatness and decline of Castile in the sixteenth and seventeenth centuries. From the other end of the spectrum, the collection by I. A. A. Thompson and Bartolomé Yun Casalilla (eds.), *The Castilian Crisis of the Seventeenth Century: New Perspectives on the Economic and Social History of Seventeenth-Century Spain* (Cambridge, 1994) does much to illuminate the sixteenth; it also offers some corrections to the notable study by David Vassberg, *Land and Society in Golden Age Castile* (Cambridge, 1984). On the Mesta and the wool trade see Carla Rahn Phillips and William Phillips, Jun., *Spain's Golden Fleece: Wool Production and the Wool Trade from the Middle Ages to the Nineteenth Century* (Baltimore and London, 1997). For town–country relations, see the specialized study by David Reher, *Town and Country in Pre-Industrial Spain: Cuenca, 1550–1870* (Cambridge, 1990). There is also a detailed study of the rise of Madrid in David R. Ringrose, *Madrid and the Spanish Economy (1560–1860)* (Berkeley, Calif., 1983). The textbook by Antonio Domínguez Ortiz, *The Golden Age of Spain 1516–1659*, tr. James Casey (London, 1971) contains more information on the economy than is usual in such works.

In the case of Italy, a knowledge of late medieval developments is especially critical for an understanding of its sixteenth-century economy. The monograph by Stephan R. Epstein, *An Island for Itself: Economic Development and Social Change in Late Medieval Sicily* (Cambridge, 1992) ranges far more widely than its title suggests, questioning the entire notion of south Italian 'backwardness', and includes reflections on the sixteenth century. It may be supplemented by Epstein's major article, 'Cities, Regions and the Late Medieval Crisis: Sicily and Tuscany Compared', *Past and Present*, 130 (1991), 3–50. A specialized case-study of rural Tuscany is by Frank McArdle, *Altopascio: A Study in Tuscan Rural Society, 1587–1784* (Cambridge, 1978). See also in this context John A. Marino, *Pastoral Economics in the Kingdom of Naples* (Baltimore and London, 1988), which discusses the Dogana. On rural manufacturing see Carlo Marco Belfanti, 'Rural Manufactures and Rural Proto-Industries in the "Italy of the Cities" from the Sixteenth through the Eighteenth Century', *Continuity and Change*, 8 (1993), 253–80. For one particular industry, see Maureen Mazzaoui, *The Italian Cotton Industry in the Late Middle Ages, 1100–1600* (Cambridge, 1981). For urban life see Richard Mackenney, *Tradesmen and Traders: The World of the Guilds in Venice and Europe, c.1250–c.1650* (London, 1987), and on Venice Brian Pullan (ed.), *Crisis and Change in the Venetian Economy in the Sixteenth and Seventeenth Centuries* (London, 1968). His various studies of credit and banking are collected in Raymond De Roover, *Business, Banking and Economic Thought in Late Medieval and Early Modern Europe: Selected Studies of Raymond De Roover*, ed. Julius Kirshner (Chicago and London, 1974).

The literature on early modern England is vast, and only a small selection of titles, excluding almost all regional or country studies, can be given here. The most convenient survey of agricultural developments remains Joan Thirsk (ed.) *The Agrarian History of England and Wales*, iv. *1500–1640* (London: Cambridge University Press, 1967). More recently, see the ambitious survey by Mark Overton, *Agricultural Revolution in England: The Transformation of the Agrarian Economy 1500–1850* (Cambridge, 1996). On enclosures see, from contrasting perspectives, the revisionist Robert C. Allen, *Enclosure and the Yeoman: The Agricultural Development of the South Midlands 1450–1850* (Oxford, 1992), and the traditionalist James A. Yelling, *Common Field and Enclosure in England, 1450–1850* (London, 1977). On agrarian problems in general see the sometimes controversial views of Eric Kerridge, *Agrarian Problems in the Sixteenth Century and After* (London, 1969), who emphasizes technological change. On the development of capitalist agriculture see Richard W. Hoyle, 'Tenure and the Land Market in Early Modern England: or a Late Contribution to the Brenner Debate', *Economic History Review*, 2nd ser. 43 (1990), 1–20, and the very important East Anglian study by Jane Whittle, *The Development of Agrarian Capitalism: Land and Labour in Norfolk, 1440–1580* (Oxford, 2000). The gentry are discussed by G. E. Chambers, *The Gentry: The Rise and Fall of a Ruling Class* (London, 1976) and their late medieval origins by Peter Coss, *The Origins of the English Gentry* (Cambridge, 2003). General surveys of industry include D. C.

Coleman, *Industry in Tudor and Stuart England* (London, 1975), and G. D. Ramsay, *The English Woollen Industry, 1500–1750* (London, 1982). To the latter now add the regional studies by Michael Zell, *Industry in the Countryside: Wealden Society in the Sixteenth Century* (Cambridge, 1994), and David Rollison, *The Local Origins of Modern Society: Gloucestershire 1500–1800* (London, 1992). More generally on rural industries see the classic article by Joan Thirsk, 'Industries in the Countryside', in F. J. Fisher (ed.), *Essays in the Economic and Social History of Tudor and Stuart England* (Cambridge, 1961), 70–88. On particular industries see, for coal, John Hatcher, *The History of the British Coal Industry*, i. *Before 1700: Towards the Age of Coal* (Oxford, 1993); for tin, his *English Tin Production and Trade before 1550* (Oxford, 1973); and for glass, Eleanor Godfrey, *The Development of English Glassmaking 1560–1640* (Chapel Hill, NC, 1975). On the rise of industries serving a consumer society see Joan Thirsk, *Economic Policy and Projects: The Development of a Consumer Society in Early Modern England* (Oxford, 1978). On coinage see J. D. Gould, *The Great Debasement: Currency and the Economy in Mid-Tudor England* (Oxford, 1970), and on inflation the pamphlet by R. B. Outhwaite, *Inflation in Tudor and Early Stuart England*, 2nd edn. (London, 1982).

Finally, on a European canvas, there are several studies of individual sectors of the economy. For the cattle-trade see the comprehensive review by Ian Blanchard, 'The Continental European Cattle Trade, 1400–1600', *Economic History Review*, 2nd ser. 39 (1986), 427–60. The mining industry is depressingly badly served in English, except for Ian Blanchard, *International Lead Production and Trade in the 'Age of the Saigerprozess' 1450–1560* (*Zeitschrift für Unternehmensgeschichte*, suppl. 85; Stuttgart, 1995), which contains vital information on silver production as well. For iron see in Hermann Kellenbenz (ed.), *Schwerpunkte der Eisengewinnung und Eisenverarbeitung in Europa 1500–1650* (Cologne and Vienna, 1974) the essays in English by D. W. Crossley, 'The English Iron Industry 1500–1650: The Problem of New Techniques', pp. 17–34, and Domenico Sella, 'The Iron Industry in Italy, 1500–1650', pp. 91–105; to these add Milan Myška, 'Pre-Industrial Iron-Making in the Czech Lands: The Labour Force and Production Relations *circa* 1350–*circa* 1840', *Past and Present*, 82 (1979), 44–72. The difficulties of European economy and society at the close of the sixteenth century are discussed in Peter Clark (ed.), *The European Crisis of the 1590s: Essays in Comparative History* (London, 1985).

2. Politics and Warfare: Mark Greengrass

Chapter 2 presupposes something of a basic understanding of the political events of Europe in the sixteenth century. The writing of general political histories of Europe has, however, been in eclipse in Anglo-Saxon historiography for several decades, so there is relatively little over the last decade within one cover that precisely serves the turn. Richard Bonney, *The European Dynastic States, 1494–1660* (Oxford, 1991) is the most recent and accessible modern account, although it covers a broader period than that considered in this chapter. It refers to others available in English before that date on p. 572 of its bibliography.

For the major individual political entities in Europe, the choice of accessible synoptic histories with good accounts of their political developments is relatively rich. For the Spanish empire, two classic texts appeared simultaneously over forty years ago and still serve well: J. H. Elliott, *Imperial Spain, 1469–1716* (London, 1963) and Henry Kamen, *Spain, 1469–1714: A Society of Conflict* (London, 1983). For this chapter, the theme of Henry Kamen, *Spain's Road to Empire: How Spain became a World Power, 1492–1763* (London, 2002) is, however, more pertinent and challenging. For Valois France, R. J. Knecht, *The Rise and Fall of Renaissance France, 1483–1610*, 2nd edn. (Oxford, 2001) is full of insights, especially on the link between political and cultural developments. J. H. M. Salmon, *Society in Crisis: France in the Sixteenth Century* (London, 1975) emphasizes that the political crises of later sixteenth-century France had deeper historical and social roots in its polity. Michael Hughes, *Early-Modern Germany 1477–1806* (London and Basingstoke, 1992) provides an overview of German lands that includes the sixteenth century, but Peter F. Wilson, *The Holy Roman Empire, 1495–1800* (New York, 1999) is more helpful on institutional and political developments. Norman Davies, *God's Playground: A History of Poland*, 2 vols. (Oxford, 1984) is the standard political history of the Polish-Lithuanian condominium, though Daniel Stone, *The Polish-Lithuanian State, 1386–1795* (Seattle, 2001) is a more recent and informative overview. For the papacy as a political organization, John A. F. Thomson, *Popes and Princes, 1416–1517* (London and Boston, 1980) sets the scene and Paulo Prodi, *The Papal Prince: One Body and Two Souls* (Cambridge, 1987) examines the ambiguities of God's vicar as the elective monarch of a secular principality. For England, Penry Williams, *The Tudor Régime* (Oxford, 1979) provides a political analysis, solidly based on its institutions. For Scotland, Jenny Wormald, *Court, Kirk and Community: Scotland, 1470–1625* (London, 1981) is an excellent broad-ranging political account.

For the more politically fragmented entities of Europe, the material in English is more mixed. Anton Schindling and Walter Ziegler (eds.), *Die Territorien des Reichs im Zeitalter der Reformation und Konfessionalisierung: Land und Konfession, 1500–1650*, 7 vols. (Münster, 1989–97) is an example of what is currently inaccessible in English, and hardly reflected in the older work of F. L. Carsten, *Princes and Parliaments in Germany, from the Fifteenth to the Eighteenth Century* (Oxford, 1959). For the Italian peninsula, Eric Cochrane, *Italy, 1530–1630* (New York and London, 1988) provides some useful synoptic accounts of individual polities with helpful bibliographies. Helmut G.

Koenigsberger, *The Government of Sicily under Philip II of Spain: A Study in the Practice of Empire* (London, 1951) remains a fine case study of informal imperial tutelage. Richard Mackenney, *The City State, 1500–1700: Republican Liberty in an Age of Princely Power* (London, 1989) is a useful comparative study of city states that is particularly good on sixteenth-century developments. James D. Tracy, *Holland under Habsburg Rule: The Formation of a Body Politic* (Berkeley, Calif., 1990) provides a much-needed overview of political developments in the Low Countries in the first half of the sixteenth century. For Hungary, Istvan G. Tóth's recently translated *History of Hungary* (Budapest, 2005) brings together various historians to place its political developments in comparison with others parts of Central Europe.

For political institutions and élites, we should start with the princely courts of Europe, where the comparative reading is at its strongest. A. G. Dickens (ed.), *The Courts of Europe: Politics, Patronage and Royalty, 1400–1800* (London, 1977) provides a well-illustrated starting-point. Ronald G. Asch, and A. M. Birke (eds.), *Princes, Patronage and the Nobility: The Court at the Beginning of the Modern Age* (London and Oxford, 1991) is an informative set of essays with an excellent introduction. Gianvittorio Signoroto and Maria Antonietta Visceglia (eds.), *Court and Politics in Papal Rome, 1492–1700* (Cambridge, 2002) provides fascinating insights into a very particular European court. For the rise of the court favourite, already prefigured in the sixteenth century, see various essays in J. H. Elliott and Lawrence W. B. Brockliss (eds.), *The World of the Favourite* (New Haven and London, 1999). On the political impact of patronage and clientage, there has been much recent work and some debate, concentrated on the French experience. See Sharon Kettering, 'Clientage during the French Wars of Religion', *Sixteenth Century Journal*, 20 (1989), 68–87, for an overview, and Mark Greengrass, 'Functions and Limits of Political Clientelism in France before Cardinal Richelieu', in Neithard Bulst, Robert Descimon, and Alain Guerreau (eds.), *L'État ou le Roi: fondations de la modernité monarchique (XIVe–XVIIIe siècles)* (Paris, 1996), 69–82, for the debate. For sixteenth-century England, too, there has been a debate about the relationship between formal institutional change and informal channels of political power. Geoffrey Elton, *The Tudor Revolution in Government* (Cambridge, 1953) provided a trenchant statement of the former. C. Coleman, and David Starkey (eds.), *Revolution Reassessed: Revisions in the History of Tudor Government and Administration* (Oxford, 1986) emphasizes the latter. On institutions and elites more generally, two collective volumes from the European Science Foundation project on 'The Origins of the Modern State in Europe' are particularly useful; Wolfgang Reinhard (ed.), *Power Elites and State Building* (Oxford, 1998) and Antonio Padoa-Schioppa (ed.), *Legislation and Justice* (Oxford, 1997). The bibliographies in these works provide excellent recent starting-points for exploring the rich veins of research in both English and other foreign languages. On the wider issues of the social basis of political power, there is just room in this very selective bibliography to mention a few studies that open up the question: Dennis Romano, *Patricians and Popolani: The Social Foundations of the Venetian Renaissance State* (Baltimore and London, 1987) examines the case of Venice. G. R. Elton, 'Tudor Government: The Points of Contact', reprinted in his *Studies in Tudor and Stuart Politics and Government*, iii (Cambridge, 1983) does the same for England.

Sixteenth-century European politics has also to be viewed in the context of a broader literature on the development of the European state. Charles Tilly, 'Reflection on the History of European State-Making', in Tilly (ed.), *The Formation of National States in Western Europe* (Princeton, 1975), 3–83, provides one such statement, based on the model-building techniques of social scientists. Wim Blockmans and Jean-Philippe Genet, *Les Origines de l'état moderne en Europe, XIIIe–XVIIIe siècles* (Paris, 2000) brings together various historians to examine the question. K. H. F. Dyson, *The State Tradition in Western Europe: A Study of an Idea and Institution* (Oxford, 1980) provides the perspective of a political theorist.

What about the great political moments and movements of sixteenth-century Europe? Mark Hansen, *The Royal Facts of Life: Biology and Politics in Sixteenth-Century Europe* (Metuchen, NJ, and London, 1980) examines the dynastic realities, emphasized in this chapter. In many respects the greatest political movements in Western Europe concerned the civil wars in France and the Netherlands. Philip Benedict, Guido Marnef, Henk van Nierop, and Marc Venard (eds.), *Reformation, Revolt and Civil War in France and the Netherlands, 1555–1585* (Amsterdam, 1999) is a comparative study of various aspects of them. N. M. Sutherland, *Princes, Politics and Religion, 1547–1589* (London, 1984) and Geoffrey Parker, *The Dutch Revolt* (London, 1977) explore other elements. On the greatest political disaster of the century, the massacre of St Bartholomew, see Robert McCune Kingdon, *Myths about the St Bartholomew's Day Massacres, 1572–1576* (Cambridge, 1988); James R. Smither, 'The St. Bartholomew's Day Massacre and Images of Kingship in France: 1572–1574', *Sixteenth Century Journal*, 22/1 (1991), 27–46; Nicola Mary Sutherland, *The Massacre of St Bartholomew and the European Conflict* (London and Basingstoke, 1973) puts the massacre into its European context.

On the political personalities of sixteenth-century Europe, we are relatively well-served in English. On Charles V, Hugo Soly (*et al.*), *Charles V, 1500–1558, and his Time* (Antwerp, 1999) is a magnificent and beautifully illustrated volume. But William S. Maltby, *The Reign of Charles V* (Basingstoke and London, 2001); James D. Tracy, *Emperor Charles V, Impresario of War: Campaign Strategy, International Finance, and Domestic Politics* (Cambridge, 2002) are both helpful studies. Mia Rodríguez-Salgado, *The Changing Face of*

Empire: Charles V, Philip II and Habsburg Authority, 1551–1559 (Cambridge, 1988) examines a crucial period of change in the light of the two personalities involved. Helmut Koenigsberger, 'Orange, Granvelle and Philip II', in Koenigsberger (ed.), *Politicians and Virtuosi: Essays in Early-Modern History* (London, 1986), 97–119, is part of a collection of essays, rich in insights on European sixteenth-century politics. It should be read alongside Mia J. Rodríguez-Salgado, 'King, Bishop, Pawn? Philip II and Granvelle in the 1550s and 1560s' in Krista De Jonge and Gustaaf Janssens (eds.), *Les Granvelle et les anciens Pays-Bas* (Leuven, 2000), 105–34. Helmut G. Koenigsberger, 'The Statecraft of Philip II', *European Studies Review*, 1 (1971), 1–21, is a forthright statement of the way he governed his empire, worth comparing with Goffrey Parker, *The Grand Strategy of Philip II* (New Haven and London, 1998); Henry Kamen, *Philip of Spain* (New Haven and London, 1997) and Geoffrey Parker, *Philip II* (Chicago, 2002) are both readable assessments of his reign. Moving away from the Spanish Habsburg court, Robert J. W. Evans, *Rudolf II and his World: A Study in Intellectual History* (Oxford, 1973) is an unbeatable study of a remarkable figure of the late sixteenth century. On the queens of sixteenth-century Europe, there are two 'profiles in power': R. J. Knecht, *Catherine de' Medici* (London, 1998) and Christopher Haigh, *Elizabeth I* (London, 1988), the latter being just one among a plethora of biographical studies currently available.

Political theatre and ritual has been the focus of a great deal of recent research, much of it concentrated on the sixteenth century. Roy Strong, *Art and Power: Renaissance Festivals, 1450–1600* (London, 1986) provides a useful starting-point. Edward Muir, *Civic Ritual in Renaissance Venice* (Princeton, 1981) is an excellent case-study. The same author's *Ritual in Early Modern Europe* (Cambridge, 1997) puts some of the issues in a broader context. Frances A. Yates, *Astrea: The Imperial Theme in the Sixteenth Century* (London, 1975) explores the intellectual justifications of power provided by the Renaissance. Allan Ellenius (ed.), *Iconography, Propaganda and Legitimation* (Oxford, 1998) has some useful studies for the sixteenth century and a good, recent bibliography. Ralph A. Giesey, *The Royal Funeral Ceremony in Renaissance France* (Geneva, 1960) and R. A. Jackson, *Vivat Rex! A History of the French Coronation Ceremony from Charles V to Charles X* (Chapel Hill, NC, 1984) are representative examples of an approach to political ritual that has brought important results for sixteenth-century Europe.

On sixteenth-century statecraft, Quentin Skinner, *The Foundations of Modern Political Thought*, 2 vols. (Cambridge, 1978) remains the best starting-point, though there are excellent synoptic chapters, with accompanying bibliography in *The Cambridge History of Political Thought, 1450–1700*, ed. J. H. Burns (Cambridge, 1991). If there is one author to engage with as a primary source on politics from this period, it has to be Machiavelli. Peter

Bondanella and Mark Musa, *The Portable Machiavelli.* (London, 1979 and reprints) provide the complete text of 'The Prince', 'The Mandrake Root', and selections from 'The Discourses'. Felix Gilbert, *Machiavelli and Guicciardini* (Princeton, 1965) is an excellent comparative study. Roberto Ridolfi, *The Life of Niccolò Machiavelli* (Chicago, 1965) remains the standard biography. J. G. A. Pocock, *The Machiavellian Moment: Florentine Political Thought and the Atlantic Republic Imaginations* (Princeton, 1975) places Florentine political thought in a longer tradition. Robert Bireley, *The Counter-Reformation Prince: Anti-Machiavellianism or Catholic Statecraft in Early-Modern Europe* (Chapel Hill, NC, 1990) is an important study of Catholic statecraft in the Counter-Reformation. Julian H. Franklin, *John Bodin and the Rise of Absolutist Theory* (Cambridge, 1973) places Bodin, too, in a longer tradition, whilst Anthony Pagden (ed.), *The Languages of Political Theory in Early-Modern Europe* (Cambridge, 1987) contextualizes the vocabulary of sixteenth-century politics.

On warfare and military conflict, John R. Hale, *War and Society in Renaissance Europe* (London, 1985) is an excellent introduction. Michael Roberts, 'The Military Revolution, 1560–1660', in Roberts (ed.), *Essays in Swedish History* (London, 1967), argued a case to which Geoffrey Parker responded in 'The Military Revolution, 1560–1660 — a Myth?', in Parker (ed.), *Spain and the Netherlands, 1559–1659* (London, 1979). The debate extended well beyond the sixteenth century, as is evident in Jeremy Black, *A Military Revolution? Military Change and European Society, 1550–1800* (London and Basingstoke, 1991) and Geoffrey Parker, *The Military Revolution: Military Innovation and the Rise of the West* (London, 1988). The same author's *The Army of Flanders and the Spanish Road 1567–1659: The Logistics of Spanish Victory and Defeat in the Low Countries' Wars* (Cambridge, 1972) is a seminal study of strategic realities in sixteenth-century Europe. M. E. Mallett, *Mercenaries and their Masters: Warfare in Renaissance Italy* (London, 1974) is a masterly analysis of a phenomenon that was still important. Michael E. Mallett and John R. Hale, *The Military Organization of a Renaissance State: Venice, c.1400–1617* (Cambridge, 1984) is a fascinating study of a state that thought military technology was the answer to its problems of security. J. R. Mulryne, and M. Shewring (eds.), *War, Literature and the Arts in Sixteenth-Century Europe* (London and Basingstoke, 1989) provides essays on the impact of military conflict on the sixteenth-century European imagination. Philippe Contamine, *War and Competition between States* (Oxford, 2000) contains some relevant studies for the sixteenth century and a bibliography of over 750 items.

3. Society: Christopher Black

Henry Kamen's latest European survey *Early Modern European Society* (London, 2000) is the best overall survey; with good bibliography, but less helpful index. Christopher Black, *Early Modern Italy: A Social History* (London, 2000) elaborates on this complex area (and justifies the verdicts and biases of this chapter), while James Casey, *Early Modern Spain: A Social History* (London, 1999) valuably elucidates Spanish social complexities. Other regional studies: Jean Bérenger, *A History of the Habsburg Empire 1273–1700* (Harlow, 1994), esp. ch. 16. Keith Wrightson, *English Society 1580–1680* (London, 1982); Natalie Zemon Davis, *Society and Culture in Early Modern France* (Stanford, Calif., 1975), for some inspirational essays, with her *The Return of Martin Guerre* (Cambridge, Mass., 1983; Harmondsworth, 1985), as the book of the film (on which she advised)! Robert Jütte, *Poverty and Deviance in Early Modern Europe* (Cambridge, 1994), and Merry Wiesner, *Women and Gender in Early Modern Europe* (Cambridge, 1993) survey two major themes touched on here, over a longer period. Carlo Ginzburg, *The Cheese and the Worms: The Cosmos of a Sixteenth-Century Miller*, tr. John and Anne Tedeschi (Baltimore, 1980; Harmondsworth, 1982) tells Menocchio's story. A translated transcript of the trial documents, with an excellent introduction, is available: Andrea Del Col, *Domenico Scandella Known as Menocchio: His Trials before the Inquisition* (Medieval and Renaissance Texts and Studies, Binghampton, NY, 1996). Guido Ruggiero (ed.), *A Companion to the Worlds of the Renaissance* (Oxford, 2002), a large multidisciplinary collection by leading scholars mainly from North America, has many chapters which are valuable for the development of points made in this chapter, as others in this book; with major composite bibliography.

4. The Mind: Charles G. Nauert

European intellectual life in the sixteenth century developed under the spell of the Italian Renaissance. There is no satisfactory survey of the cultural history of sixteenth-century Italy, but there are valuable studies of major cultural centres. On Venice, see William J. Bouwsma, *Venice and the Defense of Republican Liberty: Renaissance Values in the Age of the Counter-Reformation* (Berkeley, Calif., 1978); Oliver Logan, *Culture and Society in Venice, 1470–1790* (London, 1972); and Margaret L. King, *Venetian Humanism in an Age of Patrician Dominance* (Princeton, 1986). On Rome, see John F. D'Amico, *Renaissance Humanism in Papal Rome* (Baltimore, 1983); and Ingrid Rowland, *The Culture of the High Renaissance: Ancients and Moderns in Sixteenth-Century Rome* (Cambridge, 1998). On Naples, see Jerry H. Bentley, *Politics and Culture in Renaissance Naples* (Princeton, 1987). Two books on Florence in the late Renaissance are Eric Cochrane, *Florence in the Forgotten Centuries, 1527–1800* (Chicago, 1973), and Cochrane (ed.), *The Late Italian Renaissance, 1525–1630* (New York, 1970).

On the diffusion of the new learning to Transalpine Europe, chapter 7 of Denys Hay, *The Italian Renaissance in its Historical Background*, 2nd edn.

(Cambridge, 1977), remains a valuable introduction. Charles G. Nauert, *Humanism and the Culture of Renaissance Europe* (Cambridge, 1995), traces the growth of the new culture in Northern Europe. Several collections of essays discuss the effects of the Renaissance on native cultures: Heiko A. Oberman with Thomas A. Brady, jun. (eds.), *Itinerarium Italicum: The Profile of the Italian Renaissance in the Mirror of its European Transformations* (Leiden, 1975); vol. ii of Albert Rabil, jun. (ed.), *Renaissance Humanism: Foundations, Forms, and Legacy*, 3 vols. (Philadelphia, 1988); Anthony Goodman and Angus MacKay (eds.), *The Impact of Humanism on Western Europe* (New York, 1990); and Roy A. Porter and Mikulás Teich (eds.), *The Renaissance in National Context* (Cambridge, 1992). Most studies of the northern Renaissance deal with a single country. For France, see Franco Simone, *The French Renaissance* (London, 1969); Werner L. Gundersheimer (ed.), *French Humanism, 1470–1600* (London, 1969); Donald Stone, jun., *France in the Sixteenth Century* (Edgewood Cliffs, NJ, 1969); and A. H. T. Levi (ed.), *Humanism in France and in the Early Renaissance* (Manchester, 1970). Augustin Renaudet, *Préréforme et humanisme à Paris pendant les premières guerres d'Italie, 1494–1517*, 2nd edn. (Paris, 1952), is unsurpassed but unavailable in English. For English humanism before 1500, see Roberto Weiss, *Humanism in England during the Fifteenth Century*, 2nd edn. (Oxford, 1957). On the political use of humanist learning under Henry VIII and Edward VI, see James K. McConica, *English Humanists and Reformation Politics* (Oxford, 1965). For the period 1500–134, readers must rely on biographical studies of figures like John Colet and Thomas More. For Germany, Eckhard Bernstein, *German Humanism* (Boston, 1983), provides a brief introduction; but the most comprehensive English-language work is Lewis W. Spitz, *The Religious Renaissance of the German Humanists* (Cambridge, Mass., 1963). For Spain, the authoritative treatment is Marcel Bataillon, *Erasme et l'Espagne*, 3 vols. (Geneva, 1991), a book translated into Spanish but never into English.

'Christian' or 'biblical' humanism was essentially the creation of the French humanist Jacques Lefèvre d'Etaples and the Dutch humanist Desiderius Erasmus. Philip Edgcumbe Hughes, *Lefèvre: Pioneer of Ecclesiastical Renewal in France* (Grand Rapids, Mich., 1971) concentrates on Lefèvre's influence on the Reformation but gives some attention to his earlier career. See also the essay by Eugene F. Rice, jun., in Gundersheimer, *French Humanism*, 163–80, and Rice's introduction to *The Prefatory Epistles of Jacques Lefèvre d'Etaples and Related Texts* (New York, 1971).

Studies of Erasmus are far more numerous, including the *Collected Works of Erasmus* in course of publication by the University of Toronto Press and supplemented by a biographical dictionary, *Contemporaries of Erasmus*, 3 vols. (Toronto, 1985–7). There are many biographies of Erasmus. The best of the older ones is Johan Huizinga, *Erasmus of Rotterdam* (first English edn.,

1924; repr. Princeton, 1984). Other biographies are by Margaret Mann Phillips (London, 1949) and Roland H. Bainton (New York, 1969) and more recently by Cornelis Augustijn (Toronto, 1991), Lisa Jardine (Princeton, 1993), and James D. Tracy (Geneva, 1996). Erika Rummel, *The Confessionalization of Humanism in Reformation Germany* (Oxford, 2000), studies interaction between Erasmian humanism and the German Reformation. On other major 'Christian humanists', see *John Colet* (Berkeley, 1989) by John B. Gleason, and the many biographies of Thomas More. The standard older one is by R. W. Chambers (New York, 1935). More recent works are by Alistair Fox (New Haven, 1983), Richard Marius (New York, 1984), and Peter Ackroyd (London, 1998). On More's most famous literary work, see J. H. Hexter, *More's Utopia: The Biography of an Idea* (Princeton, 1952).

At its most basic level, humanism was a programme of classical studies. Fundamental for study of early humanist scholarship is Ronald G. Witt, *'In the Footsteps of the Ancients': The Origins of Humanism from Lovato to Bruni* (Leiden, 2000). Accounts of the recovery of ancient Greek and Latin literature include R. R. Bolgar, *The Classical Heritage and Its Beneficiaries* (Cambridge, 1954); Rudolf Pfeiffer, *History of Classical Scholarship, 1300–1850* (Oxford, 1976); and L. D. Reynolds and N. G. Wilson, *Scribes and Scholars: A Guide to the Transmission of Greek and Latin Literature*, 2nd edn. (Oxford, 1974). On the introduction of Greek, see N. G. Wilson, *From Byzantium to Italy: Greek Studies in the Italian Renaissance* (Baltimore, 1992). Ann Moss, *Renaissance Truth and the Latin Language Turn* (Oxford, 2003), traces intellectual consequences of the stylistic change from medieval to humanistic Latin. On humanist biblical scholarship, see Jerry H. Bentley, *Humanists and Holy Writ: New Testament Scholarship in the Renaissance* (Princeton, 1983). Two studies by Anthony Grafton, *Joseph Scaliger: A Study in the History of Classical Scholarship*, 2 vols. (Oxford, 1983–93), and *Defenders of the Text: The Traditions of Scholarship in an Age of Science* (Cambridge, Mass., 1991), trace the development of textual criticism.

Humanism became a powerful influence in education. For Italian schools, books by Paul F. Grendler and Robert Black are crucial, though the authors disagree on some important issues. See Grendler's *Schooling in Renaissance Italy: Literacy and Learning, 1300–1600* (Baltimore, 1989), and Black's *Humanism and Education in Medieval and Renaissance Italy* (Cambridge, 2001). Grendler's *The Universities of the Italian Renaissance* (Baltimore, 2002) shows that the new learning quietly penetrated Italian universities without precipitating much controversy.

North of the Alps, however, humanist educational reforms met more resistance. Terrence Heath, 'Logical Grammar, Grammatical Logic, and Humanism in Three German Universities', *Studies in the Renaissance*, 18 (1971), 9–64, shows how humanist curricular reforms endangered traditional education. James H. Overfield, *Humanism and Scholasticism in Late Medieval Germany* (Princeton, 1984), and Erika Rummel, *The Humanist-Scholastic Debate in the Renaissance and Reformation* (Cambridge, Mass., 1995) offer differing opinions whether conflicts over curricular reform involved a true clash between medieval and Renaissance cultures.

Mark H. Curtis, *Oxford and Cambridge in Transition, 1558–1642* (Oxford, 1959), challenged the conventional view that the English universities remained fundamentally medieval until the nineteenth century. Two newer histories confirm his conclusions: James McConica (ed.), *The Collegiate University* (Oxford, 1986), vol. iii of *The History of the University of Oxford*; and Damian Riehl Leader, *The University to 1546* (Cambridge, 1988), vol. i of *A History of the University of Cambridge*. For Paris, Renaudet, *Préréforme*, provides a detailed study of the university's intellectual life, but only to about 1517. For Spain, see Richard Kagan, *Students and Society in Early Modern Spain* (Baltimore, 1974).

Josef Ijsewijn, 'The Coming of Humanism to the Low Countries', in H. A. Oberman and T. A. Brady, jun. (eds.), *Itinerarium Italicum* (Leiden, 1975), 193–301, discusses educational reforms in the Netherlands. On the flourishing French municipal *collèges* (grammar schools), see George Huppert, *Public Schools in Renaissance France* (Urbana, Ill., 1984). For England, see Joan Simon, *Education and Society in Tudor England* (Cambridge, 1969); and Rosemary O'Day, *Education and Society, 1560–1800* (London, 1982).

The scholarly debates precipitated by Hans Baron's concept of 'civic humanism' belong to fifteenth-century historiography, but Baron's thesis concerning Florentine republicanism is important for understanding Niccolò Machiavelli. Felix Gilbert, *Machiavelli and Guicciardini: Politics and History in Sixteenth-Century Florence* (Princeton, 1965), views Machiavelli as an heir of Florentine republicanism. Peter Godman, *From Poliziano to Machiavelli: Florentine Humanism in the High Renaissance* (Princeton, 1998), also links Machiavelli to earlier Florentine humanism. J. G. A. Pocock, *The Machiavellian Moment: Florentine Political Thought and the Atlantic Revolution* (Princeton, 1975), traces the later history of Florentine republican ideology.

The French legal humanists who discovered that French laws and political institutions did not grow out of Roman law but had their roots in the Middle Ages are the subject of Donald R. Kelley, *Foundations of Modern Historical Scholarship: Language, Law, and History in the French Renaissance* (New York, 1970), and George Huppert, *The Idea of Perfect History: Historical Erudition and Historical Philosophy in Renaissance France* (Urbana, Ill., 1970).

Renaissance textual discoveries had great influence on philosophy. Two general accounts are Charles B. Schmitt and Quentin Skinner (eds.), *The Cambridge History of Renaissance Philosophy* (Cambridge, 1988), and Brian P. Copenhaver and Charles B. Schmitt, *Renaissance Philosophy* (Oxford, 1992).

On Renaissance Neoplatonism, important works include chapter 3 of P. O. Kristeller, *Renaissance Thought* (New York, 1961); Michael J. B. Allen, *The Platonism of Marsilio Ficino: A Study of his Phaedrus Commentary* (Berkeley, Calif., 1984), and *Icastes: Marsilio Ficino's Interpretation of Plato's Sophist* (Berkeley, Calif., 1989); Arthur Field, *The Origins of the Platonic Academy of Florence* (Princeton, 1988); and James Hankins, *Plato in the Italian Renaissance*, 2nd edn., 2 vols. (Leiden, 1991).

Renaissance Neoplatonism enhanced the respectability of magic, astrology, Hermetic philosophy, and other occult sciences. Surveys of Renaissance occultism include Wayne Shumaker, *The Occult Sciences in the Renaissance* (Berkeley, Calif., 1972); Ingrid Merkel and Allen G. Debus (eds.), *Hermeticism and the Renaissance: Intellectual History and the Occult in Early Modern Europe* (Washington, DC, 1988); and Gary K. Waite, *Heresy, Magic, and Witchcraft in Early Modern Europe* (New York, 2003). Two outstanding products of the 'Warburg school' of history are D. P. Walker, *Spiritual and Demonic Magic from Ficino to Campanella* (London, 1958), and Frances A. Yates, *Giordano Bruno and the Hermetic Tradition* (Chicago, 1964). On Renaissance interest in Jewish Cabbala, the best guide is Gershom Scholem, *Major Trends in Jewish Mysticism*, 3rd edn. (New York, 1944). Readers of French should consult François Secret, *Les Kabbalistes chrétiens de la Renaissance* (Paris, 1964).

Although Plato's works had a powerful influence on sixteenth-century intellectual life, they found no place in the philosophical teaching of the universities, which continued to accept Aristotle as the authority in philosophy. Charles B. Schmitt traces Aristotle's continued mastery in *Aristotle and the Renaissance* (Cambridge, Mass., 1983); *Studies in Renaissance Philosophy and Science* (London, 1981); and *The Aristotelian Tradition and Renaissance Universities* (London, 1984).

Aristotle provided the philosophical framework for university teaching of natural science and medicine. Useful introductions to Renaissance science are Marie Boas, *The Scientific Renaissance, 1450–1630* (New York, 1962), and Robert Mandrou, *From Humanism to Science, 1480–1700* (Harmondsworth, 1978). Growing awareness of the importance of mathematics is the subject of Peter Dear (ed.), *The Scientific Enterprise in Early Modern Europe: Readings from Isis* (Chicago, 1997). The crucial field for the 'scientific revolution' was astronomy, associated with the work of Nicolaus Copernicus and his successors. Useful books include Thomas S. Kuhn, *The Copernican Revolution: Planetary Astronomy in the Development of Western Thought* (New York, 1959); Alexandre Koyré, *The Astronomical Revolution: Copernicus, Kepler, Borelli* (Ithaca, NY, 1973); Robert Westman (ed.), *The Copernican Achievement* (Berkeley, Calif., 1975); Edward Rosen, *Copernicus and the Scientific Revolution* (Malabar, Fla., 1984); and Owen Gingerich, *The Eye of Heaven:*

Ptolemy, Copernicus, Kepler (New York, 1993). Two books that offer fresh perspectives on Renaissance science are Paula Findlen, *Possessing Nature: Museums, Collecting, and Scientific Culture in Early Modern Italy* (Berkeley, Calif., 1994); and Lorraine Daston and Katharine Park, *Wonders and the Order of Nature* (New York, 1998).

On Renaissance medicine, see Nancy G. Siraisi, *Medieval and Early Renaissance Medicine: An Introduction to Knowledge and Practice* (Chicago, 1990); and *Medicine in the Italian Universities, 1250–1600* (Leiden, 2001). On the Paracelsian tradition in medicine, see Allen Debus, *The Chemical Philosophy: Paracelsian Science and Medicine in the Sixteenth and Seventeenth Centuries*, 2 vols. (New York, 1977).

On Stoic moral philosophy in Renaissance Italy, see Charles Trinkaus, *Adversity's Noblemen: The Italian Humanists on Happiness* (New York, 1940). Jason L. Saunders, *Justus Lipsius: The Philosophy of Renaissance Stoicism* (New York, 1955), discusses the rise of Neostoicism during the Wars of Religion. The Wars of Religion also stimulated fresh interest in political philosophy. Literature supporting the right of rebellion against tyrannical rulers is treated in Quentin Skinner, *The Foundations of Modern Political Thought*, 2 vols. (Cambridge, 1978). On Jean Bodin, the most important political thinker of this period, see Julian Franklin, *Jean Bodin and the Sixteenth-Century Revolution in the Methodology of Law and History* (New York, 1963), and *Jean Bodin and the Rise of Absolutist Theory* (Cambridge, 1973).

Humanistic rhetoric became a rival to Aristotelian rationalism, especially after the posthumous publication of the *Disputationes dialecticae* of the Frisian humanist Rudolf Agricola in 1515. On Agricola, see F. Akkerman and A. J. Vanderjagt (eds.), *Rodolphus Agricola Phrisius, 1444–1485* (Leiden, 1988), and Peter Mack, *Renaissance Argument: Valla and Agricola in the Traditions of Rhetoric and Dialectic* (Leiden, 1993). The rhetoricians rarely attacked Aristotle's authority directly, but Aristotle did come under direct attack by the influential French philosopher Peter Ramus. The principal study is Walter J. Ong, *Ramus, Method, and the Decay of Dialogue* (Cambridge, Mass., 1958). Other discussions of Ramus and rhetoric are Wilbur Samuel Howell, *Logic and Rhetoric in England, 1500–1700* (Princeton, 1956); and Neal W. Gilbert, *Renaissance Concepts of Method* (New York, 1960).

On the growth of scepticism, Richard H. Popkin, *The History of Scepticism from Erasmus to Descartes* (Assen, 1960; rev. edn. Berkeley, Calif., 1979) is the definitive work. See also Luciano Floridi, *Sextus Empiricus: The Transmission and Recovery of Pyrrhonism* (New York, 2002); Victoria Kahn, *Rhetoric, Prudence, and Scepticism in the Renaissance* (Ithaca, NY, 1985); and Zachary Sayre Schiffman, *On the Threshold of Modernity: Relativism in the French Renaissance* (Baltimore, 1991). Although Rabelais was no sceptic, he referred to sceptical writers and delighted in paradox. See Barbara C. Bowen, *The Age of*

Bluff: Paradox and Ambiguity in Rabelais and Montaigne (Urbana, Ill., 1972). Lucien Febvre, *The Problem of Unbelief in the Sixteenth Century: The Religion of Rabelais* (Cambridge, Mass., 1982) probes intellectual unrest in French thought. On Rabelais himself, there are biographies by Marcel Tetel (New York, 1967) and M. A. Screech (Ithaca, NY, 1979). Two useful biographies of Montaigne, the most influential spokesman for scepticism before Descartes, are by Peter Burke (New York, 1982) and Donald M. Frame (New York, 1968). Paolo Rossi, *Francis Bacon: From Magic to Science* (London, 1968), shows that Platonic and occultist ideas influenced Bacon. See also Lisa Jardine, *Francis Bacon: Discovery and the Art of Discourse* (Cambridge, 1974).

5. The Turmoil of Faith: Euan Cameron

The transition from late Middle Ages to Renaissance and Reformation has received a powerful full-dress treatment by an array of authorities in Thomas A. Brady, Heiko Augustinus Oberman, and James D. Tracy (eds.), *Handbook of European History, 1400–1600: Late Middle Ages, Renaissance, and Reformation*, 2 vols. (Leiden and New York, 1994–5). For religion see especially the essays by Scribner and Van Engen in vol. i, and all of parts 1 and 2 of vol. ii. A still excellent and much shorter introduction is Steven Ozment, *The Age of Reform 1250–1550: An Intellectual and Religious History of Late Medieval and Reformation Europe* (New Haven, 1980). The older composite volume edited by E. Iserloh, J. Glazik, and H. Jedin, *Reformation and Counter Reformation*, trs. A. Biggs and P. W. Becker, forming vol. v of H. Jedin and J. Dolan (eds.), *History of the Church* (New York, 1980) suffers from its overtly pro-Catholic stance and also from its age. On the Reformation, there are multiple-author treatments in Andrew Pettegree (ed.), *The Reformation World* (London and New York, 2000) and R. Po-chia Hsia (ed.), *A Companion to the Reformation World* (Oxford, 2004). There are also single-author essays by Euan Cameron, *The European Reformation* (Oxford and New York, 1991), Carter Lindberg, *The European Reformations* (Oxford and Cambridge, Mass., 1996); more recently see the somewhat idiosyncratic but brilliant Owen Chadwick, *The Early Reformation on the Continent* (Oxford and New York: 2001) and the astonishingly wide-ranging and well-read Diarmaid MacCulloch, *Reformation: Europe's House Divided, 1490–1700* (London, 2004; American edn. *The Reformation: A History*, New York and London, 2004).

Popular belief before and during the Reformation era still awaits a fully definitive survey, such are the problems both of evidence and of method. Keith Thomas, *Religion and the Decline of Magic: Studies in Popular Beliefs in Sixteenth and Seventeenth Century England* (New York, 1997; originally publ. London, 1971), despite its age and being rather heavily influenced by post-Reformation Protestant sources, remains remarkably cogent. From an avowedly apologetic Catholic perspective is the brilliant but partisan Eamon

Duffy, *The Stripping of the Altars: Traditional Religion in England, 1400–1580* (New Haven, 1992). Both these studies are based on England, though some (not all) of what they say can be applied to Europe more generally. For continental Europe one depends on local studies, of which some of the best in English are W. A. Christian, *Local Religion in Sixteenth-Century Spain* (Princeton, 1981), J. N. Galpern, *The Religions of the People in Sixteenth-Century Champagne* (Cambridge, Mass., 1976), and perhaps most exciting of all David Gentilcore, *From Bishop to Witch: The System of the Sacred in Early Modern Terra d'Otranto* (Manchester and New York, 1992). R. W. Scribner, *Popular Culture and Popular Movements in Reformation Germany* (London and Ronceverte, WV, 1988), contains some excellent essays on this topic. Stephen Wilson, *The Magical Universe: Everyday Ritual and Magic in Pre-Modern Europe* (London, 2000) suffers from a lack of chronological and regional specificity and a poverty of theoretical reflection, though the information contained in it is copious.

On the Church before the Reformation a still excellent survey is Francis Oakley, *The Western Church in the Later Middle Ages* (Ithaca, NY, and London, 1979), as is Robert Swanson, *Religion and Devotion in Europe, c.1215–c.1515* (Cambridge and New York, 1995). Preaching is ably discussed in Larissa Taylor, *Soldiers of Christ: Preaching in Late Medieval and Reformation France* (New York, 1992), while the Eucharist is well treated in Miri Rubin, *Corpus Christi: The Eucharist in Late Medieval Culture* (Cambridge and New York, 1991). Thomas N. Tentler, *Sin and Confession on the Eve of the Reformation* (Princeton, 1977) remains a fine study of confessional theory and practice, though needing to be supplemented by the work of W. David Myers, *'Poor, Sinning Folk': Confession and Conscience in Counter-Reformation Germany* (Ithaca, NY, and London, 1996) and Anne T. Thayer, *Penitence, Preaching and the Coming of the Reformation* (Aldershot, 2002). J. A. F. Thomson, *Popes and Princes, 1417–1517: Politics and Polity in the Late Medieval Church* (London and Boston, 1980) offers a balanced and fair appraisal of the pre-Reformation papacy.

Martin Luther has probably received more biographies than anyone in history other than major political leaders. Out of hundreds the historian needs chiefly the balanced and careful Martin Brecht, *Martin Luther*, tr. James L. Schaaf, 3 vols. (Philadelphia, 1985–93), the definitive modern biography, and the whimsical but ever-brilliant Heiko A. Oberman, *Luther: Man between God and the Devil*, tr. Eileen Walliser-Schwarzbart (New Haven, 1989). Some important works study the transmission of the Reformation message through pamphlet and printed image. Robert W. Scribner, *For the Sake of Simple Folk: Popular Propaganda for the German Reformation* (Cambridge and New York: Cambridge University Press, 1981; also later edn., Oxford and New York, 1994) pioneered this subject in English; noteworthy are Mark

U. Edwards, *Printing, Propaganda, and Martin Luther* (Berkeley, Calif., 1994) and Peter Matheson, *The Rhetoric of the Reformation* (Edinburgh, 1998).

The hitherto vast literature on the reception of the Reformation in the cities of Europe has thinned out considerably in recent years (paradoxically as the amount of synthetic and evaluative material has increased). The now classic introductory essay by A. G. Dickens, *The German Nation and Martin Luther* (London, 1974) still offers accessible summaries of older monograph literature. Steven E. Ozment, *The Reformation in the Cities: The Appeal of Protestantism to Sixteenth-Century Germany and Switzerland* (New Haven, 1975) remains valid if overstated. Also still worthwhile is Bernd Moeller, *Imperial Cities and the Reformation: Three Essays*, ed. and tr. H. C. Erik Midelfort and Mark U. Edwards, jun. (Durham, NC: Labyrinth Press, 1982). Thomas A. Brady, *Turning Swiss: Cities and Empire, 1450–1550* (Cambridge and New York, 1985), while conceptually sophisticated, is very hard on the non-specialist reader. Among many local studies noteworthy are Lorna Jane Abray, *The People's Reformation: Magistrates, Clergy, and Commons in Strasbourg, 1500–1598* (Ithaca, NY, 1985), Susan C. Karant-Nunn, *Zwickau in Transition, 1500–1547: The Reformation as an Agent of Change* (Columbus, Ohio, 1987) and Lee Palmer Wandel, *Voracious Idols and Violent Hands: Iconoclasm in Reformation Zurich, Strasbourg, and Basel* (Cambridge and New York: Cambridge University Press, 1995).

A fruitful genre of historical writing on the Reformation has focused on the implementation of reforming measures at the parish level, including worship and discipline as well as the inculcation of doctrine. A good collection of essays on this topic is Andrew Pettegree (ed.), *The Reformation of the Parishes: The Ministry and the Reformation in Town and Country* (Manchester, 1993). Some fine regional studies include C. Scott Dixon, *The Reformation and Rural Society: The Parishes of Brandenburg-Ansbach-Kulmbach, 1528–1603* (Cambridge, 1996) and Bruce Tolley, *Pastors and Parishioners in Württemberg during the late Reformation, 1581–1621* (Stanford, Calif., 1995). For German-speaking Swiss territories a fine general introduction is Bruce Gordon, *The Swiss Reformation* (Manchester and New York, 2002). An interesting interpretation of the cultural changes is afforded by Susan Karant-Nunn, *The Reformation of Ritual: An Interpretation of Early Modern Germany* (London, 1997).

The evergreen subject of the peasant movements of the 1520s is now dominated, if not quite entirely, by the seminal study of Peter Blickle, *The Revolution of 1525: The German Peasants' War from a New Perspective*, tr. Thomas A. Brady, jun., and H. C. Erik Midelfort (Baltimore, 1981). For other literature the English-language reader must depend heavily on the superb survey in Tom Scott, 'The Peasants' War: A Historiographical Review', *Historical Journal*, 22 (1979), 693–720, 953–74, and on Tom Scott and Robert W. Scribner (eds.), *The German Peasants' War: A History in Documents* (Atlantic Highlands, NJ, 1991). Of the many biographies of Thomas Müntzer that appeared around the quincentenary of his birth in 1989 the most responsible are probably Hans-Jürgen Goertz, *Thomas Müntzer: Apocalyptic Mystic and Visionary*, tr. Jocelyn Jaquiery and ed. Peter Matheson (Edinburgh, 1993) and Tom Scott, *Thomas Müntzer: Theology and Revolution in the German Reformation* (New York, 1989).

On the movement associated with John Calvin we now have a magnificent and thorough survey from Philip Benedict, *Christ's Churches Purely Reformed: A Social History of Calvinism* (New Haven, 2002). This work is broader than, and in some measure supersedes, earlier multi-authored discussions of the Calvinist movements, of which the best are Menna Prestwich (ed.), *International Calvinism 1541–1715* (Oxford, 1985) and Andrew Pettegree, Alastair Duke, and Gillian Lewis (eds.), *Calvinism in Europe, 1540–1620* (Cambridge and New York, 1994). Calvin himself, perennially elusive and self-effacing, has not attracted the most convincing of recent biographies. In William James Bouwsma, *John Calvin: A Sixteenth-Century Portrait* (New York, 1988) and David Curtis Steinmetz, *Calvin in Context* (New York, 1995) the life takes second place to speculations about the relationship between his thought and intellectual trends of the age. For some stimulating thoughts on Calvin one can turn to the posthumous work of Heiko A. Oberman, *The Two Reformations: The Journey from the Last Days to the New World*, ed. Donald Weinstein (New Haven and London, 2003), chs. 7–10.

On the shape of early modern Catholicism there has been in recent years a series of survey books, including Robert Bireley, *The Refashioning of Catholicism, 1450–1700: A Reassessment of the Counter Reformation* (Basingstoke, 1999), R. Po-chia Hsia, *The World of Catholic Renewal, 1540–1770*, 2nd edn. (Cambridge, 2005), Michael A. Mullett, *The Catholic Reformation* (London, 1999), and most provocatively entitled of all, John W. O'Malley, *Trent and All That: Renaming Catholicism in the Early Modern Era* (Cambridge, Mass., 2000). The earlier literature is well abstracted in David Martin Luebke, *The Counter-Reformation: The Essential Readings* (Malden, Mass., and Oxford, 1999). The older works of Jean Delumeau, especially his *Catholicism between Luther and Voltaire: A New View of the Counter-Reformation* (London and Philadelphia, 1977) still cast an important if controversial shadow over this subject.

On the Anabaptists and their ilk much historiography remains set in an apologetic and confessional mould, though there are conspicuous exceptions. George Huntston Williams, *The Radical Reformation*, 3rd edn. (Kirksville, Mo., 1992), though radically enlarged, retains the somewhat rigid schematization of the sects and the defensive tone from the original edition, but is well abreast of modern scholarship. Michael G. Baylor (ed. and tr.), *The Radical*

Reformation (Cambridge and New York, 1991), presents some key source texts. The controversial revisionist work of Claus Peter Clasen, *Anabaptism, a Social History, 1525–1618: Switzerland, Austria, Moravia, South and Central Germany* (Ithaca, NY, 1972) is still worth reading. More recently Klaus Deppermann, *Melchior Hoffman: Social Unrest and Apocalyptic Visions in the Age of Reformation*, tr. Malcolm Wren, ed. Benjamin Drewery (Edinburgh, 1987) puts the 'untypical' Anabaptist in perspective. Hans-Jürgen Goertz, *The Anabaptists*, tr. Trevor Johnson (London and New York, 1996) is a valuable translation of this author's characteristic work. Werner O. Packull and Geoffrey L. Dipple (eds.), *Radical Reformation Studies: Essays Presented to James M. Stayer* (Aldershot, 1999) presents some of the modern debates on key issues.

6. Europe and a World Expanded: D. A. Brading

J. H. Parry, *The Age of the Reconnaissance* (London, 1963) and G. V. Scammell, *The World Encompassed* (London, 1981) are useful general accounts. Carlo M. Cipolla, *Guns, Sails and Empires* (New York, 1965) and Stuart B. Schwartz (ed.), *Implicit Understandings* (Cambridge, 1994) describe early encounters. For the Iberians in America, vols. i and ii of *Cambridge History of Latin America*, ed. Leslie Bethell, 11 vols. (Cambridge, 1984–95) offer a comprehensive account. On Columbus and the Caribbean, Samuel Eliot Morison, *The European Discovery of America: The Southern Voyages AD 1492–1616* (Oxford and New York, 1974) and Carl Ortwin Sauer, *The Early Spanish Main* (Berkeley and Los Angeles, 1966) are masterly. On the Spanish conquerors, James Lockhart, *The Men of Cajamarca* (Austin, Tex., 1972) and Rafael Varón Gabai, *Francisco Pizarro and his Brothers* (Norman, Okla., 1997) afford diverse portraits. Nobel David Cook, *Born to Die* (Cambridge, 1998) defines the demographic catastrophe. On Las Casas and subsequent historiography D. A. Brading, *The First America: The Spanish Monarchy, Creole Patriots, and the Liberal State 1492–1867* (Cambridge, 1991) is comprehensive. James Lockhart, *The Nahuas after the Conquest* (Stanford, Calif., 1992) is innovative and masterly. P. J. Bakewell, *Silver Mining and Society in Colonial Mexico* (Cambridge, 1971) is still pertinent. On Peru James Lockhart, *Spanish Peru 1532–1560* (Madison, 1968), Steve J. Stern, *Peru's Indian Peoples and the Challenge of Spanish Conquest* (Madison, 1982), and Peter J. Bakewell, *Miners of the Red Mountain* (Albuquerque, 1984) cover colonial society and economy.

Charles R. Boxer, *The Portuguese Seaborne Empire 1415–1825* (London, 1969) offers a good introduction. Sanjay Subrahmanyam, *The Portuguese Empire in Asia, 1500–1700* (London, 1993) is essential, but can be enlarged by Bailey W. Diffie and George W. Winius, *Foundations of the Portuguese Empire 1415–1580* (Minneapolis, 1977) and James C. Boyajian, *Portuguese Trade in Asia and the Habsburgs, 1580–1640* (Baltimore, 1993). There are two remarkable biographies: Peter Russell, *Prince Henry 'the Navigator': A Life* (New Haven, 2000), is essential reading, and Sanjay Subrahmanyam, *The Career and Legend of Vasco da Gama* (Cambridge, 1997) whose title says all. On the African slave trade Philip P. Curtin, *The Atlantic Slave Trade: A Census* (Madison, 1969) is still indispensable. On Africa there is John Thornton, *Africa and Africans in the Making of the Atlantic World, 1400–1800* (Cambridge, 1992). Stuart B. Schwartz, *Sugar Plantations in the Formation of Brazilian Society, 1550–1835* (Cambridge, 1985) and Robin Blackburn, *The Making of New World Slavery* (London, 1997) are both comprehensive. Gauvin Alexander Bailey, *Art on the Jesuit Missions in Asia and Latin America 1542–1773* (Toronto, 1999) covers much more than art. Adrian Hastings, *The Church in Africa 1450–1950* (Oxford, 1994) follows the Portuguese and Jesuits in Ethiopia. Stephen Neill, *A History of Christianity in India: The Beginnings to AD 1707* (Cambridge, 1984) traces the story of the St Thomas Christians.

Chronology

1492   Christopher Columbus leads expedition to the Caribbean and discovers the West Indies, believing them to be part of Asia.

Death of Lorenzo 'the Magnificent', Medici ruler of Florence.

Conquest of Muslim kingdom of Granada by Ferdinand and Isabel of Spain; Ferdinand and Isabella decree the compulsory conversion or exile of all Jews in their lands.

1493   Pietro Martire d'Anghieria writes one of the first descriptions of Columbus's discoveries for European readers, in letters sent to Cardinal Ascanio Sforza.

1494   Charles VIII leads French armies to invade Italy.

Piero di Lorenzo de' Medici expelled from Florence; theocratic republic established under Girolamo Savonarola in the city.

By Treaty of Tordesillas the newly discovered lands are shared out between Spain and Portugal.

1495   Programme of 'imperial reform' proposed by Emperor Maximilian I for the Holy Roman Empire at Imperial assembly at Worms.

1497   Vasco da Gama begins expedition to India via the Cape of Good Hope.

1498   Charles VIII dies: Louis XII succeeds as king of France.

Execution of Savonarola; Florence becomes a secular republic.

1499   Swabian war between Swiss Confederates and Maximilian I leads to the Swiss achieving *de facto* independence of the Empire.

1500   Pedro Alvares Cabral discovers what is now Brazil and claims the land for Portugal.

1503   Death of Pope Alexander VI (Rodrigo Borgia); Giuliano della Rovere elected Pope Julius II after short pontificate of Pius III; Borgia power in Papal States collapses after Alexander's death.

Erasmus of Rotterdam publishes first edition of his *Enchiridion*.

1505   Erasmus publishes Lorenzo Valla's *Annotations* on the New Testament.

1506   Julius II commissions Donato Bramante to begin the wholesale reconstruction of St Peter's basilica in Rome.

1507   Martin Waldseemüller publishes a map and a globe that name the newly discovered continent 'America'.

1508   League of Cambrai established between papacy, France, the Empire, and Aragon against Venice.

Michelangelo Buonarroti begins work on the ceiling of the Sistine Chapel.

1509   Henry VII dies; Henry VIII succeeds as king of England and marries Catherine of Aragon, his brother's widow.

Jacques Lefèvre d'Etaples publishes his *Fivefold Psalter*.

League of Cambrai's armies defeat Venice at battle of Agnadello.

Julius II issues bull *Liquet omnibus* offering special indulgence for those contributing to the rebuilding of St Peter's.

1511   Erasmus's *Praise of Folly* first published.

1512   Jacques Lefèvre d'Etaples publishes his commentary on Paul's epistles.

'Sack of Prato' leads to collapse of Florentine republic and restoration of the rule of the Medici family.

Fifth Lateran Council meets at Rome.

1513   Pope Julius II dies; Giovanni de' Medici elected pope as Leo X.

Swiss defeat the French at battle of Novara.

English defeat French at Guinegatte and Scots at Flodden.

Machiavelli drafts *The Prince* and *The Discourses* around this time.

1514   Albrecht von Hohenzollern becomes archbishop-elector of Mainz, incurring large debts to the papacy in the process.

1515   Louis XII dies; Francis I becomes king of France.

Battle of Marignano: French and Venetians defeat Swiss near Milan.

Albrecht von Hohenzollern given permission to recover some of his debts owed to the papacy by reissuing indulgences in his territories.

1516   Death of King Ferdinand of Aragon; Charles of Habsburg ('Charles of Ghent', the future Emperor Charles V) succeeds as king of Spain.

Erasmus issues his *Novum Instrumentum*, a Greek New Testament with his own Latin translation.

Thomas More's *Utopia* first published.

Pietro Martire d'Anghieria publishes first collection of his *De*

Orbe Nouo Decades, most widely read account of the
New World.

1517   Martin Luther writes his 95 theses on the power of indulgences
in response to the campaign to sell indulgences in the territory
of the archbishopric of Mainz.

1518   Luther debates with Johann von Eck at Leipzig.

1519   Maximilian I dies; Charles V elected Holy Roman Emperor.

Hernán Cortés lands in Mexico and begins to take over the
territory in the name of Spain.

Ferdinand Magellan begins his voyage that will ultimately
circumnavigate the world.

1520   Luther publishes several of his most famous pamphlets, which
are widely circulated, and is excommunicated by Pope Leo X.

Revolt of the *Comuneros* in Castile.

Accession of Suleiman I as Sultan of the Ottoman Empire.

1521   Luther appears before special hearing at the *Reichstag* in Worms
and refuses to recant his views.

Death of Pope Leo X.

Philipp Melanchthon publishes first edition of his *Common
Places*, codifying and explaining Luther's theology.

Belgrade surrenders to the Ottomans.

1522   Luther publishes the first editions of his German New
Testament.

Election of Pope Adrian VI.

Battle of Bicocca: Imperial forces defeat the French.

Rhodes surrenders to the Ottomans.

1523   Death of Adrian VI: Giulio de' Medici elected pope as
Clement VII.

Disputations at Zürich inaugurate the Reformation in the city.

Lefèvre d'Etaples publishes his New Testament in French.

Sweden establishes itself as kingdom separate from Denmark,
under Gustav I Vasa.

1524   Erasmus publishes his *Diatribe on Free Will*, signalling an open
breach with Martin Luther and his followers.

1525   Battle of Pavia: Charles V defeats and captures Francis I.

'Peasants' War' in Germany followed by widespread punitive
massacres carried out by the German nobility.

Luther marries Katharina von Bora, publishes *On the Enslaved Will* in response to Erasmus.

City reformation in Nuremberg.

1526   Battle of Mohács: most of Hungary and Balkans overrun by Ottoman Empire.

Reichstag at Speyer authorizes a temporary permissive solution to religious divisions among German princes and cities.

1527   Sack of Rome by Charles V's unpaid troops: Pope Clement VII forced to seek protection with Charles V.

Medici dynasty expelled from Florence and republic restored.

Gustav I Vasa establishes royal control over church property in Sweden at a meeting of the estates at Västerås.

Henry VIII of England begins the process of repudiating his first wife, Catherine of Aragon.

1528   Castiglione's *Book of the Courtier* first published.

City reformations in Hamburg, Konstanz, Berne.

1529   Meeting of the Reichstag at Speyer threatens reforming princes and cities: reformed states issue 'Protestation' against its decree.

Conference at Marburg between Luther and Huldrych Zwingli and their respective allies and supporters fails to bring theological agreement.

City reformations completed in Strasbourg, Basel.

Charles V by the Capitulación de Toledo authorizes Francisco Pizarro to try to conquer Peru.

1530   Meeting of the Reichstag at Augsburg fails to resolve religious dispute; *Confession of Augsburg* and *Tetrapolitan Confession* presented by Lutheran and south German reformers respectively.

François appoints first royal lecturers, beginnings of Collège Royal.

Medici rule restored in Florence.

1531   Founding of the Protestant League of Schmalkalden, led by the Lutheran princes and cities.

Battle of Kappel and death of Huldrych Zwingli.

1532   Publication of first (posthumous) edition of Machiavelli's *The Prince*.

Publication of first edition of François Rabelais's *Pantagruel*.

1533   John Calvin flees from France to Basel after associating with reformers.

Act in Restraint of Appeals estranges Henry VIII of England from the papacy.

Pizarro defeats the Inca Empire and conquers Cuzco.

1534 Act of Supremacy declares Henry VIII Supreme Head of the Church in England.

Death of Pope Clement VII: Alessandro Farnese elected as Pope Paul III.

Luther publishes complete Bible in his German translation.

1535 Siege and capture of city of Münster from the Anabaptist 'kingdom' established there by Jan Beukelszoon of Leiden.

Edict of Coucy offers temporary amnesty to Protestants in France.

First Protestant French Bible published at Neuchâtel.

Pizarro founds Lima as the capital of Spanish Peru.

1536 Francis I invades and seizes the duchy of Piedmont-Savoy.

Deaths of Erasmus of Rotterdam and Jacques Lefèvre d'Etaples.

'Wittenberg Accord' links Lutheran and south German reformers.

Lutheranism established in Denmark.

First edition of John Calvin's *Institutio* published at Basel.

Geneva resolves to adopt the Reformation; Calvin settles there.

First Helvetic Confession adopted by Swiss reformed churches.

1537 Unsuccessful summons of a General Council of the Church to Mantua.

Paul III issues bull *Sublimis Deus*: declares native Americans to be 'truly human and . . . capable of understanding the Catholic faith'.

1538 John Calvin exiled from Geneva and settles in Strasbourg.

1540 Bull of foundation issued for the Society of Jesus.

Fall of Thomas Cromwell in England.

1541 Calvin returns to Geneva at the pleading of the city council; issues the *Ecclesiastical Ordinances* for the city and revised edition of the *Institutio* in French.

Colloquy of Regensburg: failed attempt at Catholic–Protestant reconciliation in Germany.

Pedro de Valdivia founds Santiago, Chile.

1542 Defection of prominent Catholics Piermartire Vermigli and

Bernardino Ochino to the Reformation; Roman Inquisition established.

1543   First edition of Copernicus, *On the Revolutions of the Heavenly Spheres*, published.

1545   Council of Trent opens.

1546   Death of Martin Luther.

War breaks out between Charles V and League of Schmalkalden.

1547   Battle of Mühlberg: Charles V defeats League of Schmalkalden.

Council of Trent transferred to Bologna and session closed.

Death of Francis I; accession of Henri II as king of France.

Death of Henry VIII; accession of Edward VI as king of England.

1548   'Iron-clad' Reichstag at Augsburg: Charles V issues the *Interim* settlement of religion for Germany.

Lutherans divided in their responses to the *Interim*.

1549   'Zürich consensus' establishes theological accord between Zürich and Geneva.

Many continental Protestant theologians settle in England; first Book of Common Prayer issued.

Death of Pope Paul III.

1550   Giammaria Ciocchi del Monte elected Pope as Julius III.

Debate organized at Valladolid between Las Casas and Juan Ginés de Sepúlveda about morality of Spanish conquest of New World and treatment of its peoples.

1551   Council of Trent begins its second phase of deliberations.

Henri II of France and Duke Moritz of Saxony make Lochau Heath agreement to attack Emperor Charles V.

1552   'Princes' War' in Germany: Duke Moritz attacks Charles V; Henri II seizes Metz, Toul, and Verdun; Peace of Passau ends the fighting.

Closure of second phase of Council of Trent.

Second Book of Common Prayer issued in England.

Francisco López de Gómara publishes *Historia General de las Indias*.

1553   Death of Edward VI; accession of Mary I as queen of England; re-establishment of Catholic worship and exile of foreign Protestants.

1554   England restored to communion with the Roman Catholic Church.

1555 Gian Pietro Carafa elected pope as Paul IV.

Religious Peace of Augsburg agreed in the Holy Roman Empire under the leadership of Charles V's brother Ferdinand.

Perrin coup fails in Geneva: Calvin consolidates his authority and prestige in the city.

Executions of Protestants for heresy begin in England.

Charles V abdicates the Netherlands to his son Philip II.

1556 Charles V abdicates Spain to his son Philip II, the Empire and the Austrian possessions to Ferdinand I.

Thomas Cranmer, archbishop of Canterbury, tried and executed for heresy.

1557 Philip II makes first declaration of the Spanish crown's 'bankruptcy', rescheduling the crown's debts to its creditors.

1558 Death of Charles V.

Death of Mary I of England; accession of Elizabeth I.

1559 Peace of Cateau-Cambrésis brings Italian wars to an end.

Death of Henri II; Francis II succeeds as king of France as a minor.

First Protestant national synod issues Gallican Confession.

Calvin issues final definitive edition of *Institutio*.

Royal supremacy over the church and Book of Common Prayer re-established in England by parliamentary statute.

Paul IV issues Index of Prohibited Books.

Death of Pope Paul IV: Giovanni Angelo de' Medici elected as Pope Pius IV.

1560 Death of François II; Charles IX succeeds as king of France as a minor.

Scottish Reformation parliament inaugurates the Scottish reformed church.

Death of Philipp Melanchthon.

Philip II declares Spanish crown bankrupt for the second time.

1561 'Belgic Confession' prepared by reformed churches of the Netherlands.

1562 Massacre at Vassy begins first phase of French Wars of Religion.

Council of Trent enters third and final phase.

1563 Council of Trent closes its final session.

Heidelberg Confession issued for reformed church in Electoral Palatinate.

First version of Thirty-Nine Articles of Religion adopted in England.

1564　Death of Calvin.

Death of Ferdinand I: Maximilian II elected Holy Roman Emperor.

Decrees of the Council of Trent promulgated and published.

1565　Death of Pope Pius IV.

Knights of St John defeat Ottomans at Malta.

1566　Michele Ghislieri elected pope as Pius V.

Roman Catechism issued.

'Hedge-preaching' and iconoclasm in the Low Countries bring the conflict over Protestantism there to a head.

Second Helvetic Confession adopted by Swiss reformed churches.

Death of Sultan Suleiman I of the Ottoman Empire.

1567　Council of Troubles set up in Netherlands by Spanish military regime under duke of Alva to suppress the rebellion.

1568　Spanish ambush of John Hawkins's and Francis Drake's ships in San Juan de Ulúa.

Counts Egmont and Hoorn executed in Brussels by Spanish regime.

1569　Revolt of the (Catholic) 'northern earls' against Elizabeth I.

Union of Lublin unites Poland with Lithuania as a Commonwealth.

1570　Pope Pius V declares Elizabeth I of England excommunicate and deposed.

Consensus of Sandomierz unites the Trinitarian Protestants of Poland in a joint agreement against the Unitarians.

1571　Holy Alliance defeats Ottoman Empire in sea-battle at Lepanto.

Definitive version of Thirty-Nine Articles adopted for Church of England.

1572　Marriage of Henri de Navarre and Marguerite de Valois; massacre of St Bartholomew follows in Paris and other cities.

Dutch Revolt breaks out afresh in Holland and Zealand.

1573　François Hotman's *Francogallia* first published.

1574   Death of Charles IX; Henri III succeeds as king of France.

      Ottomans reconquer Tunis, previously held by Don John of Austria.

1575   'Bohemian Confession' establishes coexistence between non-Catholic churches in Bohemia.

      Philip II declares Spanish crown bankrupt for the third time.

1576   Death of Maximilian II; Rudolf II succeeds as Holy Roman Emperor.

      Peace of Monsieur offers French Protestants most favourable peace terms; enrages Catholics and prompts formation of the League.

      Sack of Antwerp by unpaid Spanish troops temporarily unites the Netherlands against Philip II's rule.

1577   Formula of Concord agreed: reunites fractured elements of the Lutheran churches (*Book of Concord* embodying the agreement was published 1580).

      'Eternal Edict' supposedly brings peace in the Netherlands but breaks down soon afterwards.

1578   Moors defeat Portuguese at battle of Al Kasr al Kebir (also Alcazarquivir) in North Africa: King Sebastian of Portugal killed, extinguishing the royal line.

      Alessandro Farnese, duke of Parma, appointed Governor-General of the Netherlands.

1579   Union of Utrecht gives rudimentary form to the alliance of the states of the northern Netherlands in revolt against Philip II.

1580   Crown of Portugal passes to Spain.

      Montaigne's *Essais* published.

      Francis Drake completes his circumnavigation of the world and returns to England with plunder from the Spanish empire.

1581   Northern provinces of the Netherlands renounce allegiance to Philip II.

1582   Gregorian calendar reform instituted, leading to a 10-day difference in dates between Catholic and Protestant countries.

1583   Catholic troops invade archbishopric of Cologne to remove a Protestant claimant to the see, threatening the religious peace in Germany.

1584   Death of François duke of Anjou leaves the Valois line without heirs.

Catholic League established in France to prevent the succession to the throne of Henri de Navarre, a Protestant.

League makes Treaty of Joinville with Philip II of Spain.

Assassination of William the Silent, leader of the Dutch Revolt.

1585   War breaks out between England and Spain following alliance between Elizabeth I and Dutch Republic by the Treaty of Nonsuch.

Duke of Parma captures Antwerp for Spain from Dutch rebels.

1587   Elizabeth I's government executes Mary Queen of Scots for conspiracy.

English ships raid Spanish fleet in Cádiz.

1588   Spanish Armada sails against England but is attacked by English at battle of Gravelines and fails to land in England.

Pope Sixtus V establishes 'congregations' of cardinals.

Henri III orders the murders of the duke and cardinal of Guise.

1589   Henri III of France assassinated: Henri de Navarre succeeds as Henri IV.

Giovanni Botero publishes *Reason of State*.

1590   Pope Sixtus V issues defective revision of the Vulgate Latin Bible.

Philip II raises new heavy domestic taxes for wartime expenses.

José de Acosta publishes *Historia Natural y Moral de las Indias*.

1592   After a series of short pontificates, Ippolito Aldobrandini elected as Pope Clement VIII.

Clement VIII's further revision of Sixtus V's Vulgate issued.

1593   Henri IV of France declares his reconversion from Protestantism to Roman Catholicism.

1594   Henri IV takes possession of Paris and is crowned king.

Earl of Tyrone's rebellion breaks out in Ireland.

1595   Henri IV declares war on Spain over its continuing support for the League.

1596   English raid against the Spanish fleet and fortifications at Cádiz.

Philip II declares Spanish crown bankrupt for the fourth time.

Johannes Kepler publishes *Mysterium Cosmographicum*.

1598   Edict of Nantes imposes an end to religious conflict in France; grants partial toleration for reformed Church in the kingdom.

Peace of Vervins ends conflict between France and Spain.

Death of Philip II; Philip III succeeds as king of Spain.

Irish rebels defeat English forces at Yellow Ford.

1601   English troops defeat the Irish rebellion at Kinsale.

1603   Death of Elizabeth I of England; James VI of Scotland succeeds as James I.

Suppression of Irish rebellion.

1604   Treaty of London: peace agreed between England and Spain.

1606   Papacy places the republic of Venice under interdict.

1607   Seizure of Donauwörth by duke of Bavaria again threatens to destabilize the religious peace in Germany.

1608   Emperor Rudolf II forced to yield control over some of his territories to Matthias I.

1609   Twelve years' truce declared in war between Dutch and Spain.

Rival Protestant and Catholic Leagues formed in Germany.

Disputed succession in duchies of Jülich-Cleves threatens religious conflict in Germany.

1610   Henri IV of France assassinated: Louis XIII succeeds as a minor.

1611   Emperor Rudolf II deposed in favour of Matthias I.

Maps

Map 1 Europe showing Habsburg territories *c.*1556

Source: Joseph Bergin ed., *Short Oxford History of Europe: The Seventeenth Century* (Oxford University Press, Oxford, 2001), p. 245.

Stable frontiers

Uncertain frontiers and regions of conflict

Boundaries within larger political units

Regions of broken frontiers and 'islands' of territory

Spanish Habsburg territories

LP   LOWER PALATINATE

UP   UPPER PALATINATE

Patrimonial territories of Austrian Habsburgs

SWEDEN

ESTONIA

INGRIA

LIVONIA

LITHUANIA

• Moscow

EAST PRUSSIA

KALMUKS

POMERANIA

RUSSIA

BURG

SILESIA

POLAND

DON COSSACKS

Vienna

HUNGARY

ZAPOROZHIAN COSSACKS

AUSTRIA

JEDISAN

OLA

MOLDOVIA

TRANSYLVANIA

KHANATE OF THE CRIMEA

SLAVONIA

DALMATIA

SERBIA

WALLACHIA

BLACK SEA

BOSNIA

KINGDOM OF NAPLES

Constantinople

TREBIZOND

OTTOMAN

ALBANIA

EMPIRE

KURDISTAN

ANATOLIA

MOREA

Crete

Cyprus

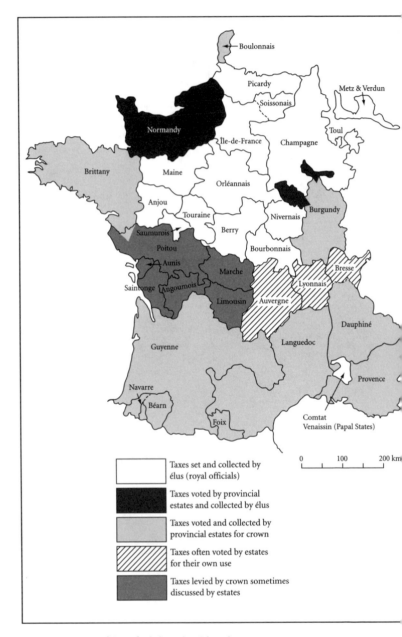

Map 2 France and its Administrative Diversity c.1600

Map 3 Italy, 1559
Source: Paul Grendler ed., *Encyclopedia of the Renaissance* (Charles Scribner's Sons, © Charles Scribner's Sons 2000. Reprinted by permission of the Gale Group).

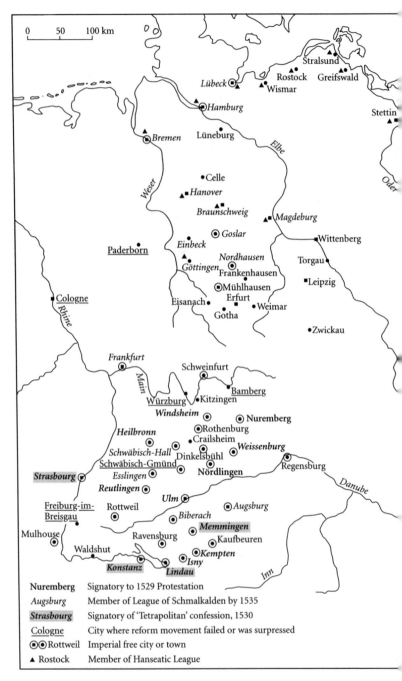

Map 4 The Cities and Towns of the Empire and the Reformation
Source: Euan Cameron, *The European Reformation* (Oxford University Press, Oxford, 1991), p. 211.

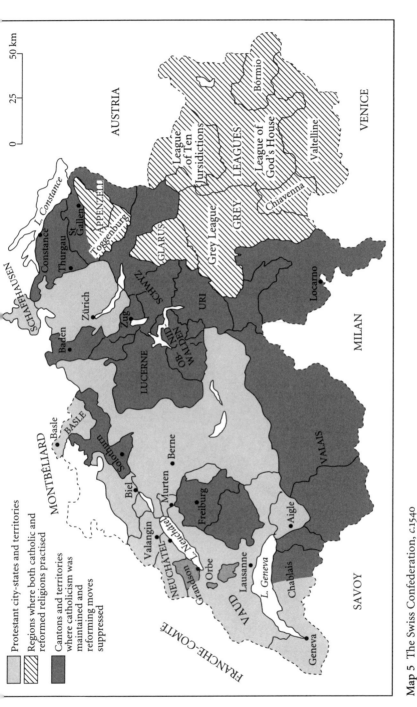

Map 5 The Swiss Confederation, c.1540

Source: Euan Cameron, *The European Reformation* (Oxford University Press, Oxford, 1991), p. 220.

Key:
- Protestant city-states and territories
- Regions where catholic and reformed religions practised
- Cantons and territories where catholicism was maintained and reforming moves suppressed

AUSTRIA
VENICE
MILAN
SAVOY
FRANCHE-COMTÉ
MONTBÉLIARD

LEAGUES
GREY
Grey League
League of Ten Jurisdictions
League of God's House
Valtelline
Bormio
Chiavenna

L. Constance
SCHAFFHAUSEN
Constance
Thurgau
St Gallen
APPENZELL
Toggenburg
Baden
Zürich
Zug
SCHWYZ
GLARUS
URI
OB- UND WALDEN
LUCERNE
Locarno

Basle
BASLE
Solothurn
Biel
Murten
Berne
Freiburg
Valangin
NEUCHÂTEL
L. Neuchâtel
Grandson
Orbe
Lausanne
VAUD
L. Geneva
Geneva
Aigle
Chablais
VALAIS

0 25 50 km

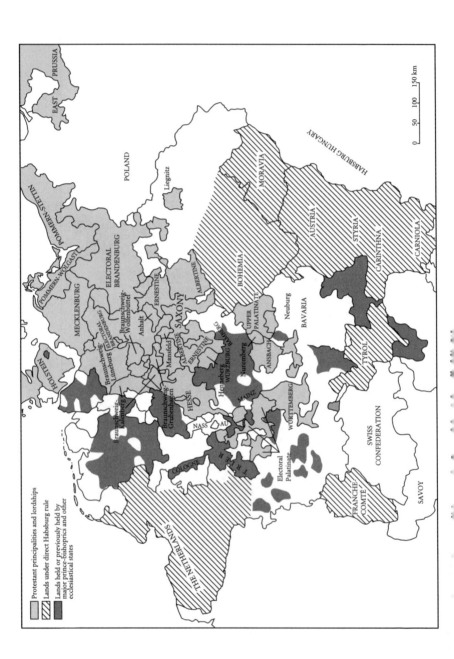

Protestant principalities and lordships

Lands under direct Habsburg rule

Lands held or previously held by
major prince-bishoprics and other
ecclesiastical states

EAST PRUSSIA

POMMERN-STETTIN

POLAND

(POMMERN-WOLGAST)

HOLSTEIN

MECKLENBURG

ELECTORAL
BRANDENBURG

Liegnitz

Braunschweig-
Lüneburg

Braunschweig
(ELECTORAL
BRANDENBURG)

Braunschweig-
Wolfenbüttel

Anhalt

ERNESTINE

ALBERTINE

SAXONY

ALBERTINE

Mansfeld

ERNESTINE

BAMBERG

BOHEMIA

MORAVIA

Braunschweig-
Kalenberg

Braunschweig-
Grubenhagen

HESSE

Henneberg

WÜRZBURG

Nuremberg

ANSBACH

UPPER
PALATINATE

Neuburg

BAVARIA

AUSTRIA

COLOGNE

NASS

AU

MAINZ

T R I E R

WÜRTTEMBERG

TYROL

STYRIA

CARINTHIA

CARNIOLA

Electoral
Palatinate

THE NETHERLANDS

FRANCHE-
COMTÉ

SWISS
CONFEDERATION

SAVOY

HABSBURG HUNGARY

0   50   100 150 km

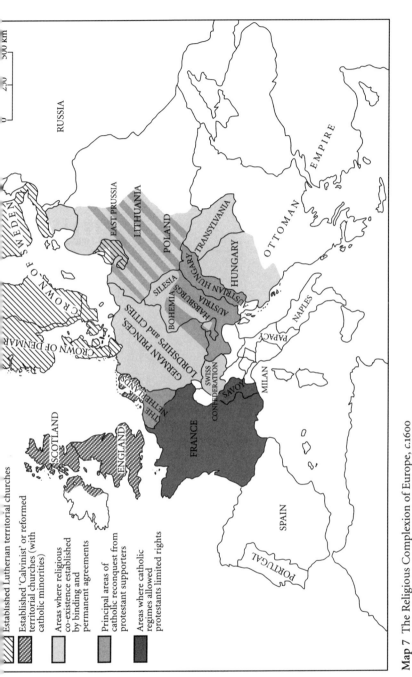

Map 7 The Religious Complexion of Europe, c.1600
Source: Euan Cameron, *The European Reformation* (Oxford University Press, Oxford, 1991), p. 362.

Legend:

- Established Lutheran territorial churches
- Established 'Calvinist' or reformed territorial churches (with catholic minorities)
- Areas where religious co-existence established by binding and permanent agreements
- Principal areas of catholic reconquest from protestant supporters
- Areas where catholic regimes allowed protestants limited rights

Map labels: SWEDEN, CROWN OF DENMARK, CROWN OF SWEDEN, RUSSIA, SCOTLAND, ENGLAND, THE NETHERLANDS, FRANCE, SPAIN, PORTUGAL, SAVOY, MILAN, NAPLES, PAPACY, SWISS CONFEDERATION, GERMAN PRINCES and CITIES, LORDSHIPS, BOHEMIA, SILESIA, HABSBURG, AUSTRIA, AUSTRIAN HUNGARY, HUNGARY, TRANSYLVANIA, POLAND, LITHUANIA, EAST PRUSSIA, OTTOMAN EMPIRE

Scale: 0 250 500 km

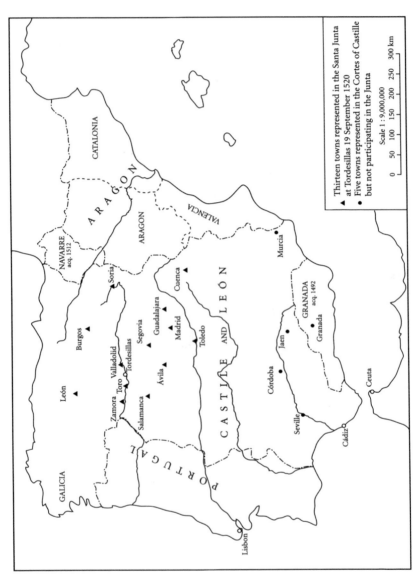

Thirteen towns represented in the Santa Junta
at Tordesillas 19 September 1520

Five towns represented in the Cortes of Castille
but not participating in the Junta

Scale 1 : 9,000,000

0   50   100 150 200 250 300 km

GALICIA

PORTUGAL

Lisbon

León

Zamora
Toro
Salamanca
Valladolid
Tordesillas

Soria

NAVARRE
acq. 1512

ARAGON

ARAGON

CATALONIA

Burgos

Ávila
Segovia
Guadalajara
Madrid
Toledo

Cuenca

VALENCIA

CASTILE AND LEÓN

Córdoba

Jaén

Seville

Cádiz

Granada

GRANADA
acq. 1492

Murcia

Ceuta

Map 8 The Iberian Peninsula

Map 9 Dutch recovery of territory from the Spanish Netherlands, 1590–1604
Source: Jonathan I. Israel, *The Dutch Republic: Its Rise, Greatness, and Fall 1477–1806* (Oxford University Press, Oxford, 1995), p. 243.

Index